THE MAKING
OF SPECIES

BY DOUGLAS DEWAR
AND FRANK FINN

Post-Darwinian books on evolution fall naturally into four classes. I. Those which preach Wallaceism, as, for example, Wallace's Darwinism, Poulton's Essays on Evolution, and the voluminous works of Weismann. II. Those advocating Lamarckism. Cope's Factors of Evolution and the writings of Haeckel belong to this class. III. The writings of De Vries, forming a group by themselves. They advocate the theory that species spring suddenly into being; that new species arise by mutations from pre-existing species. IV. The large number of books of a more judicial nature, books written by men who decline to subscribe to any of the above three creeds. Excellent examples of such works are Kellog's Darwinism To-Day, Lock's Recent Progress in the Study of Variation, Heredity, and Evolution, and T. H. Morgan's Evolution and Adaptation.

All four classes are characterised by defects.

Books of the two first classes exhibit the faults of ardent partisanship. They formulate creeds, and, as Huxley truly remarked, "Science commits suicide when it adopts a creed." The [vi] books which come under the third category have the defects of extreme youth. De Vries has discovered a new principle, and it is but natural that he should exaggerate its importance, and see in it more than it contains. But, as time wears on, these faults will disappear, and the theory of mutations will assume its true form and fall into its proper place, which is somewhere between the dustbin, to which Wallaceians would relegate it, and the exalted pinnacle on to which De Vries would elevate it.

In the present state of our knowledge, books of Class IV. are the most useful to the student, since they are unbiassed, and contain a judicial summing-up of the evidence for and against the various evolutionary theories which now occupy the field. Their chief defect is that they are almost entirely destructive. They shatter the faith of the reader, but offer nothing in place of that which they have destroyed. T. H. Morgan's Evolution and Adaptation, however, contains much constructive matter, and so is the most valuable work of this class in existence.

Zoological science stands in urgent need of constructive books on evolution—books with leanings towards neither Wallaceism, nor Lamarckism, nor De Vriesism; books which shall set forth facts of all kinds, concealing none, not even those which do not admit of explanation in the present state of our knowledge.—It [vii] has been our aim to produce a book of this description.

We have endeavoured to demonstrate that neither pure Lamarckism nor pure Wallaceism affords a satisfactory explanation of the various phenomena of the organic world. We have further, while recognising the very great value of the work of De Vries, tried to show that that eminent botanist has allowed his enthusiasm to carry him a little too far into the realm of speculation. We have followed up the exposure of the weak points of the theories, which at present occupy the field, with certain suggestions, which, we believe, throw new light on many biological problems.

Our aim in writing this book has been twofold. In the first place we have attempted to place before the general public in simple language a true statement of the present position of biological science. In the second place, we have endeavoured to furnish the scientific men of the day with food for reflection.

Even as the British nation seems to be slowly but surely losing, through its conservatism, the commercial supremacy it had the good fortune to gain last century, so is it losing, through the unwillingness of many of our scientific men to keep abreast of the times, that scientific supremacy which we gained in the middle of last century by the labours of

Charles Darwin and Alfred [viii] Russell Wallace. To-day it is not among Englishmen, but among Americans and Continentals, that we have to look for advanced scientific ideas.

Even as the Ultra-Cobdenites believe that Free Trade is a panacea for all economic ills, so do most English men of science believe that natural selection offers the key to every zoological problem. Both are living in a fool's paradise. Another reason why Great Britain is losing her scientific supremacy is that too little attention is paid to bionomics, or the study of live animals. Morphology, or the science of dead organisms, receives more than its due share of attention. It is in the open, not in the museum or the dissecting-room, that nature can best be studied. Far be it from us to deprecate the study of morphology. We wish merely to insist upon the fact, that the leaders of biological science must of necessity be those naturalists who go to the tropics and other parts of the earth where nature can be studied under the most favourable conditions, and those who conduct scientific breeding experiments. Natural selection—the idea which has revolutionised modern biological science—came, not to professors, but to a couple of field-naturalists who were pursuing their researches in tropical countries. It is absurd to expect those who stay at home and gain most of their [ix] knowledge second-hand to be the pioneers of biological science.

We fear that this book will come as a rude shock to many scientific men. By way of consolation we may remind such that they will find themselves in much the same position as that occupied by theologians immediately after the appearance of the Origin of Species.

At that time theological thought was cramped by dogma. But the clergy have since reconsidered their position, they have modified their views, and thus kept abreast of the times. Meanwhile scientific men have lagged behind. The blight of dogma has seized hold of them. They have adopted a creed to which all must subscribe or be condemned as heretics. Huxley said that the adoption of a creed was tantamount to suicide. We are endeavouring to save biology in England from committing suicide, to save it from the hands of those into which it has fallen.

We would emphasise that it is not Darwinism we are attacking, but that which is erroneously called Neo-Darwinism. Neo-Darwinism is a pathological growth on Darwinism, which, we fear, can be removed only by a surgical operation.

Darwin, himself, protested in vain against the length to which some of his followers were pushing his theory. On p. 657 of the new edition [x] of the Origin of Species he wrote: "As my conclusions have lately been much misrepresented, and as it has been stated that I attribute the modification of species exclusively to natural selection, I may be permitted to remark that in the first edition of this work, and subsequently, I placed in a most conspicuous position—namely, at the close of the Introduction—the following words: 'I am convinced that natural selection has been the main but not the exclusive means of modification.' This has been of no avail. Great is the power of steady misrepresentation; but the history of science shows that this power does not long endure."

Notwithstanding this protest the Wallaceians continue on their course, and give to the world a spurious Darwinism. It is our belief that were Darwin alive to-day his sympathies would be with us, and not with those who call themselves his followers. It was one of Darwin's strong points that he never avoided facts. If new facts came to light which were incompatible with a theory of his, he promptly modified his theory. Since his death a number of new facts have come to light which, in our opinion, plainly indicate that the theory of natural selection as enunciated by Darwin needs considerable modification.

We have in this book set forth certain of these facts and indicated the directions in [xi] which the Darwinian theory seems to require modification.

This volume originated as the result of several conversations we, the joint authors, had last summer. We discovered that we had a great many ideas in common on the subject of evolution. This seemed strange, seeing that our education had not been on the same lines. One of us took a degree in natural science at Cambridge, and subsequently entered His Majesty's Indian Civil Service, but continued his zoological studies in India as a hobby. The other, a naturalist from childhood, nevertheless took a classical degree at Oxford, then received a technical zoological training, adopted zoology as a profession, and held for some years a position in the Natural History Museum at Calcutta.

Our conversations revealed that we were both of opinion that biology is in an unhealthy condition, especially in England, and that the science sorely needs some fresh impetus. Neither of us had the time to attempt, single-handed, to give the required impetus, but as one of us happened to be home on eighteen months' leave, we thought we might undertake the task in collaboration.

We felt that we might collaborate the more successfully because the large number of facts collected by the one of us form the necessary complement to the philosophical studies of the other.

We have endeavoured, so far as possible, to [xii] avoid technical terms, and have made a special point of quoting, wherever practicable, familiar animals as examples, in order that the work may make its appeal not only to the zoologist but to the general reader.

It may, perhaps, be urged against us that we have quoted too freely from popular writings, including those of which we are the authors. Our reply to this is that the study of bionomics, the science of living animals, occupies so small a place in English scientific literature that we have been compelled to have recourse to popular works for many of our facts; and we would, moreover, point out that a popular work is not necessarily inaccurate in its information.

In conclusion, we would warn the reader against the danger of confounding Inference with Fact. The failure to distinguish between the two has vitiated much of the work of the Wallaceian school of biologists.

Facts are always to be accepted. Inferences should be scrutinised with the utmost care.

In making our deductions, we have endeavoured to act without bias. We shall, therefore, welcome any new facts, be they consistent with, or opposed to, our inferences.

D. D.
F. F.

CONTENTS

PAGE

of the theory of Natural Selection, recognises the complexity of the problems which biologists are endeavouring to solve.

The theory of protective colouration has been carried to absurd lengths—It will not bear close scrutiny—Cryptic colouring—Sematic colours—Pseudo-sematic colours—Batesian and Müllerian mimicry—Conditions necessary for mimicry—Examples—Recognition markings—The theory of obliterative colouration—Criticism of the theory—Objections to the theory of cryptic colouring—Whiteness of the Arctic fauna is exaggerated—Illustrative tables—Pelagic organisms—Objectors to the Neo-Darwinian theories of colouration are to be found among field naturalists—G. A. B. Dewar, Gadow, Robinson, F. C. Selous quoted—Colours of birds' eggs—Warning colouration—Objections to the theory—Eisig's theory—So-called intimidating attitudes of animals—Mimicry—The case for the theory—The case against the theory—"False mimicry"—Theory of recognition colours—The theory refuted—Colours of flowers and fruits—Neo-Darwinian explanations—Objections—Kay Robinson's theory—Conclusion that Neo-Darwinian theories are untenable—Some suggestions regarding the colouration of animals—Through the diversity of colouring of organisms something like order runs—The connection between biological molecules and colour—Tylor on colour patterns in animals—Bonhote's theory of pœcilomeres—Summary of conclusions arrived at.

Sexual Dimorphism

Meaning of the term—Fatal to Wallaceism—Sexual Selection—The law of battle—Female preference—Mutual Selection—Finn's experiments—Objections to the theory of Sexual Selection—Wallace's explanation of sexual dimorphism stated and shown to be unsatisfactory—The explanation of Thomson and Geddes shown to be inadequate—Stolzmann's theory stated and criticised—Neo-Lamarckian explanation of sexual dimorphism stated and criticised—Some features of sexual dimorphism—Dissimilarity of the sexes probably arises as a sudden mutation—The four kinds of mutations—Sexual dimorphism having shown itself, Natural Selection determines whether or not the organisms which display it shall survive.

The Factors of Evolution

Variation along definite lines and Natural Selection are undoubtedly important factors of evolution—Whether or not sexual selection is a factor we are not yet in a position to decide—Modus operandi of Natural Selection—Correlation an important factor—Examples of correlation—Correlation is a subject that requires close study—Isolation a factor in evolution—Discriminate isolation—Indiscriminate isolation—Is the latter a factor?—Romanes' views—Criticism of these—Indiscriminate isolation shown to be a factor—Summary of the methods in which new species arise—Natural Selection does not make species—It merely decides which of certain ready-made forms shall survive—Natural Selection compared to a competitive examination and to a medical board—We are yet in darkness as to the fundamental causes of the Origin of Species—In experiment and observation rather than speculation lies the hope of discovering the nature of these causes.

LIST OF ILLUSTRATIONS

FACING PAGE

By permission of the Avicultural Society.
From "The Modern Turbit," published by "The Feathered World," London.
On the left, the yellow-rumped finch; on the right, the chestnut-breasted; birds in state of change in the middle.

By permission of the Avicultural Society.

THE MAKING OF SPECIES

[1]

CHAPTER I

6

RISE OF THE THEORY OF NATURAL SELECTION AND ITS SUBSEQUENT DEVELOPMENT

Pre-Darwinian Evolutionists—Causes which led to the speedy triumph of the theory of Natural Selection—Nature of the opposition which Darwin had to overcome—Post-Darwinian biology—Usually accepted classification of present-day biologists as Neo-Lamarckians and Neo-Darwinians is faulty—Biologists fall into three classes rather than two—Neo-Lamarckism: its defects—Wallaceism: its defects—Neo-Darwinism distinguished from Neo-Lamarckism and Wallaceism—Neo-Darwinism realises the strength and weakness of the theory of Natural Selection, recognises the complexity of the problems which biologists are endeavouring to solve.

Darwinism and evolution are not interchangeable terms. On this fact it is impossible to lay too much emphasis. Charles Darwin was not the originator of the theory of evolution, nor even the first to advocate it in modern times. The idea that all existing things have been produced by natural causes from some primordial material is as old as Aristotle. It was lost [2] sight of in the mental stagnation of the Middle Ages. In that dark period zoological science was completely submerged. It was not until men shook off the mental lethargy that had held them for many generations that serious attention was paid to biology. From the moment when men began to apply scientific methods to that branch of knowledge the idea of evolution found supporters.

Buffon suggested that species are not fixed, but may be gradually changed by natural causes into different species.

Goethe was a thorough-going evolutionist; he asserted that all animals were probably descended from a common original type.

Lamarck was the first evolutionist who sought to show the means whereby evolution has been effected. He tried to prove that the efforts of animals are the causes of variation; that these efforts originate changes in form during the life of the individual which are transmitted to its offspring.

St Hilaire was another evolutionist who endeavoured to explain how evolution had occurred. He believed that the transformations of animals are effected by changes in their environment. These hypotheses were considered, and rightly considered, insufficient to explain anything like general evolution, so that the idea failed for a time to make headway.

[3]
Strength of Darwin's Position

As knowledge grew, as facts accumulated, the belief in evolution became more widespread. Hutton, Lyell, Spencer, and Huxley were all convinced that evolution had occurred, but they could not explain how it had occurred.

Thus, by the middle of last century, all that was needed to make evolution an article of scientific belief was the discovery of a method whereby it could be effected. This Darwin and Wallace were able to furnish in the shape of the theory of natural selection. The discovery was made independently, but Darwin being the older man, the more influential, and the one who had gone the more deeply and carefully into the matter, gained the lion's share of the credit of the discovery. The theory of natural selection is universally known as the Darwinian theory, notwithstanding the fact that Darwin, unlike Wallace, always recognised that natural selection is not the sole determining factor in organic evolution.

From the moment of the enunciation of his great hypothesis, Darwin's position was an exceedingly strong one. Everything was in his favour.

As we have seen, the theory was enunciated at the psychological moment, at the time when zoological science was ripe for it. Most of the leading zoologists were evolutionists at heart, and were only too ready to accept any theory [4] which afforded a plausible explanation of what they believed to have occurred.

Hence the rapturous welcome accorded to the theory of natural selection by the more progressive biologists.

Another point in Darwin's favour was the delightful simplicity of his hypothesis. Nothing could be more enticingly probable. It is based on the unassailable facts of variation, heredity, and the tendency of animals to multiply in numbers. Everybody knows that the breeder can fix varieties by careful breeding. Darwin had simply to show that there is in nature something to take the part played among domesticated animals by the human breeder. This he was able to do. As the numbers of species remain stationary, it is evident that only a small portion of the animals that are born can reach maturity. A child can see that the individuals most likely to survive are those best adapted to the circumstances of their life. Even as the breeder weeds out of his stock the creatures not suited to his purpose, so in nature do the unfit perish in the everlasting struggle for existence.

In nature there is a selection corresponding to that of the breeder.

It is useless to deny the existence of this selection in nature, this natural selection. The only disputable point is whether such selection can do all that Darwin demanded of it.

[5]
The man in the street, then, was able to comprehend the theory of natural selection. This was greatly in its favour. Men are usually well disposed towards doctrines which they can readily understand.

The nineteenth century was a superficial age. It liked simplicity in all things. If Darwin could show that natural selection was capable of producing one species, men were not only ready but eager to believe that it could explain the whole of organic evolution.

The simplicity of the Darwinian theory has its evil side. It has undoubtedly tended to make modern biologists superficial in their methods. It has, indeed, stimulated the imagination of men of science; but the stimulation has not in all cases been a healthy one.

So far from adhering to the sound rule laid down by Pasteur, "never advance anything that cannot be proved in a simple and decisive manner," many modern naturalists allow their imagination to run riot, and so formulate ill-considered theories, and build up hypotheses on the most insecure foundations. "A tiny islet of truth," writes Archdale Reid, "is discovered, on which are built tremendous and totally illegitimate hypotheses."

Another source of Darwin's strength was the vast store of knowledge he had accumulated. For twenty years he had been steadily amassing [6] facts in support of his hypothesis. He enunciated no crude theory, he indulged in no wild speculations. He was content to marshal a great array of facts, and to draw logical conclusions therefrom. He was as cautious in his deductions as he was careful of his facts. He thus stood head and shoulders above the biologists of his day. He was a giant among pigmies. So well equipped was he that those who attempted to oppose him found themselves in the position of men, armed with bows and arrows, who seek to storm a fortress defended by maxim guns.

Nor was this all. The majority of the best biologists of his time did not attempt to oppose him. They were, as we have seen, ready to receive with open arms any hypothesis which seemed to explain how evolution had occurred. Some of them perceived that there were weak points in the Darwinian theory, but they preferred not to expose these; they were rather disposed to make the best of the hypothesis. It had so many merits that it seemed to them but reasonable to suppose that subsequent investigation would prove that the defects were apparent rather than real.

Opponents of Darwin

We hear much of the "magnitude of the prejudices" which Darwin had to overcome, and of the mighty battle which Darwin and his lieutenant Huxley had to fight before the theory of the origin of species by natural selection [7] obtained acceptance. We venture to say that statements such as these are misleading. We think we may safely assert that scarcely ever has a theory which fundamentally changed the prevailing scientific beliefs met with less opposition. It would have been a good thing for zoology had Darwin not obtained so easy a victory.

Sir Richard Owen, a distinguished anatomist, certainly attacked the doctrine in no unmeasured terms, but his attack was anonymous and so cannot be considered very formidable. Far more important was the opposition of Dr St George Mivart, whose worth as a biologist has never been properly appreciated. His most important work, entitled the Genesis of Species, might be read with profit even now by many of our modern Darwinians.

For some time after the publication of the Origin of Species Mivart appears to be almost the only man of science fully alive to the weak points of the Darwinian theory. The great majority seem to have been dazzled by its brilliancy.

The main attack on Darwinism was conducted by the theologians and their allies, who considered it to be subversive of the Mosaic account of the Creation. Now, when one whose scientific knowledge is, to say the best of it, not extensive, attacks a man who has studied his subject dispassionately for years, and invariably expresses himself with [8] extreme caution, the onslaught can have but one result—the attacker will be repulsed with heavy loss, and the onlookers will have a higher opinion of his valour than of his common sense.

The theologians were in the unfortunate position of warriors who do not know what it is against which they are fighting; they confounded natural selection with evolution, and directed the main force of their attack against the latter, under the impression that they were fighting the Darwinian theory.

It was the misfortune of those theologians that it is possible to prove that evolution, or, at any rate, some evolution has occurred; they thus kicked against the pricks with disastrous results to themselves. When this attack had been repulsed men believed that the theory of natural selection had been demonstrated, that it was as much a law of nature as that of gravitation. What had really happened was that the fact of evolution had been proved, and the theory of natural selection obtained the credit. Men thought that Darwinism was evolution. Had the theologians admitted evolution but denied the ability of natural selection to explain it, the Darwinian theory, in all probability, would not have gained the ascendency which it now enjoys.

Evolution and Natural Selection

To us who are able to look back dispassionately upon the biological warfare of the last century, Darwin's opponents—or the majority of them—appear [9] very foolish. We must, however, bear in mind that at the time of the publication of the Origin of Species both natural selection and evolution were comparatively unknown ideas. Darwin had to fight for both. He had to prove evolution as well as natural selection. Many of the facts adduced by him supported both. It is, therefore, not altogether surprising that many of his opponents failed to distinguish between them.

A glance at the Origin of Species will suffice to show how considerable is the portion of the book that deals with the evidence in favour of evolution rather than of natural selection.

Of the fourteen chapters which make up the book no fewer than nine are devoted to proving that evolution has occurred. It has been truly said, that for every one fact biologists have found in support of the special theory of natural selection they have found ten facts supporting the doctrine of evolution. Darwin, then, was in the position of a skilled barrister who has a plausible case and who knows the ins and outs of his brief, while his opponents stood in the shoes of inexperienced counsel who had but recently received their brief, and who had not had the time to master the details thereof. In such circumstances it is not difficult to predict which way the verdict of the jury will go.

Darwin, moreover, had a charming personality. [10] Never was a man with a theory less dogmatic. Never was the holder of a theory more careful of the expressions he used. Never was a scientific man more ready to give ear to his opponents, to meet them half way, and, where necessary, to compromise. Darwin was not afraid of facts, and was always ready to alter his views when they appeared to be opposed to facts. The average scientific man of to-day makes facts fit his theory; if they refuse to fit it he ignores or denies them.

Darwin continually modified his views; when he found himself in a tight place he did not hesitate to resort to Lamarckian factors, such as the inheritance of the effects of use and disuse and of the effects of environment. He conceded that natural selection was insufficient to account for all the phenomena of organic evolution, and advanced the theory of sexual selection in order to account for facts which the major hypothesis seemed to him incapable of explaining.

Darwin, moreover, having ample private means, was not obliged to work for a living, and was therefore able to devote the whole of his time to research. The advantages of such a position cannot be over-estimated, and, perhaps, have not been sufficiently taken into account in apportioning the praise between Darwin and Wallace for their great discovery.

Huxley

To all these factors in Darwin's favour we [11] must add his good fortune in possessing so able a lieutenant as Huxley.

Huxley was an ardent evolutionist, an able writer, and a brilliant debater. A man of his mental calibre was able, like a clever barrister, to make out a plausible case for any theory which he chose to take up. While nominally a strong supporter of the Darwinian theory, he was in reality fighting for the doctrine of descent. Had any plausible theory of evolution been enunciated, Huxley would undoubtedly have fought for it equally earnestly.

A firm believer in evolution, Huxley was, as Professor Poulton says, confronted by two difficulties,—first, the insufficiency of the evidence of evolution, and, secondly, the absence of any explanation of how the phenomenon had occurred. The Origin of Species solved both these difficulties. It adduced much weighty evidence in favour of evolution, and suggested a modus operandi. Small wonder, then, that Huxley became a champion of Darwinism. But, as Poulton writes, on page 202 of Essays on Evolution, "while natural selection thus enabled Huxley freely to accept evolution, he was by no means fully satisfied with it." "He never committed himself to a full belief in natural selection, and even contemplated the possibility of its ultimate disappearance." To use Huxley's own words: "Whether the particular shape which the [12] doctrine of evolution, as applied to the organic world, took in Darwin's hands, would prove to be final or not, was, to me, a matter of indifference."

The result of the fortuitous combination of the circumstances which we have set forth was that in a surprisingly short time the theory of natural selection came to be regarded as a law of nature on a par with the laws of gravitation. Thus, paradoxical though it seems, practical certainty was given to a hitherto uncertain doctrine by the addition of a still more uncertain theory.

"At once," writes Waggett, "the theory of development leapt from the position of an obscure guess to that of a fully-equipped theory and almost a certainty."

Darwin thus became a dictator whose authority none durst question. A crowd of slavish adherents gathered round him, a herd of men to whom he seemed an absolutely unquestionable authority. Darwinism became a creed to which all must subscribe. It still retains this position in the popular mind.

Growing Opposition to Darwinism

The ease with which the theory of natural selection gained supremacy was, as we have already said, a misfortune to biological science. It produced for a time a considerable mental stagnation among zoologists. Since Darwin's day the science has not made the progress that might reasonably have been expected, because the theory has so captivated the minds of the [13] majority of biologists that they see everything through Darwinian spectacles. The wish has been in many cases the father to the observation. Zoologists are ever on the lookout for the action of natural selection, and in consequence frequently imagine they see it where it does not exist. Many naturalists, consciously or unconsciously, stretch facts to make them fit the Darwinian theory. Those facts which refuse to be so distorted are, if not actively ignored or suppressed, overlooked as throwing no light upon the doctrine. This is no exaggeration. A perusal of almost any popular book dealing with zoological theory leaves the impression that there is nothing left to be explained in the living world, that there is no door leading to the secret chambers of nature to which natural selection is not an "open sesame."

But the triumph of natural selection has not been so complete as its more enthusiastic supporters would have us believe. Some there are who have never admitted the all-sufficiency of natural selection. In the British Isles these have never been numerous. In the United States of America and on the Continent they are more abundant. The tendency seems to be for them to increase in numbers. Hence the recent lamentations of Dr Wallace and Sir E. Ray Lankester. Modern biologists are commonly supposed to fall into two schools of thought—the Neo-Darwinian and the Neo-Lamarckian.

[14]
The former are the larger body, and pin their faith absolutely to natural selection. They deny the inheritance of acquired characters, and preach the all-sufficiency of natural selection to explain the varied phenomena of nature. The Neo-Lamarckians do not admit the omnipotency of natural selection. Some of them allow it no virtue. Others regard it as a force which keeps variation within fixed limits, which says to each organism, "thus far shalt thou vary and no farther." This school lays great stress on the inheritance of acquired characters, especially on the inheritance of the effects of use and disuse.

The above statement of the recent developments of Darwinism is incomplete, for it fails to include those who occupy a middle position. If it be possible to classify a large number of men of which scarcely any two hold identical views, it is into three, rather than two, classes that they must be divided.

Speaking broadly, evolutionists of to-day may be said to represent three distinct lines of thought. For the sake of classification we may speak of them as falling into three schools, which we may term the Neo-Lamarckian, the Wallaceian, and the Neo-Darwinian, according as their views incline towards those held by Lamarck, Wallace, or Darwin.

The Neo-Lamarckian School

As adherents of the Neo-Lamarckian school, [15] we cite Cope, Spencer, Orr, Eimer, Naegeli, Henslow, Cunningham, Haeckel, Korchinsky, and a number of others. It may almost be said of these Neo-Lamarckians that each holds a totally distinct theory of evolution. So heterogeneous are their views that it is difficult to find a single article common to the evolutionary belief of all. It is commonly asserted that all Neo-Lamarckians are agreed, firstly, that acquired characters are transmissible; and, secondly, that such transmission is an important factor in the production of new species. This assertion is certainly true of the great bulk of Neo-Lamarckians, but it does not appear to hold in the case of those who believe that evolution is the result of some unknown inner force. So far as we can see, a belief in the inheritance of acquired characters is not necessary to the theories of orthogenesis held by Naegeli and Korchinsky. For that reason it would possibly be more correct to place those who hold such views in a fourth school. Since, however, a number of undoubted Neo-Lamarckians, as, for example, Cope, believe in an inner growth-force, it is convenient to regard Naegeli as a Neo-Lamarckian. His views need not detain us long. Those who wish to study them in detail will find them in his Mechanisch-physiologische Theorie der Abstammungslehre.

Naegeli believes that there is inherent in [16] protoplasm a growth-force, which makes each organism in itself a force making towards progressive evolution. He holds that animals and plants would have become much as they are now even if no struggle for existence had taken place. "To the believers in this kind of . . . orthogenesis," writes Kellog (Darwinism To-day, p. 278), "organic evolution has been, and is now, ruled by unknown inner forces inherent in organisms, and has been independent of the influence of the outer world. The lines of evolution are immanent, unchangeable, and ever slowly stretch toward some ideal goal." It is easy to enunciate such a theory, impossible to prove it, and difficult to disprove it.

It seems to us that the fact that, so soon as organisms are removed from the struggle for existence, they tend to degenerate, is a sufficient reason for refusing to accept theories of the description put forth by Naegeli. More truly Lamarckian is Eimer's theory of orthogenesis, according to which it is the environment which determines the direction which variation takes; and the variations which are induced by the environment are transmitted to the offspring.

Orr's Views

Spencer and Orr preach nearly pure Lamarckism. The former, while fully recognising the importance of natural selection, considered that sufficient weight has not been given to the effects of use and disuse, or to the direct action [17] of the environment in determining or modifying organisms.

The similarity of the views of Orr and Lamarck is best seen by comparing their respective explanations of the long neck of the giraffe. Lamarck thought that this was the direct result of continual stretching. The animal continually strains its neck in the search for food, hence it grows longer as the individual grows older, and this elongated neck has been transmitted to the offspring. Orr writes, on page 164 of his Development and Heredity: "The giraffe seems to present the most remarkable illustration of the lengthening of the bones as the result of the frequent repetition of such shocks. As is well known, this animal feeds on the foliage of trees. From the earliest youth of the species, and the earliest youth of

12

each individual, it must have been stretching upwards for food, and, as is the custom of such quadrupeds, it must have constantly raised itself off its forefeet, and, as it dropped, must have received a shock that made itself felt from the hoofs through the legs and vertical neck to the head. In the hind legs the shock would not be felt. It is impossible to imagine that an animal which, during the greater part of every day of its life (both its individual and racial life), performed motions so uniform and constant, would not be peculiarly specialised as a result. The forces acting upon such an [18] animal are widely different from the forces acting upon an animal which eats the grass at its feet like an ox, or one which must run and climb like a goat or a deer, and the resultant modifications of growth in the several cases must also be different. The principle of increased growth in the direction of the shock, resulting from superabundant repair of the momentary compression, explains how the giraffe acquired the phenomenal length of the bones of its forelegs and neck; and the absence of the shock in the hind-quarters shows why they remained undeveloped and absurdly disproportionate to the rest of the body."

Inheritance of Acquired Characters

It seems to us that a fatal objection to all these Neo-Lamarckian theories of evolution is that they are based on the assumption that acquired characters are inherited, whereas all the evidence goes to show that such characters are not inherited. In these days, when scientific knowledge is so widely diffused, it is scarcely necessary to say that all the characteristics which an organism displays are either congenital or inborn, or acquired by the organism during its lifetime. Thus a man may have naturally a large biceps muscle, and this is a congenital character; or he may by constant exercise develop or greatly increase the size of the biceps. The large biceps, in so far as it has been increased by exercise, is said to be an [19] acquired character, for it was not inherited by its possessor, but acquired by him in his lifetime. We must bear in mind that the period in the life history of an organism at which a character appears, is not necessarily a test as to whether it is congenital or acquired, for a great many congenital characters, such as a man's beard, do not appear until some years after birth. As we have seen, the Neo-Lamarckians believe that it is possible for an organism to transmit to its offspring characters which it has acquired during the course of its existence. But, as we have already said, the evidence goes to show that such characters are not inherited. For example, the tail of the young fox-terrier is not shorter than that of other breeds of dogs, notwithstanding the fact that its ancestors have for generations had the greater portion of their caudal appendage removed shortly after birth.

We do not propose to discuss at any great length the vexed question of the inheritance of acquired characters, for the simple reason that the Neo-Lamarckians have not brought forward a single instance which indubitably proves that such characters are inherited.

Mr J. T. Cunningham, in a paper of great value and interest, entitled "The Heredity of Secondary Sexual Characters in relation to Hormones: a Theory of the Heredity of Somatogenic Characters," which appeared in [20] vol. xxvi., No. 3, of the Archiv für Entwicklungsmechanik des Organismen, states: "The dogma that acquired characters cannot be inherited . . . is founded not so much on evidence, or the absence of evidence, as on a priori reasoning, on the supposed difficulty or impossibility of conceiving a means by which such inheritance could be effected." Such appears certainly to be true of some zoologists, but we trust that Mr Cunningham will do us the justice to believe that our opinion that the inheritance of acquired characters does not play an important part in the evolution of, at any rate, the higher animals, is based, not on the ground of a priori reasoning, but on facts. All the evidence seems to show that such characteristics are not inherited. If, as Mr Cunningham thinks, all secondary sexual characters are due to the inheritance of the effects of use, etc., how is it that no Neo-Lamarckian is able to bring forward a clear case of the inheritance of a well-defined acquired character? If such characteristics are habitually inherited, countless examples should be forthcoming. Fanciers in their endeavours are constantly "doctoring"

13

the animals they keep for show purposes; and it seems to us certain that if acquired characters are inherited, breeders would long ago have discovered this and acted upon the discovery. If Neo-Darwinians are [21] charged with refusing to believe that acquired characters are inherited because they "cannot conceive the means by which it could be effected," may it not be said with equal justice that many Neo-Lamarckians believe that acquired characters are inherited, not on evidence thereof, but because if such characters are not inherited it is very difficult to account for many of the phenomena presented by the organic world?

In many of the lower animals, as, for example, the hydra, the germinal material is diffused through the organism, so that a complete individual can be developed from a small portion of the creature. In such circumstances it seems not improbable that the external environment may act directly on the germinal substance, and induce changes in it which may perhaps be transmitted to the offspring. If this be so, it would seem that some acquired characters may be inherited in such organisms. Very many plants can be propagated from cuttings, buds, etc., so that we might reasonably expect some acquired characters to be hereditary in them. The majority of botanists appear to hold Lamarckian views; but on the evidence at present available, it is doubtful whether such views are the correct ones.

Plants are so plastic, so protean, so sensitive to their environment that their external structure appears to be determined by the external conditions in which they find themselves quite as [22] much as by their inherited tendencies. In this respect they differ very considerably from the higher animals. The peacock, for example, presents the same outward appearance[1] whether bred and reared in Asia or Europe, in a hot or cold, a damp or a dry climate. The same plant, on the other hand, differs greatly in outward appearance according as it is grown in a dry or a damp soil, a hot or a cold country. In his recent book The Heredity of Acquired Characters in Plants, the Rev. G. Henslow cites several examples of the celerity with which plants react to their environment. On page 32 he writes: "The following is an experiment I made with the common rest-harrow (Ononis spinosa, L.) growing wild in a very dry situation by a roadside. I collected some seeds, and also took cuttings. These I planted in a garden border, keeping this well moist with a hand-light over it, and a saucer of water, so that the air should be thoroughly moist as well. Its natural conditions were thus completely reversed. They all grew vigorously. The new branches of the first year's growth bore spines, proving their hereditary character, but instead of their being long and stout, they were not an inch long, and like needles. This proved the spines to be a hereditary feature. In the second year there were none at all; moreover, the plants [23] blossomed, and, taken altogether, there was no appreciable difference from O. repens, L."

From this experiment Professor Henslow draws the inference that acquired characters tend to be inherited in plants. In our opinion the experiment affords strong evidence against the Lamarckian doctrine. Here we have a plant which has, perhaps, for thousands of generations developed spines owing to its dry environment. If acquired characters are inherited we should have expected this spiny character to have become fixed and persisted under changed conditions, for some generations at any rate. But what do we find? By the second year the thorns have entirely disappeared. All the years during which the plant was exposed to a dry environment have left no stamp upon it. The fact that the new branches of the first year's growth bore small spines is not, as Professor Henslow asserts, proof of their hereditary character. It merely shows that the initial stimulus to their development occurred while the plant was still in its dry surroundings.

In the same way all other so-called proofs of the heredity of acquired characters break down when critically examined.

In our opinion "not proven" is the proper verdict on the question of the possibility of the inheritance of acquired characters in the higher animals. One thing is certain, and that

14

is that [24] acquired characters are not commonly inherited in those organisms in which there is a sharp distinction between the germinal and the somatic cells.

It is nothing short of a misfortune that Haeckel's History of Creation, which seems to be so widely read in England, should be built on a fallacious foundation. It seems to us that this work is calculated to mislead rather than to teach.

Our attitude is not quite that of the Wallaceian school, which denies the possibility of the inheritance of acquired characters. In practice, however, the attitude we adopt is as fatal to Lamarckism in all its forms as the dogmatic assertions of the Wallaceians. It matters not whether acquired characters are very rarely or never inherited. In either case their inheritance cannot have played an important part in evolution. All those theories which rely on use-inheritance as a factor in evolution are therefore in our opinion worthless, being opposed to facts. Our attitude, then, is that the inheritance of acquired characteristics, if it does occur, is so rare as to be a negligible quantity in organic evolution.

We may add that the position which we occupy will not be affected even if the Lamarckians do succeed eventually in proving that some acquired characters are really inherited. Such proof would [25] merely help to elucidate some of the problems which confront the biologist. Thus the question of the inheritance of acquired characters, while full of interest, has no very important bearing on the question of the making of species.

The Wallaceian School

The Wallaceians hold the doctrines which have been set forth above as those of the Neo-Darwinian school. It is incorrect to call those who pin their faith to the all-sufficiency of natural selection Neo-Darwinians, because Darwin at no time believed that natural selection explained everything. Darwin moreover was a Lamarckian to the extent that he was inclined to think that acquired characteristics could be inherited. His theory of inheritance by gemmules involved the assumption that such characters are inherited. It is Wallace who out-Darwins Darwin, who preaches the all-sufficiency of natural selection. For this reason we dub the school which holds this article of belief, and to which Weismann, Poulton, and apparently Ray Lankester belong, the Wallaceian school. Weismann has put forth a theory of inheritance, that of the continuity of the germ plasm, which makes this inheritance a physical impossibility. We believe that the Wallaceians have erred as far from the truth as the Lamarckians have, because, as we shall show hereafter, a great many of the organs and structures displayed by organisms cannot be explained on the natural selection hypothesis. Those who [26] pin their faith to this, needlessly increase the difficulty of the problem which they have to face.

There remains the third school, to which we belong, and of which Bateson, De Vries, Kellog and T. H. Morgan appear to be adherents. This school steers a course between the Scylla of use-inheritance and the Charybdis of the all-sufficiency of natural selection. It may seem surprising to some that we should class De Vries as a Neo-Darwinian, seeing that he is the originator of the theory of evolution by means of mutations, which we shall discuss in Chapter III. of this work. As a matter of fact the theory of mutations should be regarded, not as opposed to the theory of Darwin, but as a theory engrafted upon it. De Vries himself writes:—"My work claims to be in full accord with the principles laid down by Darwin." Similarly Hubrecht writes in the Contemporary Review for November 1908: "Paradoxical as it may sound, I am willing to show that my colleague, Hugo de Vries, of Amsterdam, who a few years ago grafted his Mutations Theorie on the thriving and very healthy plant of Darwinism, is a much more staunch Darwinian than either Dr Wallace himself, or the two great authorities in biological science whom he mentions, Sir William Thistleton Dyer and Professor Poulton."

Complexity of the Problem

Having classified ourselves, it remains for us [27] (the authors of the present work) to define our position more precisely. Like Darwin we welcome all factors which appear to be capable of effecting evolution. We have no axe to grind in the shape of a pet hypothesis, and consequently our passions are not roused when men come forward with new ideas seemingly opposed to some which already occupy the field. We recognise the extreme complexity of the problems that confront us. We look facts in the face and decline to ignore any, no matter how ill they fit in with existing theories. We recognise the strength and the weakness of the Darwinian theory. We see plainly that it has the defect of the period in which it was enunciated. The eighteenth century was the age of cocksureness, the age in which all phenomena were thought to be capable of simple explanation.

This is well exemplified by the doctrines of the Manchester school as regards political and economic science. The whole art of legislation was thought to be summed up in the words laissez faire. The whole sphere of legitimate government was asserted to be the keeping of order and the enforcing of contracts. Experience has demonstrated that a State guided solely by these principles is wretchedly governed. A large proportion of recent Acts of Parliament limits the freedom of contract. Such limitations are necessary in the case of contracts between the weak and [28] the strong. Similarly the earlier economists considered political economy a very simple affair. They asserted that men are actuated by but one motive—the love of money. All their men were economic men, men devoid of all attributes save an intense love of gold. Experience has shown that these premises are not correct. Love of family, pride of race, caste prejudices are more or less deeply implanted in men, so that they are rarely actuated solely by the love of money.

The Aim of the Biologist

Thus it is that the political economy of to-day as set forth by Marshall is far more complex and less dogmatic than that of Ricardo or Adam Smith. Similarly the political philosophy of Sidgwick is very different to that of Herbert Spencer. So is it with the theory of organic evolution. The theory of natural selection is no more able to explain all the varied phenomena of nature than is Ricardo's assumption that all men are actuated solely by the love of money capable of accounting for the multifarious existing economic phenomena. Even as the love of wealth is an important motive of human actions, so is natural selection an important factor in evolution. But even as the majority of human actions are the resultant of a variety of motives, so are the majority of existing organisms the resultant of a complex system of forces. Even as it is the duty of the economist to discover the various [29] motives which lead to human actions, so is it the duty of the biologist to bring to light the factors which are operative in the making of species.

[30]

CHAPTER II
SOME OF THE MORE IMPORTANT OBJECTIONS TO THE THEORY OF NATURAL SELECTION

Brief statement of Theory—Objections to the Theory fall into two classes—Those which strike at the root of the Theory—Those which deny the all-sufficiency of Natural Selection—Objections which strike at root of Theory are based on misconception—Objections to Wallaceism—The Theory fails to explain the origin of Variations—Natural Selection called on to explain too much—Unable to explain beginnings of new organs—The Theory of change of function—The co-ordination of variations—The fertility of races of domesticated animals—Missing links—Swamping effects of intercrossing—Small variations cannot have a survival value—Races inhabiting same area—Excessive specialisation—Chance and Natural Selection—Struggle for existence most severe among young animals—Natural Selection fails to explain mimicry and other phenomena of colour—Conclusion, that scarcely an organism exists which does not possess some feature inexplicable on the theory of Natural Selection as held by Wallace and his followers.

"The burden of proof is on him who asserts" is a rule of evidence which the man of science should apply as rigidly as does the lawyer.

It is therefore incumbent upon us to prove our assertion that the theory of natural selection does not afford an adequate explanation of all the varied phenomena observed in the organic world.

[31]
Theory of Natural Selection

The theory of natural selection is so generally understood, that to set it forth in detail in this place would be quite superfluous.

Darwin, it will be remembered, based his great hypothesis on the following observed facts:—

1. No two individuals of a species are exactly alike. This is sometimes called the law of variation.

2. All creatures tend in a general way to resemble their parents in appearance more closely than they resemble individuals not related to them. This may be termed the law of heredity.

3. Each pair of organisms produces in the course of a lifetime, on an average, many more than two young ones.

4. On an average the total number of each species remains stationary.

From (3) and (4) follows the doctrine of Malthus, namely, that many more individuals are born than can reach maturity.

Darwin applied this doctrine to the whole of the animal and the vegetable kingdoms.

In his introduction to The Origin of Species he writes:—"As many more individuals of each species are born than can possibly survive; and as, consequently, there is a frequently recurring struggle for existence, it follows that any being, if it vary, however slightly, in any manner profitable [32] to itself, under the complex and sometimes varying conditions of life, will have a better chance of surviving, and thus be naturally selected. From the strong principle of inheritance, any selected variety will tend to propagate its new and modified form."

In other words, the struggle for existence amongst all organic beings throughout the world, which inevitably follows from the high geometrical ratio of their increase, results in the survival of the fittest, that is to say, of those best adapted to cope with their enemies and to secure their food. Since organisms are thus naturally selected in nature, we may speak of a natural selection which acts in much the same way as the human breeder does. Darwin's theory, then, is that all the variety of organisms which now exist have been evolved from one or more forms by this process of natural selection.

Various Anti-Darwinian Views

The objections which have been urged against the theory of natural selection fall into two classes.

I. Those which strike at its root, which either deny that there is any natural selection, or declare that it is not capable of producing a new species.

II. Those which are directed against the all-sufficiency of natural selection to account for organic evolution.

Those of the first class need not detain us [33] long, although among those who formulate them are to be found some eminent men of science.

Delage alleges that selection is powerless to form species, its function is, according to him, limited to the suppression of variations radically bad, and to the maintaining of a species in its normal character. It is thus an inimical factor in evolution, a retarder rather than an accelerator of species-change. It merely acts by preserving the type at the expense of the variants, and so acts as a brake on evolution.

Korschinsky, while possibly not denying that selection occurs in nature, declares that its influence on evolution is nil, or, if it has any influence, that it is a hindering one.

Eimer similarly denies any capacity on the part of natural selection to create species.

Pfeffer urges a very different objection. He says that if such a force as natural selection existed it would transform species much more rapidly than it does!

Now, in order that the above objections can carry any weight, one of two sets of conditions must be fulfilled.

Either all organisms must be perfectly adapted to their environment, and this environment must never change, or there must be inherent in each species a kind of growth-force which impels the species to develop in certain fixed directions. [34] In either of these circumstances natural selection will be an inhibitory force, for if the normal organism is perfectly adapted to its environment, all variations from the type must be unfavourable, and natural selection will weed out the individuals that display them. No careful student of nature can maintain, either that all animals are perfectly adapted to their environment, or that this never changes. Hence those who deny that natural selection is a factor in the making of species, assume the second set of conditions, that species develop in certain fixed directions, being impelled either by internal or external forces. How far these ideas are founded on fact we shall endeavour to determine when speaking of variation. It must suffice at present to say that even if any of these views of orthogenesis be established, natural selection will have, so to speak, a casting vote, it will decide which series of species developing along preordained lines shall survive and which shall not survive.

Thus we reach by a different line of argument the conclusion we arrived at in the last chapter: namely, there is no room for doubt that natural selection is a factor in the making of species.

We must now pass on to the second class of objections, those which are urged against the all-sufficiency of natural selection. So numerous are these that it is not feasible to consider them all. A brief notice of the more important ones [35] should suffice to satisfy any unbiassed person; firstly, that natural selection is an important factor in evolution; secondly, that the position taken up by Wallace and his followers, that natural selection, acting on minute variations, is the one and only factor in organic evolution, is untenable.

Darwinism does not explain Variation

1. It has been urged that the Darwinian theory makes no attempt to explain variation, and that, until we know what it is that causes variations, we are not in a position to explain evolution. This of course is quite true, but the objection is scarcely a fair one, since, as we have seen, Darwin freely admitted that his theory made no attempt to explain the origin of variations. It is not reasonable to object to a theory because it fails to explain phenomena with which it expressly states that it is not concerned. On the other hand, the objection is one that must be reckoned with, for, as we shall see, it makes a great difference to the importance of natural selection as a factor in evolution if variations appear indiscriminately in all directions, as Darwin tacitly assumed they do, or whether, as some biologists believe, they are determinate in direction, being the result of a growth-force inherent in all organisms.

2. Very similar to the above-mentioned objection is that which points out that it is a long journey from Amoeba to man. It is difficult to [36] believe that this long course of development from the simple to the complex is due to the action of a blind force, to the survival of those whose fortuitous variations happen to be best adapted to the environment. The result seems out of all proportion to the cause. There must be some potent force inherent in protoplasm, or behind organisms, impelling them upwards. This objection is as difficult to refute as it is to establish. It is purely speculative.

3. A very serious objection to the Darwinian theory is that the beginnings of new organs cannot be explained by the action of natural selection on fortuitous minute variations, and natural selection can act on an organ only when that organ has attained sufficient size to be of practical utility to its possessor. When once an organ has come into being it is not difficult to understand how it can be improved, modified and developed by natural selection. But how can we explain the origin of an organ such as a limb by the action of natural selection on minute variations?

Theory of Change of Function

The theory of the change of function goes some way towards meeting the difficulty, for by means of it we are able to understand how certain organs, as, for example, the lung of air-breathing animals, might have come into existence. This is said to have been developed from the swimming-bladder of fishes. This bladder is, [37] to use the words of Milnes Marshall, "a closed sac lying just underneath the vertebral column. In many fish it acquires a connection by a duct with some part of the alimentary canal. It then becomes an accessory breathing organ, especially in those fish which are capable of living out of water for a time, e.g. the Protopterus of America. An interesting series of modifications exists connecting the air-bladder with the lung of the higher vertebrates, which is undoubtedly the same organ."

This theory, however, does not seem adequate to explain the origin of all organs. It does not explain, for example, how limbs developed in a limbless organism. Wallace tried to avoid the difficulty by asserting that it is unreasonable to ask a new theory that it shall reveal to us exactly what took place in remote geological ages and how it took place. To this the obvious reply is, firstly, that we ought not to give unqualified acceptance to any theory of evolution until it does afford us such explanations, and, secondly, that the theory of the origin of species by means of natural selection is no longer a new one.

Latterly, however, Wallace appears to have given up all hope of being able to account for the origin of new organs by means of natural selection, for he states on page 431 of the issue of the Fortnightly Review for March 1909: [38] "It follows—not as a theory but as a fact—that whenever an advantageous variation is needed, it can only consist in an increase or decrease of some power or faculty already existing." Now, in order for an increase or decrease to occur, there must be something in existence to be increased or diminished. Wallace, it is true, speaks here only of powers and faculties; but it can scarcely be supposed that he believes that variations as to structure are intrinsically different from those relating to powers and faculties.

4. Herbert Spencer urges, as an objection to the theory of natural selection, that favourable variations in one organ are likely to be counterbalanced by unfavourable variations in some other organ. He maintains that the chances are enormous against the occurrence of the "many coincident and co-ordinated variations" that are necessary to create a life or death determining advantage.

This objection was urged by a writer in the Edinburgh Review in January 1909, and even by Wallace himself in the Fortnightly Review last March against the mutation theory. This objection, strong though it appears on paper, exists only in the imagination of the objector.

Those who urge it display a misunderstanding of the manner in which natural selection acts, and ignorance of the phenomenon of the correlation of organs.

[39]
Correlation

Natural selection deals with an organism as a whole. Its effect is to permit those creatures to survive which, taken as a whole, are best adapted to their environment.

Physiologists insist with ever-increasing emphasis that there is more or less correlation and inter-connection between the various parts of an organism.

The several organs of an animal are not so many isolated units. It is impossible to act on one organ without affecting some or all of the others.

Variations in a given direction of one organ are usually accompanied by correlated variations in some of the other organs. If strength be of paramount importance to an animal, natural selection will tend to preserve those individuals which exhibit strength to a marked degree, and this exhibition of strength may be accompanied by other peculiarities, such as short legs or a certain colour, so that natural selection will indirectly tend to produce individuals with short legs and having the colour in question, and it may happen that this particular colour is one that renders the animal more conspicuous than the normal colour does. Nevertheless, on account of the all-needful strength which accompanies it, those animals so coloured may survive while those of a more protective hue perish. Thus, paradoxical though it seems, natural selection [40] may indirectly be responsible for characteristics which in themselves are injurious to the individual. This is probably the case as regards the decorative plumage of some male birds. The phenomenon of correlation was recognised by Darwin, and has, we believe, played an important part in the making of species. We shall deal more fully with the subject in a later chapter.

5. An oft-urged objection to the theory of natural selection, and one which weighed very strongly with Huxley, is that breeders have hitherto not succeeded in breeding a variety which is infertile with the parent species. If, Huxley asked, breeders cannot produce such a thing, how can we say we consider it proved that natural selection produces new species in nature? This objection, however, loses much of its force in view of the fact that many perfectly distinct species are quite fertile when bred together. We shall recur to this in Chapter IV.

6. The fact that palæontology has hitherto failed to yield links connecting many existing species is a classical objection to the theory of the origin of species by gradual evolution.

Missing Links

Wallace states this objection as follows, on page 376 of his Darwinism: "Many of the gaps that still remain are so vast that it seems incredible to these writers that they could ever have been filled up by a close succession of [41] species, since these must have been spread over so many ages, and have existed in such numbers, that it seems impossible to account for their total absence from deposits in which great numbers of species belonging to other groups are preserved and have been discovered."

Wallace's reply is to the effect that in the case of many species palæontology affords abundant evidence of the gradual change of one species into another, the foot of the horse being a well-known case. The genealogy of this noble quadruped can be traced from the Eocene four-toed Orohippus, through the Mesohippus, the Miohippus, the Protohippus, and the Pliohippus, until we reach the one-toed Equus.

Wallace further points out that in order that the fossil of any organism may be preserved, the "concurrence of a number of favourable conditions" is required, and against this the chances are enormous. Lastly, he urges the imperfection of our knowledge of the things that lie embedded in the earth's crust.

The objection based on the lack of "missing links" loses some of its force if we accept the theory that species sometimes arise as sports. Thus, suppose a species with well-developed horns produces as a mutation a hornless variety, which eventually replaces the horned form, we should look in vain for any forms intermediate between the parent and the daughter species. [42] On the other hand, it is significant that just where the links are most needed they are missing. For example, the splint bones of the horse, taken in conjunction with the feet of existing tapirs, which have four toes in front and three behind, would have led us to infer, without the help of the geological record, that the horse was a descendant of a polydactyle ancestor. When, however, we come to the origin of birds, bats, and whales, palæontology fails to give us any assistance, so that we are in the dark as to the origin of such really important modifications.

7. The swamping effects of inter-crossing is an objection which has been repeatedly urged against the Darwinian theory.

This objection is not so serious as it appears at first sight. Darwin and Wallace maintain, firstly, that natural selection acts by eliminating all individuals except those which present favourable variations. The favoured few alone survive and mate with one another, so that there is here no question of the swamping effects of inter-crossing, none but well-adapted individuals being left to mate with one another.

The objection gains greater force when directed against the theory that evolution proceeds by sudden jumps. But in this connection we must bear in mind that the experiments of Mendel and his followers have demonstrated that some of the offspring of crosses may resemble their [43] pure ancestors and breed true inter se. Nor is this all.

Recurrent Mutations

Experience shows that where a mutation, or sport, or discontinuous variation occurs, it frequently repeats itself; for example, the black-winged sport of the peafowl has occurred several times over and in different flocks of birds. The sport or mutation must have a definite cause. There must be something within the organism, something in the generative cells, which causes the mutation to arise; and hence, on a priori grounds, we should expect the same mutation to arise about the same time in many individuals. It seems legitimate to infer that things have been quietly working up to a climax. When this is reached there results a mutation. Therefore we should expect sudden mutations to appear simultaneously in a number of individuals. To this important subject we shall return.

8. An almost insuperable objection to the theory that species have originated by the action of natural selection on minute variations, is that such small differences cannot be of a life-or-death value, or, as it is usually called, a survival value to their possessor. But if evolution is the result of the preservation by natural selection of such slight variations, it is absolutely necessary that each of these should possess a survival value.

As D. Dewar has pointed out, on page 704 of vol. ii. of The Albany Review, it is only when the [44] beast of prey and its victim are evenly matched as regards fleetness and power of endurance that small variations in these qualities can have a survival value. But in the rough and tumble of the struggle for existence the victim and its foe are but rarely well-matched. Take as an example the case of a flycatcher. "This bird," writes D. Dewar, "will sometimes take three or four insects in the course of one flight; all are captured with the same ease, although the length of wing in each victim varies. So great is the superiority of the bird that it does not notice the difference in the flying powers of its puny quarry." It is unnecessary to labour this point.

9. Species or varieties differing considerably in colour may exist side by side, as the hooded and carrion crows, the white and dark breasted forms of the Arctic skua, the pale and dark forms of the fulmar petrel, the grey and rufous forms of the American scops owl (Megascops asio).

It is true that preponderance of one form or another in certain districts points to some advantage possessed by one over the other, but, for all we know, it may be due to heredity, and in any case the co-existence of the two types in part of their range, or at certain seasons, shows that selection is not at all rigorous.

The same argument applies to the co-existence of very differently-coloured species with generally [45] similar habits, such as that of the jaguar and puma in South America, and the five very differently-coloured flycatchers in the Nilgiri Hills.

Leaf-butterflies

In short, there is abundant evidence to show that considerable differences in colour do not appear to have any effect on the chances of survival in the struggle for existence of those that display them. Yet this is precisely what the supporters of the Darwinian hypothesis cannot afford to admit, for they then find it impossible to account for the origin of such a form as Kallima, the leaf-butterfly, by the action of natural selection. As most people are aware, this creature displays a remarkable resemblance to a decaying leaf. "These butterflies" (there are several species which show the marvellous imitation), writes Kellog, on page 53 of Darwinism To-day, "have the under sides of both fore and hind wings so coloured and streaked that when apposed over the back in the manner common to butterflies at rest, the four wings combine to resemble with absurd fidelity a dead leaf still attached by a short petiole to the twig or branch. I say absurd, for it seems to me the resemblance is over-refined. Here for safety's sake it is no question of mimicking some one particular kind of other organism or inanimate thing in nature which birds do not molest. It is simply to produce the effect of a dead leaf on a branch. [46] Leaf-shape and general dead-leaf colour-scheme are necessary for this illusion. But are these following things necessary? namely, an extra-ordinarily faithful representation of mid-rib and lateral veins, even to faint microscopically-tapering vein tips; a perfect short petiole produced by the apposed 'tails' of the hind-wings; a concealment of the head of the butterfly so that it shall not mar the outlines of the lateral margin of the leaf; and finally, delicate little flakes of purplish or yellowish brown to mimic spots of decay and fungus-attacked spots in the leaf! And, as culmination, a tiny circular clear spot in the fore-wings (terminal part of the leaf) which shall represent a worm-eaten hole, or a piercing of the dry leaf by flying splinter, or the complete decay of a little spot due to fungus growth! A general and sufficient seeming of a dead leaf, object of no bird's active interest, yes, but not a dead leaf modelled with the fidelity of the waxworkers in the modern natural history museums. When natural selection has got Kallima along to that highly desirable stage when it was so like a dead leaf in general seeming that every bird sweeping by saw it only as a brown leaf clinging precariously to a half-stripped branch, it was natural selection's bounden duty, in conformance to its obligations to its makers, to stop the further modelling of Kallima and just hold it up to its hardly won advantage. But what happens? [47] Kallima continues its way, specifically and absurdly dead-leafwards, until to-day it is a much too fragile thing to be otherwise than very gingerly handled by its rather anxious foster-parents, the Neo-Darwinian selectionists." It is obvious that if natural selection has produced so highly specialised an organism as the dead-leaf butterfly, every minute variation must be of value and have been seized upon by natural selection.

A Dilemma

Thus the Wallaceians are on the horns of a dilemma. If they assert, as they appear to do, that every infinitesimal variation has a survival value, they find it difficult to explain the existence, side by side of such forms as the hooded and carrion crows, to say why in some species of bird both sexes assume a conspicuous nuptial plumage at the very time when they stand most in need of protective coloration, why the cock paradise flycatcher is chestnut for the first two years of his life and then turns as white as snow. If, on the other hand, the Wallaceians assert that small variations are unimportant and have no survival value, they are, as Kellog points out, in trouble over the close and detailed resemblance which the Kallima butterflies bear to dead leaves.

10. An objection to the Darwinian theory which has been advanced by Conn, Henslow, D. Dewar, and others, is that the selection theory fails to take into account the effects of chance. "If," [48] writes D. Dewar on page 707 of The Albany Review, vol. ii., "the struggle for existence were of the nature of a race at a well-regulated athletic meeting, where the competitors are given a fair start, where there is no difference in the conditions to which the various runners are subjected, then indeed would every variation tell. I would rather liken the struggle for existence to the rush to get out of a crowded theatre, poorly provided with exits, when an alarm of fire is given. The people to escape are not necessarily the strongest of those present. Propinquity to a door may be a more valuable asset than strength."

Or again, we may take the imaginary case of some antelopes being pursued by wolves. The chase, being prolonged, brings the antelopes to a locality with which they are not familiar. The foremost of the herd, the most swift, and therefore the individual which should stand the best chance of survival, suddenly finds himself on soft boggy ground, which, owing to the depth to which his feet sink into the soil, seriously impedes his progress. His fellow antelopes, now outdistanced, seeing his predicament, take another course and soon leave him behind, to fall an easy prey to his foes. Here we have a case of the perishing of the most fit as regards the important point of speed.

The Effects of Chance

Writing of plants, Professor Henslow says, on page 16 of The Heredity of Acquired Characters [49] in Plants: "As the whole of the animal kingdom ultimately lives upon the vegetable, plants must supply the entire quantity of food supplied, not to add innumerable vegetable parasites as well, for both young and old. Myriads of germinating seeds perish accordingly, being destroyed by slugs and other mollusca, and 'mildews,' etc. But far more seeds and spores—about 50,000,000 of these it is calculated can be borne in a single male-fern—never germinate at all. They fall where the conditions of life are unfavourable and perish. This misfortune is not due to any inadaptiveness in themselves, but to the surrounding conditions which will not let them germinate. Thus thousands of acorns and other fruits, as of elder, drop upon the ground in and by our hedges, road-sides, copses, and elsewhere; but scarcely any or even no seedlings are to be seen round the trees."

Every year thousands of birds perish in the great migratory flight, others succumb in a cyclone, a fierce tropical storm, a prolonged drought, a severe frost. Here death overtakes multitudes, all that dwell in a locality, the weak and the strong, the swift and the slow alike.

This objection may be met by saying that in the long run it is the fittest that will survive. This is true. The objection is nevertheless of importance in showing how exceedingly uncertain must be the action of natural selection if it have but [50] small variations upon which to work. In such circumstances the mills of natural selection may grind surely, but they must grind very slowly.

11. We must bear in mind that the struggle for existence is most severe among young animals, among creatures that are not fully developed. Nature pays no attention to potentialities. The weak go to the wall in the conflict, even though, if allowed time, they might develop into prodigies of strength.

Moreover, and this is an important point, death in the case of young creatures overtakes broods and families rather than individuals.

The above-cited objections to the theory that species have originated by the action of natural selection on minute variations, are mostly of a general nature; let us now notice briefly a few more concrete objections. We shall not devote much space to these in the present chapter, since we shall be continually confronted with them when dealing with the subject of animal colouring.

The Origin of Mimicry

12. Natural selection, as we shall see, fails to account for the origin of what is known as protective mimicry. Some insects look like inanimate objects, others resemble other insects which are believed or known to be unpalatable. Those creatures displaying this resemblance to other objects or creatures, and deriving profit therefrom, are said to "mimic" the objects or creatures they copy. They are also called "Mimics." [51] It is easy to understand the profit that these mimics derive from their mimicry. When once the disguise has been assumed we can comprehend how natural selection will tend to improve it by eliminating those that mimic badly; but it seems to us that the theory fails utterly to account for the origin of the likeness.

13. Similarly, the Neo-Darwinian theory fails to explain the colours of the eggs of birds laid in open nests, why, for example, the eggs of the accentor or hedge-sparrow are blue and those of the doves are white.

14. The theory fails to give a satisfactory explanation of the phenomena of sexual dimorphism. Why, for example, in some species of doves and ducks, the sexes are alike, while in other species with similar habits they differ in appearance.

15. It fails to explain why the rook is black and why the jackdaw has a grey neck.

These and many other objections we shall deal with more fully in the chapter on animal colouration. It must suffice here to mention them, and to say that our experience teaches us that scarcely a single species of bird or beast exists which does not display some characteristic which is inexplicable on the theory that natural selection, acting on small variations, is the one and only cause of organic evolution.

CHAPTER III
VARIATION

The assumption of Darwin and Wallace that variations are haphazard in origin and indefinite in direction—If these assumptions be not correct Natural Selection ceases to be the fundamental factor in evolution—Darwin's views regarding variation underwent modification—He eventually recognised the distinction between definite and indefinite variations, and between continuous and discontinuous variations—Darwin attached but little importance to either definite or discontinuous variations—Darwin's views on the causes of variations—Criticism of Darwin's views—Variations appear to occur along certain definite lines—There seems to be a limit to the extent to which fluctuating variations can be accumulated—De Vries' experiments—Bateson on "discontinuous variation"—Views held by De Vries—Distinction between continuous and discontinuous variations—The work of De Vries—Advantages enjoyed by the botanist in experimenting on the making of species—Difficulties encountered by the animal breeder—Mutations among animals—The distinction between germinal and somatic variations—The latter, though not transmitted to offspring, are often of considerable value to their possessor in the struggle for existence.

Nature of Variation

As we have already seen, the Darwinian theory, unlike that of Lamarck, does not attempt to explain the origin of variations. It is content with the fact that variations do occur.

Although Darwin did not try to explain how it is that variation occurs, and was very guarded [53] in the expressions he used concerning it, he assumed that variations are indefinite in variety and occur indiscriminately in all directions, as the following quotations from the Origin of Species will show: "But the number and diversity of inheritable deviations of structure . . . are endless" (page 14, ed. 1902). "The variations are supposed to be extremely slight, but of the most diversified nature." "I have hitherto sometimes spoken as if the variations so common and multiform with organic beings under domestication, and in a lesser degree to those under nature, were due to chance. This, of course, is a wholly incorrect expression, but it serves to acknowledge plainly our ignorance of the cause of each particular variation" (page 164).

Wallace is far less guarded in his expressions. On page 82 of his Darwinism he speaks of "the constant and large amount of variation of every part in all directions . . . which must afford an ample supply of favourable variations whenever required."

The double assumption that variations are for all practical purposes haphazard in origin and indefinite in direction is necessary if natural selection is to be the main factor in evolution. For if variations be not haphazard, if they are definite, if there be a directive force behind them, like fate behind the classical gods, then selection is not the fundamental cause of evolution. It [54] can at most effect, not the origin of species, but the survival of certain species which have arisen as the result of some other force. Its position is changed; it is no longer a cause of the origin of new organisms, but a sieve determining which of certain ready-made forms shall survive. Evidently, then, we shall not be able to fully understand the evolutionary process until we have discovered how it is that variations are caused. In other words, we must go considerably farther than Darwin attempted to do.

Before proceeding to inquire into the true nature of variations, it behoves us to set forth briefly the ideas of Darwin on the subject. We shall then be in a position to see how much progress has been made since the days of that great biologist.

25

It is not at all easy to discover exactly what were Darwin's views on the subject of variation. A perusal of his works reveals contradictions, and gives one the impression that he himself scarcely knew his own mind upon the subject. This should not be a matter for surprise.

We must remember that Darwin had to do pioneer work, that he had to deal with altogether new conceptions. Such being the case, his ideas were of necessity somewhat hazy; they underwent considerable modification as fresh facts came to his knowledge.

Definite and Indefinite Variability

Towards the end of his life Darwin recognised [55] that variability is of two kinds—definite and indefinite. Indefinite variation is indiscriminate variation in all directions around a mean, variation which obeys what we may perhaps call the law of chance. Definite variation is variation in a determinate direction—variation chiefly on one side of the mean. Darwin believed that these determinate variations were caused by external forces, and that they are inherited. He thus accepted Lamarckian factors. "Each of the endless variations," he writes, "which we see in the plumage of our fowls, must have had some efficient cause, and if the same causes were to act uniformly during a long series of generations on many individuals, all probably would be modified in the same direction."

But Darwin was always of opinion that this definite variability, this variability in one direction as the result of some fixed cause, is far less important, from an evolutionary point of view, than indefinite variability, that it is the exception rather than the rule, that the usual result of changed conditions is to let loose a flood of indefinite variability, that it is almost exclusively upon this that natural selection acts.

Darwin also recognised that variations differ in degree, even as they do in kind. He perceived that some variations are much more pronounced than others. He recognised the distinction between what are now known as [56] continuous and discontinuous variations. The former are slight departures from the normal; the latter are considerable deviations from the mean or mode; great jumps, as it were, taken by nature, as, for example, the pea and the rose combs of fowls, which were derived from the normal single comb.

Monstrosities

"At long intervals of time," wrote Darwin, "out of millions of individuals reared in the same country and fed on nearly the same food, deviations of structure so strongly pronounced as to deserve to be called monstrosities arise, but monstrosities cannot be separated by any distinct line from slighter variations." Therefore it is evident that he regarded the difference between continuous and discontinuous variations as not one of kind, but merely of degree. To the discontinuous variations Darwin attached very little importance from an evolutionary point of view. He looked upon them as something abnormal.

"It may be doubted," he wrote, "whether such sudden and considerable deviations of structure such as we occasionally see in our domestic productions, more especially with plants, are ever permanently propagated in a state of nature. Almost every part of every organic being is so beautifully related to its complex conditions of life that it seems as improbable that any part should have been suddenly produced [57] perfect, as that a complex machine should have been invented by a man in a perfect state. Under domestication monstrosities sometimes occur which resemble normal structures in widely different animals. Thus pigs have occasionally been born with a sort of proboscis, and if any wild species of the same genus had naturally possessed a proboscis, it might have been argued that this had appeared as a monstrosity; but I have as yet failed to find, after diligent search, cases of monstrosities resembling normal structures in nearly allied forms, and these alone bear on the question. If monstrous forms of this kind ever do appear in a state of nature and are capable of reproduction (which is not always the case), as they occur rarely and singly, their preservation would depend on unusually favourable circumstances. They would, also, during the first and succeeding generations cross with the ordinary form, and thus their abnormal character would almost inevitably be lost." But, in a later edition of the Origin of Species, Darwin seems to contradict the above assertion: "It should not, however, be overlooked that certain rather strongly marked variations, which no one would rank as mere individual differences, frequently recur owing to a similar organisation being similarly acted on—of which fact numerous instances could be given with our domestic productions. In such cases, [58] if the varying individual did not actually transmit to its offspring its newly acquired character, it would undoubtedly transmit to them, as long as the existing conditions remained the same, a still stronger tendency to vary in the same manner. There can also be little doubt that the tendency to vary in the same manner has often been so strong that all the individuals of the same species have been similarly modified without the aid of any form of selection. Or only a third, fifth, or tenth part of the individuals may have been thus affected, of which fact several instances could be given. Thus Graba estimates that about one-fifth of the guillemots in the Faroe islands consist of a variety so well marked, that it was formerly ranked as a distinct species under the name Uria lacrymans. In cases of this kind, if the variation were of a beneficial nature, the original form would soon be supplanted by the modified form, through the survival of the fittest." Here we seem to have a plain statement of the origin of new forms by mutation.

Minute Variations

Again, we read (page 34): "Some variations useful to him (i.e. man) have probably arisen suddenly, or by one step; many botanists, for instance, believe that the fuller's teasel, with its hooks, which cannot be rivalled by any mechanical contrivance, is only a variety of the wild Dipsacus; and this amount of change may have suddenly [59] arisen in a seedling. This is known to be the case with the turnspit dog."[2] But, as we have already said, Darwin at no time attached much importance to these jumps made by nature as a factor in evolution. He pinned his faith to the minute, indefinite variations which he believed could be piled up, one upon another, so that, if allowed sufficient time, either nature or the human breeder could, by a continued selection of these minute variations, call into being any kind of organism. The importance of selection, he writes, "consists in the great effect produced by the accumulation in one direction, during successive generations, of differences absolutely inappreciable by an uneducated eye" (page 36). On page 132 he writes: "I can see no limit to the amount of change, to the beauty and complexity of the coadaptations between all organic beings . . . which may have been effected[3] in the long course of time by nature's power of selection." He expressly states, on page 149, that he sees no reason to limit the process to the formation of genera alone.

Although the theory of natural selection does not attempt to explain the causes of variation, [60] Darwin paid some attention to the subject. He believed that both internal and external causes contribute to variation, that variations tend to be inherited whether the result of causes within the organism or outside it. He believed that the inherited effect of use and disuse was a cause of variation, and cited, as examples, the lighter wing-bones and heavier leg-bones of the domestic duck and the drooping ears of some domestic animals. He supposed that animals showed a greater tendency to vary when under domestication than when in their natural state, attributing the supposed greater variability to the excess of food received, and the changed conditions of the life of domestic animals. Nevertheless, he was fully alive to the fact that "nearly similar variations sometimes arise under, as far as we can judge, dissimilar conditions; and, on the other hand, dissimilar variations arise under conditions which appear to be nearly uniform." In other words, the nature of organisms appeared to Darwin to be a more important factor in the origin of variations than external conditions. Evidence of this is afforded by the fact that some animals are more variable than others. Finally, he frankly admitted how great was his ignorance of the causes of variability. Variability is, he stated, governed by unknown laws which are infinitely complex.

Lines of Variation

It will be convenient to deal with each of [61] Darwin's main ideas on variation separately, and to consider to what extent they seem to require modification in the light of later research.

Firstly, Darwin believed that variations arise in what appears to be a haphazard manner, that they occur in all directions, and seem to be governed by the same laws as chance. It is our belief that we are now in a position to make more definite statements regarding variation than Darwin was able to.

Biologists can now assert definitely that variations do not always occur equally in all directions. The results of many years of the efforts of practical breeders demonstrate this. These men have not been able to produce a green horse, a pigeon with alternate black and white feathers in the tail, or a cat with a trunk, for the simple reason that the organisms upon which they operated do not happen to have varied in the required direction. It may perhaps be objected that breeders have no desire to produce such forms; had they wished to do so, they would probably have succeeded. To this objection we may reply that they have not managed to produce many organisms, which would be highly desirable from a breeder's point of view, as, for example, a blue rose, hens that lay brown eggs but do not become broody at certain seasons of the year, or a cat that cannot scratch.

As Mivart well says, on page 118 of his Genesis of Species, "Not only does it appear that there are [62] barriers which oppose change in certain directions, but that there are positive tendencies to development along certain special lines. In a bird which has been kept and studied like the pigeon, it is difficult to believe that any remarkable spontaneous variations would pass unnoticed by breeders, or that they would not have been attended to and developed by some fancier or other. On the hypothesis of indefinite variability, it is then hard to say why pigeons with bills like toucans, or with certain feathers lengthened like those of trogons, or those of birds of paradise, have never been produced."

There are certain lines along which variation seems never to occur. Take the case of the tail of a bird. Variable though this organ be, there are certain kinds of tail that are seen neither in wild species nor domesticated races. A caudal appendage, of which the feathers are alternately coloured, occurs neither in wild species nor in artificial breeds. For some reason or other, variations in this direction do not occur. Similarly, with the exception of one or two of the "Noddy" terns, whenever a bird has any of its tail feathers considerably longer than the others, it is always the outer pair or the middle pair that are so elongated. It would thus appear that variations in which the other feathers are especially lengthened do not usually occur. The fact that they are elongated in two or three wild species is the more significant, [63] because it shows that there is apparently nothing inimical to the welfare of a species in having, say, the third pair of tail feathers from the middle exceptionally prolonged.

Breeders' Boasts

This is a most important point, and one which seems to be ignored by the majority of scientific men, who appear to be misled by the boastful talk of certain successful breeders. Thus, on page 29 of the Origin of Species, Darwin quotes, with approval, Youatt's description of selection as "the magician's wand, by means of which he may summon into life whatever form and mould he pleases." Darwin further cites Sir John Sebright as saying, with regard to pigeons, that he would "produce any given feather in three years, but it would take him six years to obtain head and beak."

If it were possible absolutely to originate anything by selection, horticulturists would almost certainly ere this have produced a pure black flower. The fact that not a single mammal exists, either in nature or under domestication, with scarlet, blue, or green in its hair, appears to show that, for some reason or other, mammals never vary in any of these directions.

The fact that so few animals have developed prehensile tails seems to indicate that variation does not often occur in that direction, for obviously a prehensile tail is of the very greatest utility to its possessor; so that there can be [64] little room for doubt that it would be seized upon and preserved by natural selection, whenever it occurred.

As E. H. Aitken very truly says, "so early and useful an invention should, one would think, have been spread widely in after time; but there appears to be some difficulty in developing muscles at the thin end of a long tail, for the animals that have turned it into a grasping organ are few and are widely scattered. Examples are the chameleon among lizards, our own little harvest mouse, and, pre-eminent among all, the American monkeys" (Strand Magazine, Nov. 1908).

Even as there are many variations which seem never to occur in nature, so are there others which occur so frequently that they may be looked for in any species. Albinistic forms appear now and again in almost every species of mammal or bird; while melanistic sports, although not so common, are not by any means rare.

Every complete manual on poultry gives for each breed a note of the faults which constantly appear, and which the fancier has to watch carefully for and guard against. The fact that these "faults" occur so frequently in each breed shows how strong is the tendency to vary in certain definite directions. It is true that some of these faults are in the nature of reversions, as, for [65] example, the appearance of red hackles in the cocks of black breeds of poultry. On the other hand, some certainly are not reversions, such as the appearance of a white ring in the neck of the female of the Rouen duck, which should resemble the Mallard as regards the plumage of the neck. Again, the tendency of Buff Orpingtons to assume white in the wings and tail must be regarded as a variation which is not in the nature of a reversion. In short, the efforts of all breeders are largely directed to fighting against the tendencies which animals display towards variation in certain directions.

Albinistic Variations

This tendency to vary in the direction of whiteness may account for many of the white markings which occur in nature, as, for example, the white tails of the Sea Eagle (Haliaetus albicilla) the Nicobar Pigeon (Caloenas nicobarica), and many hornbills. Provided that such variations are not too great a handicap to their possessors in the struggle for existence, natural selection will allow them to persist.

It was the belief of Linnæus, based on experience, that every blue or red-coloured flower is likely to produce a white variety, hence he held that it is not safe to trust to colour for the identification of a botanical species.

On the other hand, white flowers are not likely to produce red varieties, and we believe we may positively assert that they never produce a blue [66] sport. Similarly, white animals appear not to give rise to colour varieties.

We are never surprised to find that an ordinary upright plant produces as a sport or mutation a pendulous, or fastigiate form. These aberrant varieties, be it noted, occur in species which belong to quite different orders.

29

De Vries points out that laciniated leaves appear in such widely separated trees and shrubs as the walnut, the beech, the hazel-nut, and the turnip.

Another example of the definiteness of variation is furnished by what Grant Allen calls the "Law of Progressive Colouration" of flowers.

On pp. 20, 21 of The Colours of Flowers, he writes, "All flowers, as we know, easily sport a little in colour. But the question is, do their changes tend to follow any regular and definite order? Is there any reason to believe that the modification runs from any one colour toward any other? Apparently there is. . . . All flowers, it would seem, were in their earliest form yellow; then some of them became white; after that a few of them grew to be red or purple; and finally a comparatively small number acquired the various shades of lilac, mauve, violet, or blue."

Over-development

So among animals there are many colour patterns and structures that appear in widely different genera, as, for example, the magpie [67] colouring in birds. With this phenomenon we shall deal more fully when speaking of animal colouration. There is certainly no small amount of evidence which seems to indicate that, from some cause or other, an impetus has been given to certain organs to develop along definite lines. The reduction of the number of digits in several mammalian families which are not nearly related is a case in point. This phenomenon is, as Cope points out, observed in Marsupials, Rodents, Insectivores, Carnivores, and Ungulates. He, being a Lamarckian, ascribes this to the inherited effects of use. Wallaceians attribute it solely to the action of natural selection. The assumption of a growth-force or tendency for the development of one digit at the expense of the others, would explain the phenomenon equally well. And it is significant that many palæontologists are believers in some kind of a growth-force. In the case of certain extinct animals we seem to have examples of the over-development of organs. "Palæontology," writes Kellog on p. 275 of his Darwinism To-day, "reveals to us the one-time existence of animals, of groups of animals, and of lines of descent, which have had characteristics which led to extinction. The unwieldiness of the giant Cretaceous reptiles, the fixed habit of life of the crinoids, the coiling of the ammonities and the nautili, the gigantic antlers of the Irish stag—all these are examples [68] of development along disadvantageous lines, or to disadvantageous degrees. The statistical studies of variation have made known numerous cases where the slight, as yet non-significant (in a life-and-death struggle) variation in pattern of insects, in dimensions of parts, in relative proportions of superficial non-active areas, are not fortuitous, that is, do not occur scattered evenly about a mean or mode according to the law of error, but show an obvious and consistent tendency to occur along certain lines, to accumulate in certain directions."

It seems to us that the only proper attitude to adopt in the present state of our knowledge is, not to call in to our aid an unknown growth-force, but simply to say that there is evidence to show that variations frequently occur along certain definite lines only.

Speed of Racehorses

Darwin's second assumption was that there is no limit to which variations may be accumulated in any direction; that by adding one minute variation to another through countless generations new species, new genera, new families may arise. This assumption, if applied to continuous or fluctuating variations, seems opposed to facts. All the evidence available goes to show that there is a definite limit to which minute variations can be accumulated in any given direction. No one has succeeded in breeding a dog as large as a horse, or a pigeon with a beak as long as that [69] of a snipe. In the case of racehorses, which have been selected so carefully through a long period of time, we seem to have reached the limit of speed which can be attained by the multiplication of insignificant variations. We do not wish to dogmatise, but we believe that of late years there has not been any material increase in the speed of our racehorses.

Mr S. Sidney says, on page 174 of Cassell's Book of the Horse: "As far as form went (pace Admiral Rous), the British racehorse had reached perfection in 1770, when 'Eclipse' was six years old." He quotes the measurements of the skeleton of "Eclipse" in the Museum of the Royal College of Surgeons as evidence of this. All the efforts of breeders, then, have failed appreciably to improve the form of the British racehorse in the course of over a century and a quarter.

Experiments of De Vries

De Vries has made some important experiments with a view to determining whether or not there is a limit to the amount of change which can be induced by the selection of fluctuating or continuous variations as opposed to mutations. "I accidentally found," he writes, on page 345 of Species and Varieties: their Origin by Mutation, "two individuals of the 'five-leaved' race (of clover); by transplanting them into my garden I have isolated them and kept them free from cross-fertilisation with the [70] ordinary type. Moreover, I brought them under such conditions as are necessary for the full development of their character; and last, but not least, I have tried to improve their character as far as possible by a very rigid and careful selection. . . . By this method I brought my strain within two years up to an average of nearly 90 per cent. of the seedlings with a divided primary leaf (such seedlings averaging five leaves in the adult). . . . This condition was reached by the sixth generation in the year 1894, and has since proved to be the limit, the figures remaining practically the same through all the succeeding generations. . . . I have cultivated a new generation of this race nearly every year since 1894, using always the strictest selection. This has led to a uniform type, but has not been adequate to produce further improvement." Similarly, De Vries found in the bulbous buttercup (Ranunculus bulbosus) a strain varying largely in the number of petals; therefore he tried by means of continuous selection of those flowers having the largest number of petals to produce a double flower, but was not able to do so. He succeeded in evolving a strain with an average number of nine petals, some individuals having as many as twenty or thirty; but even by breeding only from these last he could not increase the average number of petals in any [71] generation beyond nine. This was the limit to be obtained by the most rigorous selection of fluctuating variations.

Selection, based on fluctuating variation, does not, asserts De Vries, conduce to the production of improved races. "Only temporary ameliorations are obtained, and the selection must be made in the same manner every year. Moreover, the improvement is very limited, and does not give any promise of further increase." Notwithstanding prolonged efforts, horticulturists have not yet succeeded in breeding a biennial race of either beetroots or carrots that does not continually give rise to useless annual forms. Writing of the beet, De Vries says useless annual varieties "are sure to return each year. They are ineradicable. Every individual is in the possession of this latent quality, and liable to convert it into activity as soon as the circumstances provoke its appearance, as is proved by the increase of annuals in the early sowings"—that is to say, in circumstances favourable to the annual variety.

It will be urged perhaps that these experiments, which seem to show that there is a limit to which a species can be modified by the accumulation of fluctuating variations, cannot have been properly carried out, because all the various breeds of pigeons and other domestic animals clearly show that extraordinary differences [72] not only can, but have actually been produced by the selection of such variations. This objection is based upon the assumption that breeders have in the past dealt only with fluctuating variations. This assumption does not appear to be justified. It is exceedingly probable that most, if not all, the varieties of domesticated animals have originated in mutations. Take, for instance, the modern turbit pigeon; this has been derived from the old Court-bec, described and figured over two centuries ago by Aldrovandus.

31

De Vries goes so far as to assert that the various races of pears are all mutations; that each distinct flavour is a mutation, and that it is impossible to produce a new flavour by selecting fluctuating variations. Thus it would appear that in every case of the production of a new breed a mutation has occurred which has attracted the fancy of some breeder, and he has seized upon this and perpetuated it.

All the evidence available tends to show that there is a limit—and one which is quickly reached—to the amount of change that can be produced by the selection of fluctuating or continuous variations. We, therefore, seem driven to the belief that evolution is based on the kind of variation which Professor Bateson terms "discontinuous variation" and Professor De Vries calls "mutation."

[73]
Bateson on Variation

As long ago as 1894 Bateson published his Materials for the Study of Variation, in which he set forth a large number of cases of discontinuous variation which he had collected. He pointed out that species are discontinuous, that they are sharply separated one from another, whereas "environments often shade into one another and form a continuous series." How, then, he asked, if variations are minute and continuous, have these discontinuous species arisen? May not variation prove to be discontinuous, and thus make it clear why species are discontinuous?

On page 15 of the above-cited work we find: "The preliminary question, then, of the degree of continuity with which the process of evolution occurs has never been decided. In the absence of such a decision, there has nevertheless been a common assumption, either tacit or expressed, that the process is a continuous one. The immense consequence of a knowledge of the truth as to this will appear from a consideration of the gratuitous difficulties which have been introduced by this assumption. Chief among these is the difficulty which has been raised in connection with the building up of new organs in their initial and imperfect stages, the mode of transformation of organs, and, generally, the selection and perpetuation of minute variations. Assuming, then, that variations are minute, we are met by this familiar difficulty. We know [74] that certain devices and mechanisms are useful to their possessors; but from our knowledge of natural history we are led to think that their usefulness is consequent on the degree of perfection in which they exist, and that if they were at all imperfect, they would not be useful. Now it is clear that in any continuous process of evolution such stages of imperfection must occur, and the objection has been raised that natural selection cannot protect such imperfect mechanisms so as to lift them into perfection. Of the objections which have been brought against the theory of natural selection this is by far the most serious."

Bateson further pointed out that chemical compounds are not continuous, that they do not merge gradually each into the next, and suggested that we might expect a similar phenomenon in the organic world.

Elsewhere he says: "Let the believer in the efficacy of selection operating on continuous fluctuations try to breed a white or a black rat from a pure strain of black-and-white rats, by choosing for breeding the whitest or the blackest; or to raise a dwarf sweet pea from a tall race by choosing the shortest. It will not work. Variation leads and selection follows."

Work of Bateson and De Vries

But Bateson's views fell upon stony ground, because zoologists are mostly men of theory and not practical breeders. They laboured under the [75] delusion that mutations or

32

"sports" are rare in nature, and that when these do happen to occur they must of necessity be swamped by inter-crossing.

However, the discovery of the Abbé Mendel's account of his experiments on breeding mongrel sweet peas has opened the eyes of many zoologists, so that they have at last learned what practical breeders have known for untold years—namely, that sports have a way of perpetuating themselves. Moreover, Mendel was able to give a theoretical explanation of his discoveries, with the result that the believers in discontinuous variation have largely increased in number of late.

While we are unable to see eye to eye with Professor Bateson in all things, we gladly recognise the immense value of his work. Had his statements in 1894 received the attention they merited, zoological theory would to-day be considerably more advanced than it actually is.

Professor De Vries has gone farther than Bateson, having engrafted upon the Darwinian hypothesis the theory of mutations. He has done no small amount of experimental work, and has undoubtedly thrown much new light on the ways in which species arise. He is purely a botanist, so that he argues only from plants. Nevertheless, we believe that some of his conclusions are applicable to animals. We are far [76] from accepting his theory of mutations in toto. We are, however, convinced that he, like Bateson, is on the right track. There can be no doubt that a great many new forms have originated suddenly, by jumps, and not by imperceptibly slow degrees. Before giving a list of the names of some of the races, both plant and animal, which appear to have come into existence suddenly, it will be of advantage to consider for a little some of the more important conceptions of De Vries.

Varieties and Elementary Species

That eminent botanist, as we have already seen, insists on the distinction between fluctuating variations and mutations. The former correspond, for all practical purposes, to the continuous variations of Bateson, and the latter seem to be equivalent to his discontinuous variations.

According to De Vries, all plants display fluctuating variation, but only a small percentage exhibit the phenomenon of mutation. The most daring of his conceptions is, that the history of every species is made up of alternating periods of inactivity, when only fluctuating variations occur, and of activity when "swarms of species" are produced by mutation, and of these only a few at the most survive; natural selection, which De Vries likens to a sieve, determining which shall live and which shall perish.

[77]
As we have seen, De Vries does not believe that new species can arise by the accumulation of fluctuating variations. By means of these the race may be greatly improved, but nothing more can be accomplished. These variations follow Quetelet's law, which says that, for biological phenomena, deviations from the average comply with the same laws as the deviations from the average in any other case, if ruled by chance alone.

Very different in character are mutations. By means of these, new forms, quite unlike the parent species, suddenly spring into being. Mutations are said by De Vries to be of two kinds—those that produce varieties and those which result in new elementary species.

According to De Vries, those species of plants which are in a state of mutation (he refers to the species of the systematic botanists) are of a composite nature, being made up of a collection of varieties and elementary species. His conception of a variety is a plant that differs from the parent plant in the loss or suppression of one or more characters, while an elementary species differs from the parent form in the possession of some new and additional character. But we will allow him to speak for himself: "We can consider (page 141 Species and Varieties) the following as the principal difference between elementary species and varieties: that the first arise by the [78] acquisition of entirely new characters, and the latter by the loss of existing qualities, or by the gain of such peculiarities as may already be seen in other allied species. If we suppose elementary species and varieties originated by sudden leaps and bounds, or mutations, then the elementary species have mutated in the line of progression, some varieties have mutated in the line of retrogression, while others have diverged from the parental types in a line of digression or in the way of repetition. . . . The system (of the vegetable kingdom) is built up of species; varieties are only local and lateral, never of real importance for the whole structure."

De Vries asserts that these elementary species, when once they arise, breed true, and show little or no tendency to revert to the ancestral form. We can, says De Vries, ascertain only by experiment which plants are in the mutating state and which are not. The great majority, however, are not at present in the mutating state.

Mutations

The distinction between fluctuating variation and mutation has been roughly illustrated by the case of a solid block of wood having a number of facets, on one of which it stands. If the block be tilted slightly it will, when the force that has tilted it is removed, return to its old position. Such a gentle tilt may be compared to a fluctuating variation in an organism. If, however, the block be tilted to such an angle that when left to [79] itself the block does not return to its old position, but tips over and comes to rest on another facet, we have a representation of the kind of change indicated by a mutation.

The analogy is far from perfect, for it makes it appear that the smallest mutation must of necessity involve a departure from the normal type more considerable than that of the largest fluctuating variation. Now, although mutations ordinarily consist in considerable deviations from the mean or mode of the type, while continuous variations are usually minute deviations, it sometimes happens that the extreme fluctuations are more considerable than some mutations. Hence "fluctuating" describes this latter kind of variation more accurately than "continuous" does.

The test, then, of a mutation is not so much the amount of deviation as the degree in which it is inherited. Mutations show no tendency to a gradual return to the mean of the parent species; fluctuating variations do display such a tendency. A mutation consists, as M. E. East says, in the production of a new mode or centre for linear fluctuation; it is, as it were, a shifting of the centre of gravity; the centre about which those fluctuations which we call continuous variations occur.

As it is of considerable importance thoroughly to grasp the true nature of mutations or discontinuous [80] variations, and as some writers do not appear to realise wherein lies the essential difference between the two kinds of variation, we will, at the risk of appearing tedious, give a further illustration. Let A be a species of bird of which the average length of the wing is 20 inches, and let us suppose that individuals belonging to that species occur in which the length of the wing varies as much as 3 inches each side of the mean; thus it is possible to find individuals of this species with a wing as short as 17 inches, or as long as 23 inches. Let B be another species of which the average length of the wing is 17 inches, and let us suppose that a 3-inch variation on each side of the mean be found to occur. Individuals belonging to species B will occur which have a wing as short as 14 inches, or as long as 20 inches. Thus some individuals of the short-winged species will have longer wings than certain individuals of the long-winged species. Similarly, certain individuals of a species which display a mutation may show less deviation from the mean than some individuals showing a very pronounced fluctuating variation. In other words, even as by measuring the length of wing in the above example it was not always possible to say whether a given individual belonged to species A or B, so is it not always possible to say by looking at an individual that shows a considerable departure from the [81] mean whether that departure is due to a mutation or a fluctuating variation.

Law of Regression

It is only by watching the effect of the peculiarity on the offspring of its possessor that we are able to determine the nature of the variation. Where the peculiarity is due to a fluctuating variation the offspring will display the peculiarity in a diminished degree; but if the peculiarity be due to a mutation, the offspring are likely to display it in as marked a degree as the parent.

Fritz Müller and Galton conducted independently enquiries into the amount of the regression shown by the progeny of parents which have deviated from the average by fluctuating variation.

Müller experimented with Indian corn; Galton with the sweet pea.

Each found that where the deviation of the parents is represented by the figure 5, that of their offspring is usually 2, that is to say, the deviation they display is, on the average, less than half that of their parents.

Applying this rule to the hypothetical case given above, if two individuals of species A having a length of wing of 20 inches be bred together, their offspring will, on an average, have a length of wing of 20 inches, since neither parents showed any deviation from the mean. On the other hand, the offspring of 20-inch-wing individuals of species B would show, on an [82] average, a length of wing of only about 18¼ inches. They tend to return to that mode from which their parents had departed.

But suppose that the deviation of the parents in this case had been due, not to fluctuating variation, but to a mutation; this would mean that, owing to some internal change in the egg that produced each parent, 20 inches became the normal length of wing; that the normal length of wing had suddenly shifted from 17 inches to 20 inches.

The result of this would be that their offspring would have on an average a wing-length of 20 inches instead of 18¼ inches, that the centre of variation as regards length of wing had suddenly shifted from 17 to 20, that, in future, all fluctuating variations would occur on either side of 20 inches, instead of on either side of 17 inches as heretofore.

Thus a variation is a fluctuating one or a mutation according as it does or does not obey Galton's Law of Regression.

De Vries's Dictum

De Vries says that it is of the essence of mutations that they are completely inherited. This statement, although substantially true, fails to take into consideration the factor of fluctuating variation. For example, in the above instance if the two individuals of species B had mutated into forms with a 20-inch wing, their offspring will nevertheless vary inter se, some of them [83] will have wings shorter than 20 inches and others wings more than 20 inches in length. But the average wing-length of the offspring of the two mutating individuals will be 20 inches.

So much, then, for the practical difference between a mutation and a fluctuating variation. In Chapter V. we shall discuss the possible causes of the difference. By way of anticipation we may say that the suggestion we shall make is that a mutation is due to some rearrangement in the particles which represent that part of the organism in the fertilised egg, whereas a fluctuating variation is caused by variations in the particles themselves.

De Vries, it should be noted, bases his theory largely on experimental evidence. His dictum is "the origin of species is an object of experimental observation." He has, we consider, proved conclusively that among plants mutations sometimes occur, and, further, that in a mutating plant the same mutation tends to occur again and again. This latter is a most important fact, because it goes some way towards overcoming the difficulty urged by Darwin that isolated sports must be swamped by continual crossing with the normal type. If mutations arise in swarms, as De Vries asserts they do, then any particular mutation is likely, sooner or later, to cross with a similar mutation and so be able to perpetuate itself.

[84]
Mutating Plants

The classical example of a mutating plant is the evening primrose of the species Oenothera lamarckiana. This is described by De Vries as a stately plant, with a stout stem, attaining often a height of 1.6 metres or more. The flowers are large and of a bright yellow colour, attracting immediate attention, even from a distance. "This striking species," he writes, in Species and Varieties (p. 525), "was found in a locality near Hilversum, in the vicinity of Amsterdam, where it grew in some thousands of individuals. Ordinarily biennial, it produces rosettes in the first, and stems in the second year. Both the stems and the rosettes were seen to be highly variable, and soon distinct varieties could be distinguished among them.

"The first discovery of this locality was made in 1886. Afterwards I visited it many times, often weekly or even daily, and always at least once a year up to the present time. This stately plant showed the long-sought peculiarity of producing a number of new species every year. Some of them were observed directly in the field, either as stems or rosettes. The latter could be transplanted into my garden for further observation, and the stems yielded seeds to be sown under like control. Others were too weak to live a sufficiently long time in the field. They were discovered by sowing seed from indifferent plants of the wild locality in the garden. A third [85] and last method of getting still more new species from the original strain was the repetition of the sowing process, by saving and sowing the seed which ripened on the introduced plants. These various methods have led to the discovery of over a dozen new types, never previously observed or described." Some of these De Vries regards as varieties, in the sense in which he uses the words; others, he maintains, are real progressive species, some of which are strong and healthy, others weaker and apparently not destined to be successful. All these types proved absolutely constant from seed. "Hundreds of thousands of seedlings may have arisen, but they always come true and never revert to the original O. lamarckiana type. But some of them, however, are, like their parent form, liable to mutations." The case of the evening primrose is by no means an isolated one. De Vries cites several other instances of plants in a mutating state. "The common poppy," he says (p. 189), "varies in height, in colour of foliage and flowers; the last are often double or laciniated. It may have white or bluish seeds, the capsules may open themselves or remain closed, and so on. But every single variety is absolutely constant, and never runs into another when the flowers are artificially pollinated and the visits of insects excluded." Similarly the garden carnation sometimes gives rise to the wheat-ear form. "In this [86] variety," writes De Vries (p. 228), "the flower is suppressed, and the loss is attended by a corresponding increase in the number of pairs of bracts. This malformation results in square spikes, or somewhat elongated heads, consisting only of the greenish bracts. As there are no flowers, the variety is quite sterile, and, as it is not regarded by horticulturists as an improvement on the ordinary bright carnations, it is seldom multiplied by layering. Notwithstanding this it appears from time to time, and has been seen in different countries and at different periods, and what is of great importance for us, in different strains of carnations. Though sterile, and obviously dying out as often as it springs into existence, it is nearly two centuries old. It was described

36

in the beginning of the eighteenth century by Volckamer, and afterwards by Jaeger, De Candolle, Weber, Masters, Magnus, and many other botanists. I have had it twice at different times and from different growers." Similarly, the long-headed green dahlia arose twice over some years ago in the nursery of Messrs Zocher & Co.

Further, the peloric Toad-flax (Linaria vulgaris peloria) is, De Vries informs us, "known to have originated from the ordinary type at different times and in different countries under more or less divergent conditions." And, as this variety is wholly barren, it must in each instance have had an independent origin. Lastly, the [87] purple beech seems to be a mutation which has originated at least three times over.

Mutation Theory Criticised

Every one interested in biological theory should read both Species and Varieties and Plant Breeding by De Vries, works which are of incalculable value to the horticulturist and agriculturist as well as to the biologist.

While not wishing to detract in any way from the truly splendid work done by De Vries, we feel constrained to bring several charges against him.

Firstly, he suffers from the complaint that seizes nine out of ten originators of new theories. He pushes his theory to extreme lengths; he allows his imagination to run away with him. We do not think that on the evidence available he is justified in asserting that every species passes through alternating periods of comparative quiescence and periods in which it throws off, as mutations, swarms of elementary species. He is justified in asserting that discontinuous variation is by no means an uncommon phenomenon, but further than this it does not seem safe to go at present.

Secondly, he ought to lay more stress on the fact that Oenothera lamarckiana is a plant which does not appear to be known in the wild state, and that it is therefore possibly a hybrid plant, and the so-called elementary species which it gives off may be merely the varieties out of [88] which it has been built up. Boulenger and Bailey have both studied this plant, and they have not been able to witness all the mutations of which De Vries speaks, so that the former says, "The fact that Oenothera lamarckiana was originally described from a garden flower, grown in the Paris Jardin des Plantes, and that, in spite of diligent search, it has not been discovered wild anywhere in America, favours the probability that it was produced by crossing various forms of the polymorphic Oenothera biennis, which had been previously introduced in Europe."

Definition of a Species

It has further been objected that, even if these various forms which Lamarck's evening primrose throws off are true mutations, they ought not to be called new species, for they do not differ sufficiently from the parent species to deserve the name of new species. The reply to this criticism is that De Vries asserts that mutations produce new elementary species, which are not the same things as new species in the ordinary sense of the term. Most Linnæan species differ from one another to a far greater extent than do elementary species. It seems to us quite plain that new species arise, not by a single mutation, but by two or three successive mutations which occur in various parts of an organism.

First arises a well-marked variety, by a single mutation. Subsequent mutations follow, so that [89] a distinct race is produced. And, finally, fresh mutations occur, so that a new species is eventually produced.

What De Vries calls an elementary species the majority of systematists would call a well-marked variety.

We may take this opportunity of remarking that the definition of a species is one on which naturalists seem unable to agree.

So vast is the field of biology, that now-a-days biologists are compelled to specialise to some extent. Thus we have botanists, ornithologists, those who devote themselves to the study of mammals, those who confine themselves to reptiles, or insects, or fishes, or crustaceans, or bacteria, etc.

Now each class of systematists has its own particular criterion of what constitutes a species. Ornithologists do not seem very exacting. Most of them appear to consider a constant difference of colour sufficient for the formation into a species of the birds that display such a variation. Those who study reptiles, on the other hand, do not allow that a mere difference in colour is sufficient to promote its possessor to specific rank. Into these nice questions we cannot enter. For our purpose a species is a group of individuals that differ from all other individuals in displaying certain well-marked and tolerably constant characters, which they transmit to their offspring.

[90]
Our contention, then, is that new species, in the ordinarily-accepted use of the term, do not arise as a rule by one sudden bound (although they may sometimes do so), but are the result of the accumulation of several mutations or discontinuous variations. Some of these mutations are exceedingly well marked, while others are so small as to be indistinguishable from the more extreme fluctuating variations. Before passing on to consider some cases of well-marked mutations which have occurred among animals and plants, we should like to take this opportunity of pointing out that as regards experiments in evolution the botanist is far more favourably situated than the zoologist.

The botanist is able to reproduce many species vegetatively, e.g. by cuttings, and is thus easily able to multiply examples of mutation. He can also reproduce the great majority of plants by self-fertilisation, and so experiences no difficulty in "fixing" a new form. Again, plants are far easier to control than animals; as a rule they can be transplanted without any impairment of their capacity for breeding. Moreover, they produce a greater number of offspring than the most prolific of the higher animals. The animal breeder is thus at an obvious disadvantage as compared with the horticulturist. It is only with great difficulty that he can fix the mutations which appear in his stock.

[91]
"Scatliff Strain" of Turbit

The history of the production of the "Scatliff strain" of turbit affords a good example of the kind of difficulties that confront the breeder.

Pigeon fanciers require that the ideal turbit shall have, among other things, an unbroken "sweep," that is to say the line of the profile from the tip of the beak to the back of the head should be the arc of a circle. As a rule this line is broken by the overgrowth of the wattle at the base of the beak. Mr Scatliff, however, has succeeded in breeding a strain which possesses the required description of profile.

"In the year 1895," writes Mr H. P. Scatliff on page 25 of The Modern Turbit, "I visited Mr Houghton's lofts and purchased three or four extra stout and short-beaked stock birds. . . . The following year I mated one of these to one of my own black hens, and reared one of the most successful show birds ever bred, viz. 'Champion Ladybird,' a black hen. . . . Most of the leading judges and many turbit breeders remarked upon this hen's wonderful profile, which seemed to improve as she got older instead of getting worse, as is usual in rather coarse-wattled birds. I, too, had remarked this, and it opened my eyes to a point in turbit breeding which I had never heard mentioned by any turbit judges or breeders, and which I believe I am now pointing out for the first time in print, viz. that the feathers over her beak wattle which formed [92] her front grew from the top and right to the front of her wattle, and not from slightly behind, as in almost every other turbit of her day; thus, as the wattle developed and grew coarser, the front became more developed, and made her head larger without in any way spoiling the sweep of the profile.

"The same year 'Ladybird' was bred I bred eight others from the same pair, and with one exception all turned out to be hens. There was only one other hen, however (a dun), that had this same point, but in a lesser degree than 'Ladybird,' and from these two hens nearly all my blacks, and several of my blues are descended."

A TURBIT BELONGING TO MR. H. P. SCATLIFF
A TURBIT BELONGING TO MR. H. P. SCATLIFF

Mr Scatliff, having "spotted" this point, looked about him for another bird having the peculiarity, with the object, if possible, of fixing the same in his strain. He discovered this point in a pigeon belonging to Mr Johnston of Hull, and purchased the bird for £20. But it died in the following spring without producing for Mr Scatliff a single young one. The next year Scatliff found that a bird belonging to a Mr Brannam had the required peculiarity and so purchased him for £20. But that cock, too, died before anything was bred from him. Nothing daunted, Scatliff found that another of Brannam's cocks displayed the same peculiarity, so purchased him in 1899 for £15, but he also died before the [93] year was out. Meanwhile Scatliff had, by mating up "Ladybird" with the most likely of his own cocks, succeeded in producing one or two young cocks with the desired point. By breeding these with their mother "Ladybird" and their offspring again with "Ladybird," Scatliff eventually succeeded in breeding some turbits, both blacks and duns, with the required peculiarity fully developed, but not before he had spent a further sum of £55 on two other cocks, both of which died before they could be mated with the famous "Ladybird." However, amid all his misfortunes, Scatliff informs us that he bought one bird, by name "Amazement," which did assist him in fixing his strain. Thus Scatliff spent considerably over £100 in purchases, and took eight years fixing the peculiarity in question. Had "Ladybird" been a flower, the peculiarity could probably have been fixed in one generation by self-fertilisation.

This furnishes an excellent example of the trouble which breeders will take, and the expense to which they will go in order to produce a desired result. Nevertheless, it appears to be the fashion for scientific men to decry the work of the breeder.

Let us now pass on to consider the cases of mutations which are known to have occurred among animals.

[94]
Mutations among Animals

Some instances of great and sudden variation in domesticated animals have become classical, and been detailed in almost every work on evolution. These are, firstly, the celebrated hornless Paraguay cattle. This hornless breed, or rather the ancestor of the breed, arose quite suddenly.

Many domestic horned breeds of animals, especially sheep and goats, throw off hornless sports. Were a hornless breed of buffalo found in nature, it would undoubtedly be ranked a new species, and the Wallaceians would doubtless exercise much ingenuity in explaining how natural selection had brought about the gradual disappearance of the horns; and palæontologists, being baffled in their search for intermediaries between the hornless species and their horned ancestors, would complain of the imperfection of the geological record.

It may, perhaps, be argued that this hornless mutation was a direct result of the unnatural conditions to which the Paraguay cattle were subjected, it may be asserted that since there are no species of hornless cattle in nature, such mutations have never occurred under natural conditions, and hence the Paraguay cattle prove nothing. As a matter of fact, we know that in nature a great many mutations occur which are [95] not perpetuated because not beneficial to the species. A hornless individual in the wild state would stand but little chance in fighting for females against his horned brethren. We must keep clearly in mind that the theory of mutation does not seek to abolish natural selection; it merely affords that force something substantial to work upon.

The second classical example of a leap taken by nature is furnished by the Franqueiro breed of long-horned cattle in Brazil. These furnish us with an example of a mutation in the other direction. Then there is the Niata or bull-dog breed of cattle, which are also South American. These instances would seem to indicate that cattle are what De Vries would call "in a mutating state" in that part of the world.

The other classical examples of great and sudden variations are the Ancon sheep of Massachusetts, the Mauchamp breed of Merino sheep, the tufted turkeys, and the long-haired race of guinea-pigs.

The "wonder horses," whose manes and tails grow to an extraordinary length, so as to trail on the ground, may perhaps be cited as a race which originated in a sudden mutation. They are all descendants of a single individual, Linus I., whose mane and tail were respectively eighteen and twenty-one feet long. But in this case it is important to note that the parents and [96] grandparents of Linus I. had exceptionally long hair.

Mutations among Birds

Coming now to birds we find several undoubted examples of mutations, or new forms which have come suddenly into being.

The black-winged peafowl, whose peculiarities were commented on by Darwin, afford a striking example of this phenomenon. These birds breed true when mated together, and are known to have arisen from common peafowl in no less than nine instances. The cocks have the wings (except the primary quills), black glossed with blue and green, and have the thighs black, whereas, in the ordinary peacock, the same part of the wing is nearly all mottled black and pale buff, and the thighs are drab. The black-winged hen, on the other hand, is nearly white, but has a black tail and black speckling on the upper surface of the body, while her primary quills are cinnamon coloured as in male peafowl, not drab as in the normal hens. The young are white when hatched, the young cock gradually assuming the dark colour as he matures.

This mutation, which, in one case quoted by Darwin, increased among a flock of peafowl until the black-winged supplanted the ordinary kind, is so distinct in appearance in all stages that it was formerly supposed to be a true species (Pavo nigripennis), of which the wild habitat was unknown.

[97]
The Golden Pheasant (Chrysolophus pictus) produces, in domestication, the dark-throated form (C. obscurus), in which the cock has the throat sooty-black instead of buff, and the scapulars or shoulder feathers black instead of red. Moreover, the two middle-tail-feathers are barred with black and brown like the lateral ones, while in the ordinary form they are spotted with brown on a black ground. The hens have a chocolate-brown ground-colour instead of yellow-ochre as in the normal type. The chicks are likewise darker.

The common duck, in domestication, when coloured like the wild mallard, sometimes produces a form in which the chocolate breast and white collar of the drake are absent, the pencilled grey of the abdomen reaching up to the green neck. In this mutation the duck has the head uniformly speckled black and brown, and lacks the light eye-brow and cheek-stripes found in the normal duck. Both sexes have the bar on the wing dull black instead of metallic blue.

The ducklings which ultimately bear this plumage are sooty-black throughout, not black and yellow like normal ones.

The phenomenon of mutation is not confined to animals in a state of domestication. The common Little Owl of Europe (Athene noctua) has produced the mutation A. chiaradiæ in the wild state. In this the irides are dark, instead of [98] yellow as in the normal type, and the plumage of the back of the wings is longitudinally streaked with white instead of barred. Several examples of this form were found, along with normal young, in the nest of one particular pair of little owls in Italy, but the whole family were foolishly exterminated by local ornithologists.

The reed bunting (Emberiza schœniclus) exists in two distinct forms—one having a much stouter bill than the other (E. pyrrhuloides). This probably is an example of a mutation.

The rare yellow-rumped Finch (Munia flaviprymna), of Australia, has displayed a tendency to change into the allied and far commoner chestnut-breasted Finch (M. castaneithorax) during the lifetime of the individual (Avicultural Magazine, 1907). Conversely, the male of the common Red-billed Weaver (Quelea quelea) of Africa has been found in its old age to assume the characters of the comparatively rare Q. russi, its black throat becoming pale buff as in that form.

Everyone is familiar with the chequered variety of the common blue-rock pigeon, in which the wings are regularly mottled with black instead of being barred. This form sometimes occurs among wild birds, so that it has been described as a distinct species. It is important to note that there are red, dun, and silver chequers as well as blue ones.

YELLOW-RUMPED AND CHESTNUT-BREASTED FINCHES, WITH TRANSITIONAL SPECIMENS
YELLOW-RUMPED AND CHESTNUT-BREASTED FINCHES, WITH SPECIMENS IN TRANSITIONAL STATE

On the left, the yellow-rumped finch; on the right, the chestnut-breasted; birds in state of change in the middle.

[99]
A well-marked mutation which appears regularly in nature is the red-headed variety of the beautiful Gouldian Finch (Pöephila mirabilis) of North Australia. Normally the head of the cock is black, but in about ten per cent. of the individuals the cock has a crimson head, while that of the hen is dull crimson and black.

Mutations which occur with such regularity are certainly rare. On the other hand, there are certain mutations which we may expect to see appear in any species of plant or animal.

Albinistic forms are a case in point, and less frequently we see white varieties which are not pure albinos, because the eye retains some at least of the normal pigment. As examples, we may cite white dogs, cats, fowls, horses, ducks, geese, and Java sparrows

41

among domesticated animals, and the white forms of the Amazonian dolphin and of the giant Petrel of the South seas (Ossifraga gigantea) among wild creatures.

In a white mutation the eye may lose all its pigment, and then we have a true albino. Such forms on account of their imperfect vision cannot survive in a state of nature, hence no wild pink-eyed species are known.

Or the eye may display a partial loss of pigment, as, for example, in the white domestic forms of the common goose, the Chinese goose, and the Muscovy duck. Finn saw a case in which the eyes of a pink-eyed rabbit changed [100] after death into this type of eye—that is, with the pupil black and the iris blue. It is to be observed that this kind of eye sometimes occurs in coloured horses, rabbits, and dogs. Finally, we have white mutations in which the eye loses none of the pigment. These are abundant in nature, and probably most of the white species of birds—as, for example, some egrets, swans, etc.—arose in this way.[4] Pure white species are comparatively uncommon in nature, because, except in snow-clad regions, white creatures are easily seen by their adversaries. Most white birds are of considerable size, and well able to look after themselves.

Similarly black mutations occur frequently among animals, both under domestication and in a state of nature. All are familiar with black dogs, cats, horses, fowls, ducks, pigeons. Black mutations, however, do not occur nearly so frequently as white ones. So far as we are aware no black mutation has been recorded among canaries, geese, guinea-fowl, ferrets, Java sparrows or doves, all of which produce white mutations.

On the other hand, in the wild state black species occur more frequently than normal-eyed white forms. This is probably because such [101] creatures are less conspicuous than white ones. As examples of black mutations which occur in nature, we may cite black leopards, water rats, squirrels, foxes, barking deer (Cervulus muntjac), hawk-eagles, harriers, peppered moth (Amphidasys betularia), etc.

That many black species have arisen as sudden mutations from lighter-coloured animals seems tolerably certain from the facts that in Malacca the black leopard forms a local race; that some of the Gibbon apes are as often black as light coloured; that the American black bear is sometimes brown, while the other bears, when not brown, are almost invariably black.

Color Mutations

Not uncommon, although rarer than black or melanistic forms, are reddish or chestnut varieties. These occur both among tame and wild animals. Among domesticated creatures, sandy cats, "red" pigeons, buff fowls, chestnut horses, red guinea pigs afford examples of this mutation. Among wild animals many of the species of squirrel, not naturally red, produce red mutations; and some of the grey owls—as, for example, the Indian race of the Scops (Scops giu)—throw off a red or chestnut form. As everyone knows, some species are normally red.

Green or olive species not unfrequently throw off yellow mutations. As examples of these we may cite yellow canaries, yellow budgerigars (Melopsittacus undulatus), goldfish, golden tench, [102] and the golden form of the common carp among captive animals; and among animals in a state of nature, yellow forms have been recorded of the rose-ringed Paroquet (Palæornis torquatus), the green woodpecker, the pike, and the eel. These lutinistic forms usually have normally coloured eyes. Sometimes, but only very rarely, these yellow forms throw off white sports—as, for example, the "silver" form of the goldfish. Finn has seen a white variety of the common carp. White canaries are excessively rare, while white budgerigars are unknown.

It is worthy of note that entirely yellow species of birds and fish are unknown. We would suggest that the explanation of this is that yellowness is correlated with some physical characteristic unfavourable to an organism exposed to the struggle for existence; hence individuals which are yellow are not permitted to survive. In some species of moths individuals occur in which the parts normally red are yellow. According to Bateson, a chalk pit at Madingly, near Cambridge, has long been known to collectors as a habitat of a yellow-marked form of the six-spot Burnet Moth (Zygæna filipendulæ). These lutinistic forms are not confined to one genus of Butterflies. Moreover, in the Pin-tailed Nonpareil Finch (Eythrura prasina) of the Eastern Archipelago the red tail and other red parts of the plumage are not infrequently replaced by [103] yellow in wild individuals of either sex and of any age. In the blue-fronted Amazon parrot (Chrysotis æstiva)—a most variable bird—the normally red edge of the pinion is sometimes yellow. Bateson, in his Materials for the Study of Variation, gives other examples of this kind of variation.

Mutations among Invertebrates

As further instances of mutations among animals which have been observed in nature, we may mention the valezina form of the female of the Silver-washed Fritillary Butterfly (Argynnis paphia) and the helice form of the female Clouded-yellow Butterfly (Colias edusa).

The common jelly-fish is an organism which frequently throws off sports, and some zoologists are of opinion that the medusoid Pseudoclytia pentata arose by a discontinuous variation from Epenthesis folleata or a closely allied form. Thomson discusses this particular case at some length on pages 87-89 of his Heredity, and gives it as his opinion that the evidence in favour of this latter having arisen as a mutation is "exceedingly strong."

Mutating Species

It is our belief that many species of birds which occur in nature have been derived from other species which still exist, but as no one has ever seen the mutation take place, we cannot furnish any proof thereof. We merely rely on the fact that the species in question differ so slightly from one another that there seems every [104] likelihood that they have suddenly arisen and managed to establish themselves alongside of the parent species.

The Curassows, Crax grayi, C. hecki, each of which is only known by a very few specimens, appear to be mutations of the female of the globose Curassow, Crax globicera. The fact that when a female hecki bred in the London Zoological Gardens with a male globicera, the solitary young one which lived to grow up was a pure globicera, renders the assumption almost certain.

The Chamba Monaul (Lophophorus chambanus) seems to be a mutation of the male of the common Monaul or Impeyan Pheasant (Lophophorus impeyanus), the common species of the Himalayas.

The Three-coloured Mannikin (Munia malacca) of South India is probably simply a white-bellied form of the widely-ranging Black-headed Mannikin (M. atricapilla), which has the abdomen chestnut like the back. Intermediate wild-caught forms have been recorded.

The African Cordon-bleu (Estrelda phœnicotis) and Blue-bellied Waxbill (E. cyanogastra) would also seem to be mutations, as almost the only difference between them lies in the fact that the male of the former has a crimson cheek-patch, which is wanting in the latter.

The Ringed Finch (Stictoptera annulosa) of [105] Java, and Bicheno's Finch (S. bichenovii) of Australia, only differ in the former having the rump black, while in the latter it is white, and this difference appears to be of the nature of a mutation.

So, it might be urged, is the pure white breast of the male Upland Goose (Chloëphaga magellanica), which part, in the very similar C. dispar, is barred as in the females, the latter form being probably the ancestor.

The differences between the silver-grey-necked Crowned Crane of the Cape (Balearica chrysopelargus) and the dark-necked species of West Africa (B. regulorum) seem also to be not more than could be accounted for by mutation.

Peculiar forms, such as a rabbit with a convoluted brain or a mouse with a peculiar pattern of molar teeth, have been come upon by anatomists.

The above-cited mutations are all very considerable ones, and we do not profess to have mentioned a tenth part of those which have actually been recorded.

We trust that we have collected and set forth sufficient evidence to show that the phenomenon of discontinuous variation is a very general one, and this would seem to tell against the hypothesis of De Vries that species pass through alternate periods of comparative stability and periods when swarms of mutations appear. We [106] think it more probable that all species throw off at greater or less intervals discontinuous variations, and that it is upon these that natural selection acts.

We further hope that we have succeeded in making clear what we believe to be the very sharp distinction between continuous and discontinuous variations, even when the latter are inconsiderable, as frequently happens.

Somatic and Germinal Variations

Before leaving the subject of variation it is necessary to notice the distinction, which Weismann was the first to emphasise, between somatic and germinal variations.

Every adult organism must be regarded as the result of two sets of forces; inherited tendencies or internal forces, and the action of environment or external forces. The differences which the various members of a family show are due in part to the initial differences in the germinal material of which they are composed, and in part to the differences of their environment. The former differences are the result of what we may call germinal variations, and the latter the result of somatic variations. It is scarcely ever possible to say of any particular variation that it is a germinal or a somatic one, because even before birth a developing organism has been subjected to environmental influences. One of a litter may have received more nourishment than the others. Nevertheless, any marked variation which appears [107] at birth is probably largely germinal. According to Weismann and the majority of zoologists, there is a fundamental difference between these germinal and somatic variations, in that the former tend to be inherited, while the latter are never inherited. Weismann believes that very early in the formation of the embryo the cells which will form the generative organs of the developing organism are separated off from those cells which will go to build up the body, and become as much isolated from them as if they were contained in a hermetically-sealed flask, so that they remain totally unaffected by any changes which the environment effects in the somatic cells. Therefore, says Weismann, acquired characters cannot be inherited.

While the majority of zoologists believe that acquired characters are not inherited, probably not many will go so far as Weismann and declare that the environment cannot exercise any effect whatever on the germ cells.

Somatic Variations

Even though acquired characters or variations are not inherited, it does not follow that they do not play an important part in evolution. Acquired variations are the result of the way in which an organism reacts to its environment. If an organism is unable to react to its environment it must inevitably perish. If it is able to react, it matters not, so far as the chances of survival of the organism are concerned, whether the adaptation [108] is the result of a congenital variation or a somatic one. This will be rendered clear by a hypothetical example. Let us suppose that a certain mammal is forced, owing to the intensity of the struggle for existence, to migrate into the Arctic regions. Let us further suppose that this organism is preyed upon by some creature that hunts by sight rather than by scent. Let us yet further imagine that this predacious species is swifter than our animal, on which it preys. It is obvious that, other things being equal, the more closely the creature preyed upon assimilates to its surroundings the more likely is it to escape the observation of its foes, and so to survive and give birth to offspring. Now suppose that the glare from the snow-covered ground bleaches its coat. This whitening of the fur is a somatic variation, one which is induced by the environment. Such an animal will be as difficult to see, if the bleaching is such as to render it snow-white, as if its whiteness were due to a germinal variation. Thus, as regards its chances of survival, it matters not whether its whiteness be the result of germinal or somatic variation. But if the whiteness is due to a somatic variation, its offspring will show no tendency to inherit the variation; they will have in turn to undergo the bleaching process. If, on the other hand, the whiteness is due to a germinal variation, the offspring will tend to inherit this peculiarity and [109] to be born white. In such a case, it is unlikely that the fur of an organism which is naturally coloured will be completely bleached by the snow, and, even if it be, the bleaching process will take time, meanwhile the creature will be comparatively conspicuous. So that those which are naturally whiter than the average, that is to say, those in which the tendency to whiteness appears as a germinal variation, will be less conspicuous than those which tend to be the ordinary colour. Thus the former will enjoy a better chance of survival, and will be likely to transmit their whiteness to their offspring in so far as it is due to a germinal or congenital variation.

Thus, although none of the whiteness due to somatic variations is transmitted to the offspring, such variations are of considerable importance to the species, as they enable it to survive and allow time for the germinal variations in the required direction to appear.

That this case need not be purely hypothetical is shown by the fact that dun domestic pigeons, which are of an earthy-brown colour when fresh moulted, soon fade in the sun to a dull creamy hue. Thus a coloration adapted to an ordinary soil could soon be suited to a desert environment. The ruddy sheldrake also, normally a bright chestnut-coloured bird, and one that haunts exposed sunny places, in many cases fades very much, becoming almost straw-coloured.

[110]
Many variations which organisms display are of a mixed kind, being in part the result of inner forces and in part due to the action of the environment. In so far as they are due to this latter they do not appear to be inherited.

Thus, although we cannot say of many variations whether they are germinal, or somatic, or of a mixed kind, it is of great importance to keep continually in mind the fundamental differences between the two kinds.

Some somatic variations are due to the direct action of the environment; they are merely the expression of the manner in which an organism responds to external stimuli.

45

What is the cause of germinal variations? This is a question to which we are not yet in a position to give a satisfactory answer.

The attempt to explain their origin plunges us into the realm of theory. This doubtless is a realm full of fascination, but it is an unexplored region of extreme darkness, in which, we believe, it is scarcely possible to take the right road until more of the light of fact has been shed upon it.

In the chapter dealing with inheritance we shall indicate the lines along which it is likely that future progress will be made.

[111]

CHAPTER IV
HYBRIDISM

The alleged sterility of hybrids a stumbling-block to evolutionists—Huxley's views—Wallace on the sterility of hybrids—Darwin on the same—Wallace's theory that the infertility of hybrids has been caused by Natural Selection so as to prevent the evils of intercrossing—Crosses between distinct species not necessarily infertile—Fertile crosses between species of plants—Sterile plant hybrids—Fertile mammalian hybrids—Fertile bird hybrids—Fertile hybrids among amphibia—Limits of hybridisation—Multiple hybrids—Characters of hybrids—Hybridism does not appear to have exercised much effect on the origin of new species.

The alleged sterility of the hybrids produced by crossing different species has long proved a great stumbling-block to evolutionists. Huxley, in particular, felt the force of this objection to the Darwinian theory. If the hybrids between natural species are sterile, while those of all the varieties which the breeder has produced are perfectly fertile, it is obviously quite useless for evolutionists to point with pride to the results obtained by the breeder, and to declare that his products differ from one another to a greater extent than do many well-recognised species.

[112]
"After much consideration, and with no bias against Mr Darwin's views," wrote Huxley to the Westminster Review in 1860, "it is our clear conviction that, as the evidence now stands, it is not absolutely proven that a group of animals having all the characters exhibited by species in nature, has ever been originated by selection, whether natural or artificial. Groups having the morphological nature of species, distinct and permanent races, in fact, have been so produced over and over again; but there is no positive evidence at present that any group of animals has, by variation and selective breeding, given rise to another group which was in the least degree infertile with the first. Mr Darwin is perfectly aware of this weak point, and brings forward a multitude of ingenious and important arguments to diminish the force of the objection. We admit the value of these arguments to the fullest extent; nay, we will go so far as to express our belief that experiments, conducted by a skilful physiologist, would very probably obtain the desired production of mutually more or less infertile breeds from a common stock in a comparatively few years; but still, as the case stands at present, this little 'rift within the lute' is not to be disguised or overlooked."

Alleged Sterility of Hybrids

Similarly Wallace writes, at the beginning of chapter vii. of his Darwinism: "One of the greatest, or perhaps we may say the greatest, of [113] all the difficulties in the way of accepting the theory of natural selection as a complete explanation of the origin of species, has been the remarkable difference between varieties and species in respect of fertility when crossed. Generally speaking, it may be said that the varieties of any one species, however different they may be in external appearance, are perfectly fertile when crossed, and their mongrel offspring are equally fertile when bred among themselves; while distinct species, on the other hand, however closely they may resemble one another externally, are usually infertile when crossed, and their hybrid offspring absolutely sterile. This used to be considered a fixed law of nature, constituting the absolute test and criterion of a species as distinct from a variety; and so long as it was believed that species were separate creations, or at all events had an origin quite distinct from that of varieties, this law could have no exceptions, because if any two species had been found to be fertile when crossed and their hybrid offspring to be also fertile, this fact would have been held to prove them to be not species but varieties. On the other hand, if two varieties had been found to be infertile, or their mongrel offspring to be sterile, then it would have been said—These are not varieties, but true species. Thus the old theory led inevitably to reasoning in a circle, and what might be [114] only a rather common fact was elevated into a law which had no exceptions."

Thus the sterility of hybrids was a zoological bogey which had to be demolished. The plan of campaign adopted by Darwin and Wallace was, firstly, to try to disprove the assertion that the hybrids between different species are always sterile, and secondly, to find a reason for the alleged sterility of these hybrids.

Fertile Hybrids

Darwin succeeded in obtaining some examples of crosses between botanical species which were said to be fertile. These he quotes in chapter viii. of The Origin of Species. As regards animals, he met with less success. "Although," he writes, "I do not know of any thoroughly well-authenticated cases of perfectly fertile hybrid animals, I have some reason to believe that the hybrids from Cervulus vaginalis and reevesii, and from Phasianus colchicus and P. torquatus and with P. versicolor are perfectly fertile. There is no doubt that these three pheasants, namely, the common, the true ring-necked, and the Japan, intercross, and are becoming blended together in the woods of several parts of England. The hybrids from the common and Chinese geese (A. cygnoides), species which are so different that they are generally ranked in distinct genera, have often been bred in this country with either pure parent, and in one single instance they have [115] bred inter se. This was effected by Mr Eyton, who raised two hybrids from the same parents but from different hatches; and from these two birds he raised no less than eight hybrids (grandchildren of the pure geese) from one nest. In India, however, these cross-bred geese must be far more fertile; for I am assured by two eminently capable judges, namely, Mr Blyth and Captain Hutton, that whole flocks of these crossed geese are kept in various parts of the country; and as they are kept for profit, where neither pure parent species exists, they must certainly be highly fertile.[5] . . . So again there is reason to believe that our European and the humped Indian cattle are quite fertile together; and from facts communicated to me by Mr Blyth, I think they must be considered as distinct species."

Darwin does not seem to have been very satisfied with the evidence he had collected, for he said: "Finally, looking to all the ascertained facts on the intercrossing of plants and animals, it may be concluded that some degree of sterility, [116] both in first crosses and in hybrids, is an extremely general result; but that it cannot, under our present state of knowledge, be considered as absolutely universal."

Similarly Wallace writes: "Nevertheless, the fact remains that most species which have hitherto been crossed produce sterile hybrids, as in the well-known case of the mule; while almost all domestic varieties, when crossed, produce offspring which are perfectly fertile among themselves."

Darwin resorted to much ingenious argument in his attempt to explain what he believed to be the almost universal sterility of hybrids, as opposed to mongrels or crosses between varieties. He pointed out that changed conditions tend to produce sterility, as is evidenced by the fact that many creatures refuse to breed in confinement, and believed that the crossing of distinct wild species produced a similar effect on the sexual organs. He expressed his belief that the early death of the embryos is a very frequent cause of sterility in first crosses.

Wallace thus summarises Darwin's conclusions as to the cause of the sterility of hybrids: "The sterility or infertility of species with each other, whether manifested in the difficulty of obtaining first crosses between them or in the sterility of the hybrids thus obtained, is not a constant or necessary result of species difference, but is incidental [117] on unknown peculiarities of the reproductive system. These peculiarities constantly tend to arise under changed conditions owing to the extreme susceptibility of that system, and they are usually correlated with variations of form or of colour. Hence, as fixed differences of form and colour, slowly gained by natural selection in adaptation to changed conditions, are what essentially characterise distinct species, some amount of infertility between species is the usual result."

A Biological Bogey

But Wallace has not been content to let the matter remain where Darwin left it. He has boldly tried to make an ally of this bogey of the infertility of hybrids. On page 179 of Darwinism he argues, most ingeniously, that the sterility of hybrids has been actually produced by natural selection to prevent the evils of the intercrossing of allied species. We will not reproduce his argument for the simple reason that it is now well-known, or should be well-known, that hybrids between allied species are by no means always sterile. The doctrine of the infertility of hybrids seems to have been founded on the fact that the hybrids best known to breeders, namely the cross between the ass and the horse, and those between the canary and other finches, are sterile.

[118]
Fertile Crosses between Species of Plants

In the case of plants the number of fertile hybrids between species is so large that we cannot attempt to enumerate them. De Vries cites several instances in Lecture IX of his Species and Varieties: Their Origin by Mutation.

One of these—the hybrid between the purple and the yellow species of Lucerne which is known to botanists as Medicago media is, writes De Vries, "cultivated in some parts of Germany on a large scale, as it is more productive than the ordinary lucerne." Other examples of perfectly fertile plant hybrids cited by De Vries are the crosses between Anemone magellanica and A. sylvestris, between Salix alba and Salix pentandra, between Rhododendron hirsutum and R. ferrugineum.

He gives an instance of a hybrid—Ægilops speltæformis, which, though fertile, is not so fertile as a normal species would be. It is worthy of note that Burbank of California has obtained a hybrid between the blackberry and the raspberry, which is not only fertile, but quite popular as producing a novel fruit.

Sterile Plant Hybrids

De Vries does not cite nearly so many examples of sterile hybrids, presumably because they are not so easy to find. He mentions the sterile [119] "Gordon's currant," which is considered to be a hybrid between the Californian and the Missouri species. He also gives Cytisus adami as an absolutely sterile hybrid, this being a cross between two species of Labernum—the common and the purple.

48

In the case of animals the known hybrids are so much less numerous that we are able to furnish a list which may be taken as fairly exhaustive.

Fertile Mammalian Hybrids

Taking the mammals first, we find that, in addition to those cited by Darwin, there are several recorded cases of crosses between well-defined species which are fertile.

There is the hybrid between the brown bear and the polar bear, which is perfectly fertile. In the London Zoological Gardens there is a specimen of this hybrid, also one of this individual's offspring by a pure polar bear.

The stoat has been crossed with the domestic ferret, a descendant of the polecat, a very distinct species; the resulting hybrids have nevertheless proved fertile.

The bull American bison produces with the domestic cow hybrids known as "cataloes," which are fertile. The reverse cross of the domestic bull with the bison cow does not, however, succeed at all, which reminds us of what happens in the case of finch-hybrids.

[120]
Bird fanciers when crossing the canary with wild species of finch, almost invariably use a hen canary as the female parent, because domesticated female animals breed more readily than do captive wild ones.

The domestic yak breeds frequently in the Himalayas with the perfectly distinct zebu or humped cow of India, and the hybrids are fertile. Yet the zebu and the Indian buffalo, living constantly side by side in the plains of India, never interbreed at all.

Among wild ruminants of this hollow-horned family, the Himalayan Argali (Ovis ammon) ram, a giant sheep of the size of a donkey, has been known to appropriate a herd of ewes of the Urial (O. vignei), a very distinct species of the size of a domestic sheep. Many hybrids were born, and these, in turn, bred with the pure urials of the herd.

In our parks the little Sika deer of Japan (Cervus sika), a species about the size of the fallow-deer, with an even more marked seasonal change of colouration and antlers having only three tines, breeds with the red deer, and the hybrids are fertile.

In certain parts of Asia Minor the natives cross the female one-humped camel with the male of the bactrian or two-humped species. The hybrids (which are one-humped) will breed with the pure species; but, although the hybrids are [121] strong and useful, the three-quarter bred beasts are apparently of little value.

Fertile Bird Hybrids

Coming to birds, we are confronted by a longer list of fertile hybrids. This is the natural outcome of the fact that a greater number of bird species have been kept in captivity.

The oldest known fertile hybrid is that between the common and Chinese geese above cited, but many others have since been recorded. Even among birds so seldom bred, comparatively, as the parrot family, a fertile hybrid has been produced, that between the Australian Rosella Parrakeet (Platycercus eximius) and Pennant's Parrakeet (P. elegans). The hybrid was first described as a distinct species, the Red-mantled Parrakeet (P. erythropeplus). These two parrakeets, though nearly allied, are very distinct; Pennant's being coloured red, blue, and black, with a distinct young plumage of uniform dull green; the rosella in addition to the above colours displays much yellow and some white and green. It is, moreover, considerably smaller and has no distinct youthful dress.

The Amherst Pheasant (Chrysolophus amherstiæ) and the Gold Pheasant (C. pictus) have long been known as producing hybrids which are fertile either inter se or with the parents. Here the species are still more distinct; not only [122] are the leading colours of the Amherst white and green, instead of red and gold, but it is a bigger bird with a larger tail and smaller crest, and a bare patch round the eyes.

The Pintail Duck (Dafila acuta) and the Mallard or Wild Duck and its domestic descendants (Anas boscas), when bred together, produce hybrids which have been proved fertile between themselves and with the pure pintail. Any sportsman or frequenter of our parks can see for himself the distinctness of the species concerned.

The Pied Wagtail (Motacilla lugubris) and the Grey Wagtail (M. melanope) have produced hybrids in aviaries, which have proved fertile. The two species are distinct in every way, as all British ornithologists know.

The Cut-throat Finch (Amadina fasciata) and Red-headed Finch (A. erythrocephala) of Africa have hybridised in aviaries, and the produce has proved fertile. The red-headed finch, among other differences, is far larger than the cut-throat, and the males have the head all red, not merely a throat-band of that colour.

The Japanese Greenfinch (Ligurinus sinicus) which is not green, but brown and grey, with bolder yellow wing- and tail-markings than our larger European greenfinch, has produced fertile hybrids with this latter bird.

MALE AMHERST PHEASANT
MALE AMHERST PHEASANT

The chief colours of this species (Chrysolophus amherstiæ), are white and metallic green, so that it is very different in appearance from its near ally the gold pheasant.

The Red Dove of India (Oenopopilia tranquebarica) has produced hybrids with the tame [123] Collared Dove (T. risorius) and these have bred again when paired with the red species. O. tranquebarica, although presenting a general similarity to the collared dove, is truly distinct, being much smaller, with a shorter tail, and displaying a marked sex-difference (the male only being red, and the female drab). Its voice is also utterly unlike the well-known penetrating and musical coo of the Collared Dove.

There is a large class of fertile wild hybrids produced between forms differing only in colour, such as those between the Hooded Crow (Corvus cornix) and Carrion Crow (Corvus corone), the various species of Molpastes bulbuls, and the Indian Roller (Coracias indica) and Burmese Roller (C. affinis). Indeed, it may be said that wherever two such colour-species meet they hybridize and become more or less fused.

In this connection sportsmen, as mentioned by Darwin, performed unconsciously a most interesting experiment when, more than a century ago, they introduced largely into their coverts the Chinese Ring-necked Pheasant (Phasianus torquatus) and the Japanese P. versicolor. So freely has the former bred with the common species already present there (Phasianus colchicus) that nowadays nearly all our English pheasants show traces of the cross in the shape of white feathers on the neck, or the green tinge of the plumage of the lower back. The influence of the Japanese [124] Green Pheasant (P. versicolor) has been very slight.

It is, of course, open to anyone to assert that such crosses are not true hybrids, as the species are not fully distinct, but mere colour-mutations.

The fact of the intermingling, however, is a fatal blow to the theory of recognition marks, since it demonstrates that merely distinctive colouring is not a preventative of cross-breeding. To this matter we shall return later.

Fertile Hybrids among Amphibia

Our Crested Newt (Molge cristata) and the Continental Marbled Newt (M. marmorata) interbreed in France, in the wild state, and the resulting hybrid was at first described as a distinct species, under the name of Molge blasii. These two newts differ greatly in appearance. In the Marbled Newt the colouration is brilliant green and black above, and shows no orange below, thus differing much from that of the Crested Newt, which is black above and mottled with orange beneath, while the crest of the breeding-male of this species lacks the notches which are so conspicuous in that of the Crested Newt.

HARLEQUIN QUAIL (Coturnix delegorguei)
HARLEQUIN QUAIL
(Coturnix delegorguei)

RAIN QUAIL (Coturnix coromandelica)
RAIN QUAIL
(Coturnix coromandelica)

The markings on the throats of these quails are of the type usually put down as "recognition marks," but as the Harlequin Quail is African and the Rain Quail Indian, the two species cannot possibly interbreed. The pattern, then, can have no "recognition" significance.

Insects

Among insects, M. de Quatrefages states that the hybrid progeny of the silk-moths Bombyx [125] cynthia and B. arrindia are fertile for eight generations when bred inter se.

Limits to the Possibilities of Hybridisation

Hybrids can apparently only be produced between species of the same natural family. The stories of cat-rabbits, deer-ponies, fowl-ducks, and similar distant crosses invariably break down on close examination. A belief in such remote crosses characterized the ancient "bestiaries," and still lingers, as witness the falsely-reputed crosses alluded to above.

This belief has no doubt arisen from the fact that the domestic breeds of dogs, fowls, etc., are popularly confounded with truly distinct species. Mongrels are well known to be readily produced, and hence the notion arises that hybrids between the most widely-separated species are possible.

In practice, the most remote cross of which authenticated specimens exist is that between the red grouse and the domestic fowl (bantam cock). It is true that the grouse are commonly ranked by ornithologists as a family distinct (Tetraonidae) from that of the pheasants and partridges (Phasianidae), to which the fowl belongs; but the relationship is admittedly very close, and we doubt if general zoologists would countenance the maintenance of the families as distinct. Ornithologists are notoriously apt to [126] over-rate small differences when drawing up a classification. It would be therefore safe to say, in the present state of our knowledge, that species belonging to different natural families cannot hybridize.

In some cases multiple hybrids have been produced. Thus, at the London Zoological Gardens, many years ago, a hybrid between the Gayal of India (Bos frontalis) and the Indian humped cow mentioned above was put to an American bison, and produced a double hybrid calf.

M. G. Rogeron of Angers bred many hybrids from a male pochard and a duck bred from a Mallard and a Gadwall.

More recently, Mr J. L. Bonhote has succeeded in combining the blood of five wild species of ducks in one individual.

Mr J. T. Newman has also bred turtle-doves containing the blood of three distinct species.

A cross, which usually results in sterile offspring, may in very rare cases produce a fertile individual; thus, Mr A. Suchetet once succeeded in obtaining a three-quarter-bred bird from the not uncommon hybrid of the tame pigeon and tame collared dove (Turtur risorius), which is usually barren, by pairing it with a dove; but the bird thus produced, when again paired with a dove, was itself sterile. Some of the cases here given seem to encourage [127] Darwin's view that domestication tends to eliminate sterility; but it is doubtful if this can be upheld. The hybrid between the Muscovy duck (Cairina moschata) and common duck is usually, at all events, sterile, like that between the pigeon and dove; yet all these birds have been long domesticated. The hybrid between the fowl and the guinea-fowl is likewise barren, nor has the long domestication of the horse and ass lessened the sterility of the mule.

Characters of Hybrids

Some facts may be noted respecting the characters of hybrids. In the first place, it is important to notice that the characters of the hybrid vary according to the sexes of the species concerned; thus, the "hinny," which is bred from a horse and a she-ass, is a different animal from the true "mule," which is bred from the jackass and mare, and is inferior to it.

Similarly, Mr G. E. Weston, a great authority on British cage-birds and their hybrids, informs us that when hybrids are bred from a male canary and a hen goldfinch or siskin— contrary to the almost universal practice of using the hen canary for crossing—the progeny are inferior in size and colour to the hybrids obtained in the ordinary way.

Hybrids, in animals at all events, differ from crosses between mutations or colour-variations in not exhibiting the phenomenon of alternative inheritance; they do not follow one parent or [128] the other exclusively, but always exhibit some blending of the characters of both, which is, after all, what might have been expected, since well-defined species usually differ in more than one character.

Thus, the cross between the Amherst and gold pheasants chiefly resembles the latter, but has the ruff white as in the Amherst, while the crest, though in form it resembles that of the gold species, is not yellow as in that species, nor red as in the Amherst, but of an intermediate tint, brilliant orange.

The mule between the horse and ass, as all know, combines the shapes of the two parents, though in colour it follows the horse rather than the ass.

When two remote species, one or each of which possesses some distinctive structural peculiarity, are crossed, the hybrid does not inherit such points. The guinea-fowl has a helmet, and a pair of wattles on the upper jaw; the common fowl a comb, and a pair of wattles on the lower jaw; but in the hybrid no comb, helmet, or wattles are present.

The Muscovy drake has a bare red eye-patch, and the male of the common duck curled middle-tail feathers; in the hybrid neither of these peculiarities is reproduced.

In a cross between nearly-related forms, the peculiarity of one species may be reproduced in [129] a modified form in the hybrid; for instance, in that between the blackcock (Tetrao tetrix) and the capercailzie (T. urogallus), the forked tail of the former reappears to a small extent in the hybrid.

Very interesting are those cases in which the hybrid resembles neither parent, but tends to be like an altogether distinct species, or to have a character of its own. Thus the hybrids between the pied European and chestnut African sheldrakes (Tadorna cornuta and Casarca cana), now in the British Museum, bear a distinct resemblance to the grey Australian sheldrake (C. tadornoides). In pheasants, also, the crosses between the common and gold, common and Amherst, gold and Japanese, and gold and Reeves' pheasants, widely different as all these birds are in colouration, are remarkably alike, being all chestnut-coloured birds with buff median tail-feathers. These may be seen in the British Museum. This phenomenon, together with the above-noted disappearance of specialised features in hybrids, is possibly comparable to the "reversion" observed when widely-distinct domestic breeds are crossed, and so may give us an idea of the appearance of the ancestors of the groups of species concerned.

In the few cases wherein several generations of hybrids have been bred inter se, there seems to have been no reversion to the original pure [130] types, such as happens when colour-forms are crossed.

M. Suchetet bred hybrid gold = Amherst pheasants for four generations, and they retained the hybrid character. The young bred by Darwin from a pair of common = Chinese geese hybrids "resembled," he says, "in every detail their hybrid parents."

Wild Hybrids

When hybrids have been—as has far more usually been the case—bred back to one of the pure stocks, the hybrid characters have shown, as might be expected, a tendency quickly to disappear. The three-quarter-bred polar bear now in the London Zoological Gardens is a pure polar save for a brown tinge on the back. A three-quarter Amherst = gold pheasant in the British Museum is a pure Amherst save for the larger crest, and a patch of red on the abdomen. When three-quarter-bred pintail = common duck hybrids were bred back to the pintail, the offspring "lost all resemblance to the common duck." In the case of the Argali-urial herd of wild sheep above-mentioned, after the usurping Argali ram had been killed by wolves, the hybrids bred with the urials, with the result that the herd renewed the appearance of pure urial.

Thus, except in the very improbable case of a family of hybrids going off and starting a colony by themselves, the effect of hybridism on the evolution of species seems likely to have been [131] nil. It is, however, curious that three-quarter-bred animals have rarely, if ever, been recorded in a state of nature, though a good many wild-bred hybrids are on record.

This points to some unfitness for the struggle for existence even in a fertile hybrid. It is necessary to emphasise the fact that wild hybrids are always exceedingly rare as individuals, in spite of what has been said as to the number of recorded crosses.

More hybrid unions have been noted among the duck family than anywhere else in the animal kingdom. Nevertheless Finn never once saw a hybrid duck for sale in the Calcutta market, although for seven years he was constantly on the look-out for such forms; nor does Hume record any such specimen in his Game Birds and Wild Fowl of India.

The hybrid which occurs most commonly as an individual is that between the blackcock and capercailzie, which is recorded yearly on the Continent; but it appears to be sterile, and so has no influence on the species.

Wild hybrids between mammals are far rarer even than bird hybrids, the only ones which seem to be on record being those between the Argali and Urial above alluded to; those between the brown and blue hares and the common and Arctic foxes.

A consideration of the phenomena of hybridism [132] thus leads us to the conclusion that, although many hybrids are fertile, the crossing of distinct species has exercised little or no effect on the origin of species. Even where allied species, like the pintail and the mallard ducks, whose hybrid offspring is known to be fertile, inhabit the same breeding area and occasionally interbreed in nature, such crossing does not, for some reason or other, appear to affect the purity of the species.

Very different, of course, is the effect of crossing a mutation within a species with the parent form; the offspring are, as we shall see, likely to resemble one or other of the parents; so that, if the mutation occur frequently enough and be favourable to the species, the new form may in course of time replace the old one.

[133]

CHAPTER V
INHERITANCE

Phenomena which a complete theory of inheritance must explain—In the present state of our knowledge it is not possible to formulate a complete theory of inheritance—Different kinds of inheritance—Mendel's experiments and theory—The value and importance of Mendelism has been exaggerated—Dominance sometimes imperfect—Behaviour of the nucleus of the sexual cell—Chromosomes—Experiments of Delage and Loeb—Those of Cuénot on mice and Castle on guinea pigs—Suggested modification of the generally-accepted Mendelian formulae—Unit characters—Biological isomerism—Biological molecules—Interpretation of the phenomena of variation and heredity on the conception of biological molecules—Correlation—Summary of the conception of biological molecules.

We have seen that variations may be, firstly, either acquired or congenital, and, secondly, fluctuating or discontinuous. We have further seen that acquired variations—at all events in the higher animals—do not appear to be inherited, and therefore have not played a very important part in the evolution of the animal world. Discontinuous congenital variations or mutations are the usual starting points of new species. It is not unlikely that fluctuating congenital variations, although they do not appear to give rise directly to new species, may play a [134] considerable part in the making of new species, inasmuch as they may, so to speak, pave the way for mutations.

We are now in a position to consider the exceedingly difficult question of inheritance. We know that offspring tend to resemble their parents, but that they are always a little different both from either parent and from one another. How are we to account for these phenomena? What are the laws of inheritance, whereby a child tends to inherit the peculiarities of its parents, and what are the causes of variation which make children differ inter se and from their parents?

Scores of theories of inheritance have been advanced. It is scarcely exaggerating to assert that almost every biologist who has paid much attention to the subject has a theory of inheritance which differs more or less greatly from the theory held by any other biologist.

As regards the phenomena of heredity we may say Tot homines tot sententiæ.

Phenomena of Inheritance

For this state of affairs there is a good and sufficient reason. We are not yet in possession of a sufficient number of facts to be in a position to formulate a satisfactory theory of inheritance. A complete theory of heredity must explain, among other things, the following phenomena:—

1. Why creatures show a general resemblance to their parents.

[135]
2. Why they differ from their parents.

3. Why the members of a family display individual differences.

4. Why the members of a family tend to resemble one another more closely than they resemble individuals belonging to other families.

5. Why "sports" sometimes occur.

6. Why some species are more variable than others.

7. Why certain variations tend to occur very frequently.

8. Why variations in some directions seem never to occur.

9. Why a female may produce offspring when paired with one male of her species and not when paired with another male of the species.

10. Why organisms that arise by parthenogenesis appear to be as variable as those which are sexually produced.

11. Why certain animals possess the power of regenerating lost parts, while others have not this power.

12. Why most plants and some of the lower animals can be produced asexually from cuttings.

13. Why mutilations are not inherited.

14. Why acquired characters are rarely, if ever, inherited.

15. Why the ovum puts forth the polar bodies.

16. Why the mother-cell of the spermatozoa produces four spermatozoa.

[136]
17. Why differences in the nature of the food administered to the larvæ of ants determines whether these shall develop into sexual or neuter forms.

18. Why the application of heat, cold, etc., to certain larvæ affects the nature of the imago, or perfect insect, to which they will give rise.

19. Why the females in some species lay eggs which can produce young without being fertilised.

20. Why some species exhibit the phenomena of sexual dimorphism, while others do not.

21. In addition to all the above, a satisfactory theory of inheritance must account for all the varied phenomena which are associated with the name of Mendel. It must explain the various facts with which we have dealt in the chapter on hybridism, why some species produce sterile hybrids when intercrossed, while others give rise to fertile hybrids, and yet others form no offspring when crossed; why the hinny differs in appearance from the mule, etc.

22. It must explain all the facts which constitute what is known as atavism.

23. It must account for the phenomenon of prepotency.

24. It must explain the why and the wherefore of correlation.

25. It must tell us the meaning of the results of the experiments of Driesch, Roux, and others.

[137]
26. It must render intelligible the effects of castration on animals.

Existing Theories Unsatisfactory

Now, no existing theory of heredity can give anything approaching a satisfactory explanation of all these phenomena.

It is for this reason that we refrain from critically examining, or even naming, any of them.

We are convinced that in the present state of our knowledge it is not possible to formulate anything more than a provisional hypothesis.

It must not be thought that we consider the various theories that have been enunciated to be of no value. Erroneous hypotheses are often of the greatest utility to science, for they set men thinking and suggest experiments by means of which important additions to knowledge are made.

We now propose to set forth certain facts of inheritance, and from these to make a few deductions—deductions which seem to be forced upon us.

We would ask our readers to distinguish carefully between the facts we set forth, and the conclusions we draw therefrom. The former, being facts, must be accepted.

The interpretations we suggest should be rigidly examined, we would say regarded with suspicion, and all possible objections raised. It is only by so doing that any advance in knowledge can be made.

[138]
By inheritance we mean that which an organism receives from its parents and other ancestors—all the characteristics, whether apparent or dormant, it inherits or receives from its parents. Professor Thomson's definition—"all the qualities or characters which have their initial seat, their physical basis, in the fertilised egg cell"—seems to cover all cases except those where eggs are parthenogenetically developed.

The first fact of heredity which we must notice is that inheritance may take several forms. This is apparent from what was set forth in the chapter dealing with hybrids.

Types of Crosses

In considering the phenomena of inheritance it is convenient to deal with crosses in which the parents do not closely resemble one another, because by so doing we are able readily to follow the various characters displayed by each parent. It may, perhaps, be urged that such crosses occur but rarely in nature. This is true. But we should bear in mind that any theory of inheritance must explain the various facts of cross-breeding, so that, from the point of view of a theory of inheritance, crosses are as important as what we may term normal offspring. As inheritance is so much easier to observe in the former, it is but natural that we should begin with them. Our deductions must, if they be valid ones, fit all cases of ordinary inheritance, i.e. all cases where the offspring results from the [139] union of parents which closely resemble one another. Now, when two unlike forms inter-breed, their offspring will fall into one of six classes.

I. They may exactly resemble one parent, or rather the type of one parent, for, of course, they will never be exactly like either parent; they must of necessity display fluctuating variations. The cases in which the offspring exactly resemble one parent type in all respects are comparatively few. They occur only when the parents differ from one another in one, two, or at the most three characters. Thus when an ordinary grey mouse is crossed with a white mouse the offspring are all grey, that is to say, they resemble the grey parent type. Although they are mongrels or hybrids, they have all the appearance of pure grey mice. This is what is known as unilateral inheritance.

II. The offspring may resemble one parent in some characters and the other in other characters. They may have, for example, the colour of one parent, the shape of the other, and so on. Thus if a pure, albino, long-haired, and rough-coated male guinea-pig be crossed with a coloured, short-haired and smooth-coated female, all the offspring are coloured, short-haired, and rough-coated. That is to say, they take after [140] the father in being rough-coated, but after the mother in being pigmented and short-haired. This form of inheritance is usually seen only in crosses between two types which differ in but few of their characters.

III. The offspring may display a blend of the characters of the two parents. They may be intermediate in type. They are not of necessity midway between the two parents; one of the parents may be prepotent. The crosses between the horse and the ass show this well. Both the mule, where the ass is the sire, and the hinny, where the horse is the sire, are more like the ass than like the horse; but the hinny is less ass-like than the mule. The offspring between a European and a native of India furnishes a good case of blended inheritance; Eurasians are neither so dark as the Asiatic nor so fair as the European.

IV. The offspring may show a peculiarity of one parent in some parts of the body and the peculiarity of the other parent in other parts of the body. This is known as particulate inheritance. The piebald foal, which is the result of a cross between a black sire and a white mare, is a good example of such inheritance. This does not appear to be a common form of inheritance.

V. The usual kind of inheritance is perhaps a combination between the forms II. and III. [141] In such cases the offspring display some paternal characters and some maternal ones, and some characters in which the maternal and paternal peculiarities are blended. An example of inheritance of this description is furnished by a cross between the golden and the amherst pheasants.

VI. The offspring may be quite unlike either parent. For example, Cuénot found that sometimes a grey mouse when crossed with an albino produces black offspring.

Mendel's Experiments

The first two kinds of inheritance were carefully investigated by Gregor Johann Mendel, Abbot of Brunn. The results of his experiments were published in the Proceedings of the Natural History Society of Brunn, in 1854, but attracted very little notice at the time.

Mendel experimented with peas, of which many varieties exist. He took a number of varieties, or sub-species, which differed from one another in well-defined characters, such as the colour of the seed coat, the length of the stem, etc. He made crosses between the various varieties, being careful to investigate one character only at a time. He found that the offspring of such crosses resembled, in that particular character, one only of the parents, the other parent apparently exerting no influence on it. Mendel [142] called the character that appeared in the off-spring dominant, and the character which was suppressed, recessive. Thus when tall and short varieties were crossed the offspring were all tall. Hence Mendel said that tallness is a dominant character, and shortness a recessive character. Mendel then bred these crosses among themselves, and found that some of the offspring resembled one grandparent as regards the character in question while some resembled the other, and he found that those that showed the dominant character were three times as numerous as those that displayed the recessive character. He further found that all those of the second generation of crosses which displayed the recessive character bred true; that is to say, when they were bred together all their descendants exhibited this characteristic. The dominant forms, however, did not all breed true; some of them produced descendants that showed only this dominant character, others, when crossed, gave rise to some forms having the dominant character and some having the recessive character.

It is thus evident that organisms of totally different ancestry may resemble one another in external appearance. In other words, part of the material from which an organism is developed may lie dormant.

Mendelism

From the above results Mendel inferred, in [143] the case of what he called alternating characters, that only one or other of the pair can appear in the offspring, that they will not blend. If both parents display one of the opposing characters, the offspring will of course show it. But if one parent display one character and the other the opposing character, the hybrid offspring will display one only, and that which is dominant. The other character is suppressed for the time being. When, however, these hybrids are bred inter se, their gametes or sexual cells split up into their component parts, and then the recessives are free to unite with other recessives and thus produce offspring which show the recessive character.

His results can be set forth in symbols.

Let T stand for the tall form and D for the dwarf form. Since the offspring are composed of both the paternal and maternal gamete, we may represent them as TD. But dwarfness is, as we have seen, recessive, so that the offspring all look as though they were pure T's. When, however, we come to breed these TD's inter se, the gamete or sex-cell of each individual crossed breaks up into its component parts T and D, which unite with other free T or D units to form TD's or TT's or DD's. What are the possible combinations? A D of one parent may meet and unite with a D of the other parent, so that the resulting cells will be pure D, i.e. DD, and will give rise to pure dwarf [144] offspring. Or the D gamete from one parent may unite with a T gamete from the other parent, and the result will be a TD cross, but this, as we have seen, will grow up to look like a pure T, i.e. will become a tall organism. Similarly, a T gamete from one parent may unite with a T gamete of the other, and produce a pure tall form, or it may unite with a D and produce a hybrid TD, which gives rise to a tall form. Thus the possible combinations of offspring are DD, DT, TD, TT, but all these three last contain the dominant T gamete, and so develop into tall offspring; therefore, ex hypothesi, we shall have three tall forms produced to one dwarf form, but of these three tall forms two are not pure, and do not breed true. Mendel's experimental results accorded with what we should expect to obtain if the above explanation were correct. Hence the inference that there is such a splitting of the gametes in the sexual act seems a legitimate one.

Mendel's experiments are of great importance, for they give us some insight into the nature of the sexual act. But, as is usual in such cases, Mendel's disciples have greatly exaggerated the value and importance of his work. It is necessary to bear in mind that Mendel's results apply only to a limited number of cases—to what we may call balanced characters. In the case of characters which [145] do not balance one another, which are, so to speak, not diametrically opposed to one another, Mendel's law does not hold. A second important point is, that the dominance is in many cases not nearly so complete as it should be if the Mendelian formula correctly represented what actually occurs in nature. Further, the segregation of the gametes does not appear to be so complete as the above hypothesis requires it to be. The phenomena of inheritance seem to be far more complex than the thorough-going Mendelian would have us believe.

Let it be noted that it is not to the facts of Mendelism, but to some portions of what we may call the Mendelian theory, that we take exception.

Maturation of the Germ-cells

Before passing on to consider some of the later developments of Mendelism, it is necessary for us to set forth briefly certain of the more important facts regarding the sexual act which the microscope has brought to light. We propose to state these only in the merest outline. Those who are desirous of pursuing the subject farther are referred to Professor Thomson's Heredity.

The germ cells, like all other cells, consist of a nucleus lying in a mass of cytoplasm. The nucleus is composed of a number of rod-like bodies, which are called chromosomes, because they are readily stainable.

[146]
These chromosomes appear, under ordinary circumstances, to be joined together end to end, and then look like a rope in a tangle.

When a cell is about to divide into two, these chromosomes become disjoined and can then be counted, and it is found that each cell of each species of animal or plant has a fixed number of these chromosomes. Thus the mouse and the lily have twenty-four chromosomes in each cell, while the ox is said to have sixteen of them per cell.

When a cell divides into two, each of these chromosomes splits by a longitudinal fissure into two halves, which appear to be exactly alike. One-half of every chromosome passes into each of the daughter cells, so that each of these is furnished with exactly half of each one of the rod-like chromosomes. In the cell division, which takes place immediately before the male gamete or generative cell meets the female gamete, the chromosomes do not divide into equal halves, as is usually the case. In this division half of them pass into one daughter cell and half into the other daughter cell, so that, prior to fertilisation both the male and the female gametes contain only half the normal number of chromosomes. In the sexual act the male and the female chromosomes join forces and then the normal number is again made up, each parent contributing exactly one half.

[147]
Experiments of Delage and Loeb

59

Biologists, with a few exceptions, seem to be agreed that these chromosomes are the carriers of all that which one generation inherits from another. Thus the cardinal facts of the sexual act are, firstly, prior to fertilisation the male and the female gamete each part with half their chromosomes; and, secondly, the fertilised cell is composed of the normal number of chromosomes, of which one-half have been furnished by each parent. Thus the microscope shows that the nucleus of the fertilised egg is made up of equal contributions from each parent. This is quite in accordance with the observed phenomena of inheritance.

But Delage has shown that a non-nucleated fragment of the ovum in some of the lower animals, as, for example, the sea-urchin, can give rise to a daughter organism with the normal number of chromosomes when fertilised by a spermatozoon. Conversely, Loeb showed that the nucleus of the spermatozoon can be dispensed with. Thus it seems that either the egg or the spermatozoon of the sea-urchin contains all the essential elements for the production of the perfect larva of a daughter organism. We are, therefore, driven to the conclusion that the fertilised ovum contains two sets of fully-equipped units. Only one of these seems to contribute to the developing organism. If this set happens to be composed of material derived from one only of the parents, [148] we can see how it is that we get unilateral inheritance in the case of a cross. Where, however, the units from the two parents intermingle, although only one set is active in development, the result will be blended inheritance. Thus, we may regard the fertilised egg as made up of two sets of characters—a dominant set, which is active in the production of the resulting organism, and a recessive set, which appears to take little or no part in the production of the organism.

This is quite in accordance with Mendelian conceptions.

Let X be an organism having the unit characters A B C D E F G, and let Y be another organism having the unit characters a b c d e f g.

Now suppose that these behave as opposed Mendelian units, and that the unit characters in italics are dominant ones. Then the resulting individual will resemble each parent in certain unit characters. It may be represented by the formula a B c d E f G, but it will contain the characters A b C D e F g in a recessive form, so that its complete formula may be written a B c d E f G $\quad$ } $\qquad$ A b C D e F g

When these hybrids are paired together it will be possible to get such forms as A B C D E F G $\quad$ A B C D E F G and a b c d e f g a b c d e f g which exactly resemble the [149] respective grandparents, and these should breed absolutely true, if the segregation of the gametes is as pure as the Mendel's law seems to require.

Experiments of Cuénot and Castle

There are, however, certain facts, which recent experimenters have brought to light, that seem to show that the segregation is not so complete as the law requires. For example, the so-called pure extracted forms may be found, when bred with other varieties, to have some latent characters. Thus Cuénot observed that extracted pure albino mice, that is to say, those derived from hybrid forms, did not all behave alike when paired with other mice. Those which had been bred from grey × white hybrids behaved, on being crossed, differently to those that had been bred from black × white hybrids; and further, those derived from yellow × white hybrids yielded yet other results on being intercrossed. Castle records similar phenomena in the case of guinea-pigs, and accordingly draws a distinction between recessive and latent characters. Recessive characters are those which disappear when they come into contact with a dominant character, but reappear whenever they are separated from the opposing dominant character. Latency is defined by Castle as "a condition of activity in which a normally dominant character may exist in a recessive individual or gamete."

[150]

The ordinary Mendelian pictures a unit character in a cross that obeys Mendel's law, as follows:— D   R, the dominant character only showing. It seems to us that each unit character should be represented as a double entity, thus D(D), the portion within the bracket being latent. The cross would appear to be represented by the formula D(R)

R(D), since the union appears to take the form of the transfer of the dormant latent characters. Now an extracted pure recessive will, on this hypothesis, bear the formula R(D)   R(D). When such recessives are crossed the two dormant portions will ordinarily change places, and never appear, so that these extracted recessives will, under ordinary circumstances, appear to be as pure as the true pure recessives, which are represented by the formula R(R)   R(R). Now, suppose that, from some cause or other, it is possible for the latent D to change places with the visible R, it is obvious that the impure nature of the extracted and hitherto apparently pure recessives will become manifest. This seems to be what happens under certain circumstances to the extracted albino mice. They [151] possess latent the character of their dominant ancestor.

Unit Characters

Mendelian phenomena force upon us the conclusion that organisms display a number of unit characters, each of which behaves in much the same way as a radicle does in chemistry, inasmuch as for one or more of these characters others can be substituted without interfering with the remaining unit characters. For example, it is possible to replace the chemical radicle NH_3 by the radicle Na_2; e.g. $(NH_3)_2SO_4$ (ammonium sulphate) may be transformed into Na_2SO_4 (sodium sulphate).

The conclusion that each organism is composed of a number of unit characters, which sometimes behave more or less independently of one another, is one which most biologists who have studied the phenomena of inheritance appear to have arrived at. Zoologists are mostly of opinion that these characters, or rather their precursors, exist as units in the fertilised egg. Very varied have been the conceptions of the nature of these biological units. Almost every biologist has given a name to his particular conception of them. Thus we have the gemmules of Darwin, the unit characters of Spencer, the biophors of Weismann, the micellæ of Naegeli, the plastidules of Haeckel, the plasomes of Wiesner, the idioblasts of Hertwig, the pangens of De Vries, and so on. It is unnecessary to [152] extend this list. It must suffice that almost every investigator of the phenomena of inheritance believes in these units, and calls them by a different name. Moreover, each clothes them with characteristics according to his taste or the fertility of his imagination.

Chemical Molecules

These units behave in such a way as to suggest to us an analogy between them and the chemical molecules. The sexual act would appear to resemble a chemical synthesis in some respects. One of the most remarkable phenomena of chemistry is that of isomerism. It not infrequently happens that two very dissimilar substances are found, upon analysis, to have the same chemical composition, that is to say, their molecules are found to be composed of the same kind of atoms and the same number of these. Thus chemists are compelled to believe that the properties of a molecule are dependent, not only on the nature of the atoms which compose it, but also on the arrangement of these within the molecule. To take a concrete example: Analysis shows that both alcohol and ether are represented by the chemical formula C_2H_6O. In other words, the molecule of each of these compounds is made up of two atoms of the element Carbon, six of the element Hydrogen, and one of the element Oxygen. Now, every chemical atom possesses the property which chemists term valency, in other words, the number of other atoms with which [153] it can directly unite is strictly limited. All atoms of the same element have the same valency. Monovalent atoms are those which can, under no circumstances, unite with more than one other atom. The Hydrogen atom is an example of such an atom. Divalent atoms, as, for example, that of Oxygen, can unite with one other atom of similar valency or with two monovalent atoms. Similarly, a trivalent atom, such as that of Nitrogen, can unite with three monovalent atoms.

A tetravalent atom, such as that of Carbon, can combine with four monovalent atoms. There are also pentavalent and hexavalent atoms. Now, by indicating the valency of any given atom by a stroke for each monovalent atom with which it is able to combine, chemists have been able to represent the molecule of every compound, or, at any rate, of every inorganic compound, by what is known as a graphic or structural formula. Thus, ethylic alcohol is represented by the formula:—

```
    H              H
    |              |
    H   —     C       —     C    —     O    —
      H = C2H6O,
    |              |
    H              H
```

and methylic ether by the structural formula:—

```
    H                        H
    |                        |
    H   —     C     —     O     —     C    —
      H = C2H6O.
    |                        |
    H                        H
```
[154]

The formulæ indicate a very different arrangement of the nine atoms which compose the molecule in each case. And to this different arrangement the differing properties of the two compounds are supposed to be due. A rough illustration of the phenomenon of isomerism is furnished by written language. Thus, three different words can be made from the letters t, a, and r, e.g. tar, art, and rat. They also form tra, which does not happen to be an English word, although it might have been one.

Experiments of Gräfin von Linden

Among organisms we sometimes observe a phenomenon which looks very like isomerism. The classical example of this is furnished by the butterflies Vanessa prorsa and Vanessa levana.

At one time these were supposed to belong to different species, since they differ so greatly in appearance. Vanessa levana is red, with black and blue spots. Vanessa prorsa is deep black, with a broad yellowish-white band across both wings. It is now known that the levana is the spring form and the prorsa the summer and autumn form of the same species. The pupæ of levana produce the prorsa form, but Weismann found that after being placed in a refrigerator they emerged, not as prorsa, but partly as levana and partly as another form intermediate in many respects between levana and prorsa. Weismann also succeeded, by exposing the winter pupa to a [155] high temperature, in making it give rise to the prorsa form, and not to the levana form, as it would ordinarily do.

Similar results have been obtained with the seasonally dimorphic Pieris napi. Standfuss, the Gräfin von Linden, and others have obtained like results in the case of other seasonally dimorphic butterflies. In some instances it has been proved that the change in the pigment is a purely chemical one; a similar transformation can be effected in the extracted pigment. But, we must bear in mind that the changes which are induced in this way are not confined to colour; they occur in the marking and shape of the wing.

Even more remarkable is the fact that in some sexually dimorphic species a change of temperature alters the female, so as to cause her to have the outward appearance of the male. For example, it has been found that warmth changes the colours of the female Rhodocera rhamni and Parnassius apollo into the colours of the male.

62

By applying rays of strong light, electric shock, or centrifuge, the Gräfin von Linden was able to change the colours of the butterflies to which the caterpillars gave rise. Pictet experimented on twenty-one species of butterflies, or rather on their caterpillars, and found that in nearly all cases when the caterpillars ate unusual food, they developed into butterflies with abnormal [156] colouring. Schmankewitsch made the discovery that, in the case of the crustacean Artemia, he could produce either of two species according to the amount of salt in the water in which these creatures were placed. He declared that the anatomical differences between the species Artemia salina and Artemia milhausenii depended solely on the percentage of the salt in the surrounding water. He further stated that by adding still more salt he could change the Artemia into a new genus—Branchipus. More recent observers have cast doubt upon these results of Schmankewitsch. They, however, admit that the degree of salinity of the water has some effect on the form of the Artemia, although they suggest that factors other than concentration affect the result. In any case, it is now well-known that changes in the environment effect changes in the colouring of many crustacea. Pictet has shown that the alternating wet and dry seasons in some tropical countries are the cause of, or stimulus that induces, seasonal dimorphism in some butterflies. He was able to effect changes in the colouring of certain species by means of humidity.

The most important cases, from our point of view, are those in which the application of heat or cold to a pupa has affected the colour, shape, etc., of the emerging butterfly. Here we have but one factor, that of temperature. All [157] the material for the formation of the butterfly is already stored up in the pupa. The unit characters, or their precursors, are all there, and they take one form or another according to the stimulus applied.

Biological Isomerism

Phenomena of this kind can, we think, be accounted for only on the assumption that the unit characters affected are each developed from a definite portion of the fertilised egg, that each of these portions, these precursors of the unit characters, is, like a chemical molecule, made up of a number of particles, and that upon the arrangement of these particles in its precursor in the egg depends the form that the unit character derived from it will take. One arrangement of these particles gives rise to one form of unit character, while another arrangement will give rise to a totally different form of unit character.

Thus, some organisms seem to display a biological isomerism akin to chemical isomerism, save that the particles which in organisms take the place of chemical atoms are infinitely more complex.

In other words, the precursors in the fertilised egg of each of these unit characters behave in some respects like chemical molecules.

In order to avoid the manufacture of fresh terms we may speak figuratively of the germ cells as being composed of biological molecules, [158] which in their turn are built up of biological radicles and atoms. These behave in some ways like chemical molecules, radicles, and atoms, as the case may be.

Biological Molecules

It seems legitimate to regard each unit character in the adult as the result of the development of one or more of the biological molecules which compose the nucleus of the fertilised egg. These biological molecules are, of course, a million-fold more complex than chemical molecules. Each biological atom must contain within itself a number of the very complex protoplasmic molecules. This view of the structure of the germ cell seems to force itself upon the observer. Notwithstanding this, the conception will have no value unless it seems to throw light on the various phenomena of heredity, variation, etc.

Let us then try to interpret some of these.

Each chemical element is made up of atoms which are all of the same kind, but no two elements are made up of the same kind of atoms, although chemists are now inclined to conceive of all the various kinds of atoms as made up of varying amounts of some primordial substance. In any case, the molecules of chemical compounds are made up of various kinds of atoms. With biological atoms the case would seem to be different. All would appear to be made up of the same kind of substance, and the differences shown by the various unit characters that go to [159] make up an organism would seem to be due to the different numbers and the varying arrangement of the biological atoms which compose the molecules from which unit characters are derived. This would be quite in accordance with the chemical notion of allotropy. Thus, the graphite and the diamond molecules are both made up of the same kind of atoms.

But the biological atoms are living, that is to say, they are continually undergoing anabolism and katabolism, growth and decay. They exhibit all the phenomena of life, they must grow and divide, and they must absorb nourishment; hence it is not surprising that they should differ slightly among themselves, that they should exhibit the phenomenon of variation. Although probably all are composed of the same living material, no two are exactly alike, hence the molecules formed by them will also differ from one another. Thus we can see why it is that all organisms exhibit fluctuating variations.

Very different are the discontinuous variations or mutations. These would seem to be due to either a rearrangement of the biological atoms in the biological molecule or the splitting up of the latter into two or more molecules. This, of course, is pure hypothesis. Let us take an imaginary example. Suppose that a biological molecule contains eighteen biological atoms, and that these are arranged in the form of an equilateral [160] triangle, six of them going to each side. Suppose now, that from some cause or other they rearrange themselves to form an isosceles triangle, so that only four form the base and seven go to each of the remaining sides. Such an arrangement would give rise to a mutation. Suppose now that, from some cause or other, this triangular biological molecule were to split up into two triangles, each having three atoms to each side, we should obtain a still more marked mutation. We are far from saying that the atoms in the organic molecule ever take such forms. We have merely attempted to give rough but simple illustrations of the kind of processes which on this hypothesis might be expected to take place in the germ cells or the fertilised eggs.

Let us now consider the sexual act from this aspect. The various molecules (we speak, of course, of biological molecules) of the male parent meet those of the female parent, and a synthesis occurs, which results in the formation of a new organism. When these two sets of gametes meet one another, one of several events may happen. The gametes may refuse to combine. This will occur whenever they are of very different constitution; thus it is that widely differing species will not interbreed. But it may even happen that gametes of individuals of the same species may refuse to coalesce on account of some peculiarity in the composition of one or [161] other of them. Secondly, they may be able to form some sort of a union, but, owing to their diverse nature, the resulting molecules may be so complex that they cannot be broken up into equal halves, and as this seems to be necessary for the sexual act, the resulting organism will be sterile. Thirdly, the two sets of gametes may enter into a proper union, that is to say, form new molecules, but these may be of such different structure to the molecules of the gametes, that the resulting offspring will be quite unlike their parents in appearance. Fourthly, some or all the groups of radicles in each gamete may be united so closely that in the sexual act they do not break up, but enter bodily into the new resulting organism. In these circumstances the inheritance of the offspring will follow Mendel's law. Fifthly, there may be some slight disturbance of the molecule, perhaps one or only a few atoms will be replaced by those of the other gamete. This would give us impure dominance.

Thus this hypothesis appears to be compatible with the various modes of inheritance.

The curious phenomenon known as prepotency would seem also to be quite in accordance with the conception.

In chemical reactions the tendency is for the most stable combinations to be formed, so in nature.

We may probably go farther and say, not [162] only will the most stable biological molecules be formed, but the most stable radicles will dominate the molecule. Hence, if any two animals are crossed and the offspring show alternate inheritance, the resulting organism will, in the case of each unit character, display the most stable of the pair; in other words, it will take after the parent which happens to have the greater stability as regards that particular character. The difference between the mule and the hinny would seem to be explicable on this supposition. If the union were like a simple chemical synthesis it should not make any difference which way the cross were made. But if the species crossed are of varying stability, and if their respective degrees of stability vary with the sex, it is easy to see that it will make a difference how the animals are crossed.

In the cases of creatures that obey Mendel's law, the most stable form of a unit character will presumably be the dominant one.

One of the most curious of the phenomena of inheritance is that of correlation. We shall deal with this more fully in Chapter VIII. It will suffice here to say that certain characters appear to be linked together in organisms. Such seem to be transmitted in pairs. The offspring never exhibits one of such a correlated couple without exhibiting the other also.

It would thus seem that certain combinations [163] of biological atoms, certain molecules, can only exist in conjunction with certain other combinations. This is quite in accordance with the teaching of physiologists regarding the interdependence of the various organs of the body. We have now reached the stage of the fertilised ovum. According to our conception it is a series or conglomeration of the precursors of the unit characters of the adult. These precursors we call biological molecules. Each is of a very complex nature. Each seems to be composed of several portions, only one of which will take part in the building up of the body of the offspring, the other portions remaining latent. We further conceive that it is possible for the various radicles which compose these molecules to arrange themselves in various manners, and with each new arrangement a different form of unit character will be developed. These molecules, then, are built up from radicles derived from both parents, the most stable combinations being formed and one portion of the molecule dominating the whole. Under normal circumstances this dominant portion of the molecule will give rise to a character of a definite type. But it seems that other factors may come into play and cause a rearrangement of the radicles which compose it, and this will result in the formation of a unit character different from that to which it would ordinarily give rise.

[164]
But, it may be objected, if the colour of an organism be derived from one of these so-called biological molecules, how is it that it affects the whole organism, or, at any rate, several of the other unit characters? The objection may be met in several ways. In the first place, the colour-forming molecules may split up into as many portions as there are units which it affects, and each portion may attach itself to a unit. Or the property which we call colouration may not be derived from a molecule, it may be an expression in the relative positions of the various molecules in the fertilised egg. Or the colour-determining molecule

may secrete a ferment or a hormone, and this may be the cause of the particular colouring of the resulting organism. We do not pretend to say which (if any) of these alternative suppositions is the correct one. But it seems to us that some such conception as that which we have set forth is forced upon us by observed facts. This conception should be regarded not as a theory, but rather as an indication of the lines along which we believe the study of inheritance could best be made.

The fertilised ovum has nothing of the shape of the creature to which it will give rise. It is merely a potential organism, a something which under favourable conditions will develop into an organism.

Phenomenon of Sex

In the higher animals each individual is either [165] of the male or the female sex. A vast amount of ingenuity has been expended by zoologists in the attempt to ascertain what it is that determines sex. Many theories have been advanced, but no one of them has obtained anything like general acceptance, because its opponents are able to adduce facts which appear to be incompatible with it.

It is tempting to try to interpret the phenomenon of sex on the assumption that the female-producing biological molecule or unit is an isomeride of the male-producing cell. Certain facts, however, seem to negative the idea, as, for example, the occasional appearance in an individual of one sex of characteristics of the other sex.

Possibly the attempts to explain the phenomena of sex-production on a Mendelian basis may prove to be more successful. It seems not impossible that each fertilised egg contains material which is capable of developing into male generative organs and material which is capable of developing into female generative organs, but that only one kind of material, that which dominates, succeeds in developing. The number of what are known as "X-elements" that happen to be present in the fertilised egg appear to decide which kind of material is to be dominant.

But the problem of the determination of sex, [166] fascinating though it be, is not one that can be discussed adequately in a general work on evolution. Those interested in the subject are referred to Professor Thomson's Heredity, and to the address given by Professor E. B. Wilson, of Columbia University, before the American Association for the Advancement of Science, which was fully reported in the issue of Science, dated January 8, 1909.

Stated briefly, then, our conception is, that the fertilised egg is composed of a number of entities, to which we have given the name "biological molecules," because in certain respects their behaviour is not unlike that of chemical molecules.

The units which compose these molecules, being made up of protoplasm, are endowed with all the properties of life, including the inherent instability which characterises all living matter.

We suggest that the continuous or fluctuating variations that appear in the adult organism may be the result of individual differences in the biological "atoms" that compose the molecule.

Discontinuous variations, or mutations, on the other hand, may be the result of a rearrangement of the atoms within the biological molecule. Upon what causes this rearrangement it would not be very profitable to speculate in the present state of our knowledge. To do this would be to inquire into the cause of a re-grouping of entities [167] of the existence of which we are not certain! For aught we know there may be an intracellular struggle for nourishment among the various molecules and among the atoms which compose the molecules. If one molecule enjoys any special advantage over the others the result may be an unusual degree of development of the resulting unit character; in other words, the result will be a variation in the organism. This variation may prove favourable or unfavourable to its possessor.

Struggle for Nourishment

Certain phenomena seem to point to a struggle for nourishment between the germinal and the somatic portions of the egg, between the parts from which the sexual cells of the resulting organism are produced and those which give rise to the body of the organism. Each molecule may strive, so to speak, to increase at the expense of the others. Thus, great size in an organism is likely to be produced at the expense of the germinal cell-forming molecules. In other words, great size in an organism would be incompatible with excessive fecundity. This is what we observe in nature. On the other hand, poor development of bodily tissue, as in the case of intestinal parasites, would be correlated with great fecundity. Some organisms are mere sacs full of eggs.

Success in the struggle for nourishment of one molecule might be shared by the other molecules near to it, hence the phenomena of correlation.

[168]
It is thus conceivable that, in a brood consisting of several individuals, a particular molecule or set of molecules in one of the individuals may receive more than its share of nourishment, and this will result in the organs of that individual which spring from the well-nourished molecules being exceptionally well developed. Thus arises the phenomenon of differences between the members of a litter or brood.

Natural selection will tend to eliminate those individuals in which the resulting variation is an unfavourable one. If the environment is such, as in the case of an internal parasite, that the production of germ cells is the most necessary function of the organism, then those individuals in which the germ-forming molecules increase at the expense of the body-forming ones will tend to be preserved. This would cause the phenomenon which biologists term degeneration. The nourishment of the various biological molecules may possibly depend on their relative positions in the egg. Those in a favourable position will then tend to develop at the expense of the others. This will result in variation along definite lines. Each succeeding generation will tend to an increased development of that particular organ to which the favourably-situated molecule gives rise. This process may continue, as in the case of the horns of the Irish elk, until the development of that particular organ becomes [169] so excessive as to be positively injurious; then natural selection will step in and eliminate the species. But before this happens, something may cause a rearrangement of the biological molecules in the fertilised egg, and thus a mutation may arise, which, so to speak, strikes out a new line.

Origin of Mutations

Finally, on this conception there may be some sort of connection between fluctuating variations and mutations. We can picture the fluctuating variations being piled up, one upon the other, until there results a rearrangement of the atoms in one or more of the biological molecules which, in turn, causes a mutation.

Occasionally this remodelling, as it were, of one biological molecule may affect certain of the other molecules, and thus lead to correlated mutations.

[170]

CHAPTER VI
THE COLOURATION OF ORGANISMS

The theory of protective colouration has been carried to absurd lengths—It will not bear close scrutiny—Cryptic colouring—Sematic colours—Pseudo-sematic colours—Batesian and Müllerian mimicry—Conditions necessary for mimicry—Examples—Recognition markings—The theory of obliterative colouration—Criticism of the theory—Objections to the theory of cryptic colouring—Whiteness of the Arctic fauna is exaggerated—Illustrative tables—Pelagic organisms—Objectors to the Neo-Darwinian theories of colouration are to be found among field naturalists—G. A. B. Dewar, Gadow, Robinson, F. C. Selous quoted—Colours of birds' eggs—Warning colouration—Objections to the theory—Eisig's theory—So-called intimidating attitudes of animals—Mimicry—The case for the theory—The case against the theory—"False mimicry"—Theory of recognition colours—The theory refuted—Colours of flowers and fruits—Neo-Darwinian explanations—Objections—Kay Robinson's theory—Conclusion that Neo-Darwinian theories are untenable—Some suggestions regarding the colouration of animals—Through the diversity of colouring of organisms something like order runs—The connection between biological molecules and colour—Tylor on colour patterns in animals—Bonhote's theory of pœcilomeres—Summary of conclusions arrived at.

Since the publication of The Origin of Species, naturalists have paid much attention to the colouration of animals and plants, with the result that a large majority of scientific men to-day hold the belief that all, or nearly all, the colours displayed [171] by animals are of direct utility to them, and are therefore the direct result of natural selection; a few would add, "and of sexual selection."

"Among the numerous applications of the Darwinian theory," writes Wallace, "in the interpretation of the complex phenomena, none have been more successful than those which deal with the colours of animals and plants."

Robinson on Protective Colouring

We readily admit that the Darwinian theory has thrown a great deal of light on the phenomenon of animal colouration; it has reduced to something like order what was before Darwin's time chaos. While admitting this we feel constrained to say that many naturalists, especially Dr Wallace and Professor Poulton, have pushed the various theories of animal colouration to absurd lengths. As Dr H. Robinson truly says (Knowledge, January 1909), "It seems to have been taken for granted, and some even of Dr Wallace's writings may be interpreted in this sense, that protective colouring is necessary to the continued existence of every species, and that, sexual colouration apart, it is incumbent on naturalists to offer ingenious speculations in this sense to account for the appearance even of the most bizarre and conspicuous beasts. Thence it has been but a short step to the announcement of those speculations as further evidence in favour of natural selection, and of various assumptions [172] made in the speculative process as indisputable facts."

The result of this is that men have ceased to regard the Neo-Darwinian[6] theories of protective colouration, mimicry, and recognition markings as mere hypotheses which seem to throw light on certain phenomena in the organic world. These theories have assumed the rank of laws of nature. To dispute them would seem to be as futile as to assert that the earth is flat. To take exception to them would appear to be as ridiculous as to object to Mont Blanc. To dare to criticise them is heresy of the worst type.

Be this as it may, scientific dogma or no scientific dogma, scientific opinion or no scientific opinion, we have dared to weigh these theories in the balance of observation and reason, and have found them wanting. We have examined these mighty images of gold, and silver, and brass, and iron, and found that there is much clay in the feet.

We shall devote this chapter to lifting the hem of the garment of sanctity that envelopes each of these images, and so expose to view the clay that lies concealed.

We propose, first, to set forth in outline what [173] we trust will be considered a fair statement of the various theories of animal colouration which are generally accepted to-day, then to show up the various weak points in these, and lastly, to endeavour to ascertain whether there are not some alternative explanations in certain cases to which the generally-accepted theory does not apply.

Cryptic Colouring

Neo-Darwinians divide the various forms of colouration into three great classes:—(1) Cryptic colouring, or protective and aggressive resemblances; (2) sematic colours, or warning and recognition colours; and (3) pseudo-sematic colours, or mimicry. A tabular statement of this scheme of colouring will be found on pp. 293-7 Professor Poulton's Essays on Evolution.

As regards class (1), Neo-Darwinians point out that the great majority of animals are so coloured as to make them very difficult to see in their natural environment, hence the whiteness of the creatures which inhabit the snow-bound Arctic regions, the sandy colour of desert animals, the spotted coats of creatures which live among trees, the striped markings of animals which spend their lives amid long grass, and the transparent blueness of pelagic animals. The theory is that all kinds of animals, whether those that hunt or those that are hunted, derive much advantage from being coloured like their environment. [174] The hunted creatures are thereby the better able to elude the vigilance of their foes, while those that hunt are in a position to take their quarry by surprise; so that natural selection has caused them all to assimilate to the hues of their surroundings. Neo-Darwinians point to the fact that some Arctic animals are brown in the summer to match the ground from which the snow has melted, and turn white in winter to assimilate with their snowy background. Naturalists further cite, as evidence in favour of this theory, the case of those creatures which imitate inanimate objects, such as leaves and twigs, and thereby escape the observation of their foes.

Thus, the great majority of animals are supposed to be cryptically coloured, that is to say, coloured so as to be, if not quite invisible, at least very inconspicuous in their natural habitat.

Warning Colouration

It is, however, generally admitted that many creatures are not cryptically coloured. Some, indeed, seem to be coloured in such a way as to render them as conspicuous as possible. The Neo-Darwinians declare that there is a reason for this. "If," writes Professor Milnes Marshall (page 133 of his Lectures on the Darwinian Theory), "an animal, belonging to a group liable to be eaten by others, is possessed of a nauseous taste, or if an animal, such as a wasp, is specially [175] armed and venomous, it is to its advantage that it should be recognised quickly, and so avoided by animals that might be disposed to take it as food.

"Hence arises warning colouration, the explanation of which is due to Wallace. Darwin, who was unable to explain the reason for the gaudy colouration of some caterpillars, stated his difficulty to Wallace, and asked for suggestions. Wallace thought the matter over, considered all known cases, and then ventured to predict that birds and other enemies would be found to refuse such caterpillars if offered to them. This explanation, first applied to caterpillars, soon extended to adult forms, not only of insects, but of other groups as well. . . . Insects afford many admirable examples of warning colours, and many well-known instances occur among butterflies. The best examples of these are found in three great families of butterflies—the Heliconidæ, found in South America, the Danaidæ, found in Asia and tropical regions generally, and the Acræidæ of Africa. These have large but rather weak wings, and fly slowly. They are always very abundant, all have conspicuous colours or markings, and often a peculiar form of flight, characters by which they can be recognised at a glance. The colours are nearly always the same on both upper and under surfaces of the wings; they never try to conceal [176] themselves, but rest on the upper surfaces of leaves and flowers. Moreover, they all have juices which exhale a powerful scent; so that, if they are killed by pinching the body, a liquid exudes which stains the fingers yellow, and leaves an odour which can only be removed by repeated washing. This odour is not very offensive to man, but has been shown by experiment to be so to birds and other insect-eating animals.

"Warning colours are advertisements, often highly coloured advertisements, of unsuitability as food. Insects are of two kinds—those which are extremely difficult to find, and those which are rendered prominent through startling colours and conspicuous attitudes. Warning colours may usually be distinguished by being conspicuously exposed when the animal is at rest. Crude patterns and startling contrasts in colour are characteristically warning, and these colours and patterns often resemble each other; black combined with white, yellow, or red, are the commonest combinations, and the patterns usually consist of rings, stripes, or spots."

We trust that we shall be forgiven for this lengthy quotation. Our object in reproducing so large an extract is to allow the Neo-Darwinians to speak for themselves. Were we to state their theory in our own words, we might perhaps be charged with stating it inaccurately. We should [177] add that, even as natural selection is supposed to have been the cause of conspicuous colouring in some organisms, so has it caused others to assume intimidating attitudes or emit warning sounds, such as a hiss, when attacked.

Batesian Mimicry

We now come to the third great class of animal colours—mimetic colours. Mimicry is of two kinds, known respectively as Batesian and Müllerian mimicry, after their respective discoverers.

It has been found that some apparently warningly coloured butterflies and other creatures are palatable to insectivorous animals. The explanation given of this is that these showy but edible butterflies "mimic," that is to say, have the appearance of, show a general resemblance to, species which are unpalatable. This is known as Batesian mimicry. "Protective mimicry," writes Professor Poulton (Essays on Evolution, p. 361), "is here defined as an advantageous superficial resemblance of a palatable defenceless form to another that is specially defended so as to be disliked or feared by the majority of enemies of the groups to which both mimic and model belong—a resemblance which appeals to the senses of animal enemies . . . but does not extend to deep-seated characters, except when the superficial likeness is affected thereby."

As Wallace has pointed out, five conditions [178] must be satisfied before such protective mimicry can occur:—

"1. That the imitative species occur in the same area and occupy the same station as the imitated. 2. That the imitators are always the more defenceless. 3. That the imitators are always less numerous in individuals. 4. That the imitators differ from the bulk of their allies. 5. That the imitation, however minute, is external and visible only, never extending to internal characters or to such as does not affect the external characters." (Darwinism, Chap. ix.)

Thus the mimic is supposed to deceive his enemies by deluding them into the belief that he is the inedible species which they once tried to eat and vowed never again to touch, so nasty was it. The mimic, then, may be compared to the ass in the lion's skin. Needless to say, this mimicry is quite unconscious. It is supposed to have been developed by natural selection. Every popular book on Evolution cites many examples of such mimicry. We may therefore content ourselves with mentioning but a few.

Examples of Mimicry

Our common wasps are copied by a beetle (Clytus arietis), active in movement and banded black and yellow, and by several yellow-barred hover-flies (Syrphidæ); and the bumble-bee by a clear-winged moth (Sesia fuciformis). [179] There is, indeed, a whole group of these clear-winged moths, resembling bees, wasps, and other stinging hymenoptera. The common Indian Danaid butterfly, Danais chrysippus, is marvellously reproduced by the female of Hypolimnas misippus, a form allied to our Purple Emperor. The male of this is black, with white blue-bordered patches, the female chestnut, edged with black and with white spots at the tips of the wings, as in the Danais. Finn has shown experimentally that this species is liked by birds.

Another common Indian Danaid (D. limniace), black, spotted with pale green, is imitated, though not very closely, by the female of one of the "white" group, Nepheronia hippia. Finn found that this insect was eaten freely by birds, and that the common jungle-babbler (Crateropus canorus) was deceived by the mimicry of the female. The very nauseous Indian swallow-tail (Papilio aristolochiæ) is closely imitated by another swallow-tail (P. polites), both having black wings marked with red and white; P. aristolochiæ, however, has a red abdomen. This difference was not noticed by two species of Drongo-shrikes (Dicrurus ater and Dissemurus paradiseus), to which the butterflies were offered; but the Pekin robin (Liothrix luteus)—a very intelligent little bird—did not fail to pick out and eat the mimic, though it was deceived by the marvellously [180] perfect imitation of Danais chrysippus, by the female of the Hypolimnas.

Such resemblances can therefore be effective.

The cases of mimicry usually quoted include very few among mammals, probably, as Beddard suggests, because the species of that class are relatively few.

The insectivorous genus Tupaia is supposed to mimic the squirrels, which it much resembles as regards form in all respects save the long muzzle; the idea being that squirrels are so active that carnivorous animals find it hopeless to pursue them.

On the other hand, there is a squirrel (Rhinosciurus tupaioides) which is supposed to mimic the tupaias! It has a similar long muzzle, and the light shoulder-stripe which is a common marking in tupaias. But why the squirrel, one of the group imitated, should in turn become an imitator is not explained.

The true interpretation of the resemblance is probably that both squirrels and tupaias are adapted to a life in trees. Like profession begets like appearance: the ground-living shrews much resemble mice, and the moles find representatives in mole-like rodents.

Another case, however, wherein true mimicry may have come into play is that of the South American deer (Cervus paludosus) which singularly resembles in colouration the long-legged [181] wolf or Aguara-guazu (Canis jubatus). Both these species are chestnut in colour, with the front of the legs black, and the ears lined with white hair; both inhabit the same regions in South America.

Müllerian Mimicry

The second kind of mimicry—Müllerian mimicry—is where one unpalatable creature resembles another. This form of mimicry is named after Fritz Müller, who suggested the explanation now usually accepted, namely, that "Life is saved by a resemblance between the warning colours in any area, inasmuch as the education of young inexperienced enemies is facilitated, and insect life saved in the process." "It is obvious," writes Poulton (p. 328 of Essays on Evolution), "that the amount of learning and remembering, and consequently of injury and loss of life involved in these processes, are reduced when many species in one place possess the same aposematic colouring, instead of each exhibiting a different danger signal. . . . The precise statement of advantage was made by Mr Blakiston and Mr Alexander, of Tokio. 'Let there be two species of insects equally distasteful to young birds, and let it be supposed that the birds would destroy the same number of individuals of each before they were educated to avoid them. Then if these insects are thoroughly mixed and become undistinguishable to the birds, a proportionate advantage accrues to each over its former state of existence. [182] These proportionate advantages are inversely in the duplicate ratio of the respective percentages that would have survived without the mimicry.'"

This is rather a cumbrous method of saying that if there are in a locality a number of young birds, and each of these has to learn by experience which insects are edible and which are not, each will, if it learns by one example, devour one insect of any given pattern. Now, if two species of inedible insects have this pattern, they will between them lose only one member in the educating process of each bird, whereas if each species of insect had a colouration peculiar to itself, each species would lose a whole individual instead of half a one. There can be no doubt that such a livery of unpalatability is of some advantage to its possessors.

It has been shown experimentally that hand-reared young birds have to acquire their knowledge of flavours and colours by experiment.

It is well known that in many species the male and the female are not coloured alike. Such species are said to exhibit sexual dimorphism. In these cases it is usually the male that is more conspicuously coloured. Darwin felt that the theory of natural selection could not satisfactorily account for this phenomenon, so put forward the supplementary theory of sexual selection. On this hypothesis the females are supposed to be able to pick and [183] choose their mates, and to select the most beautiful and ornamental ones, hence the greater showiness of these in most sexually dimorphic species. Wallace does not accept this theory. He thinks it unnecessary. He looks upon the brilliant colouring of the males as due to their superior vigour; moreover, he says that it is the hen that sits upon the eggs, and so requires a greater degree of protection than the male, and therefore natural selection has not permitted her to develop all the ornaments displayed by the cock. With the phenomenon of sexual dimorphism we shall deal at length in the next chapter.

Danger Signals

Dr Wallace recognizes yet another exception to the rule that animals are cryptically coloured. Many creatures possess on the body markings which tend to render them conspicuous rather than difficult to see. Where such markings occur on gregarious animals, Wallace believes that they have been evolved by natural selection, either to enable their possessors to recognize one another, or to act as a danger signal to their fellows. The white tail of the rabbit is believed by Wallace to serve as a danger signal. The first member of the company to espy the approaching foe takes to his heels, and, as he moves, his white tail catches the eye of his neighbour, who at once follows him, so that, in less time than it takes to tell, the whole company of rabbits is [184] scampering towards the burrow, thanks to the white under-surface of the tail.

Even as Wallace out-Darwin's Darwin, so does Mr Abbott Thayer, an American naturalist and artist, out-Wallace Wallace. That gentleman seems to be of opinion that all animals are cryptically or, as he calls it, concealingly or obliteratively coloured. Even those schemes of colour which have hitherto been called conspicuous are, he asserts, "purely and potently concealing" when looked at properly, that is to say, with the eye of the artist.

Lest it be thought unnecessary to criticize a hypothesis which appears to be based upon the assumption that animals see with the eye of the artist, we may say that Professor Poulton writes approvingly of Thayer's theory. He frequently alludes to it in his Essays on Evolution, and he published an account of it in the issue of Nature, dated April 24, 1902. Moreover the hypothesis has been enunciated in such scientific journals as The Auk (1896) and The Year-Book of the Smithsonian Institution (1897).

Thayer asserts that all animals, or at any rate the great majority, including many that are usually supposed to be conspicuously coloured, are in reality obliteratively coloured— that is to say, coloured in such a way that the effects of light and shade are completely counteracted, with the result that they are invisible.

[185]
Obliterative Colouring

It is possible, says Mr Thayer, to almost obliterate a statue in a diffused light, by putting white paint on the surfaces in darkest shadow and dark paint on the most brightly lighted parts, all in due proportion. Now this is precisely what nature is supposed by Mr Thayer to have done for all her creatures.

It is well known that a great many animals, as for example the Indian black-buck and the hare, are coloured on the upper side and white below. This is called by Mr Thayer the principle of the gradation of colour. It runs, he declares, all through the animal world, and is "the main essential step toward making animals inconspicuous under the descending light of the sky."

Animals, he contends, are not protectively coloured to look like clods or stumps or like surrounding objects, they are simply obliteratively coloured—coated, as it were, with invisible paint.

To quote from The Century Magazine (1908): "Whales, lions, wolves, deer, hares, mice; partridges, quails, sandpipers, larks, sparrows; frogs, snakes, fishes, lizards, crabs; grasshoppers, slugs, caterpillars—all these animals, and many thousands more, crawl, crouch, and swim about their business, hunting and eluding, under cover of this strange obliterative mask, the smooth and perfect balance between shades of colour and degrees of illumination."

[186]
Nature having thus visually unsubstantialized the bodies of animals, so that, if seen at all, they look flat and ghostly, does not stop there. From solid-shaded bodies they have been converted, as it were, into flat cards or canvases, and, to complete the illusion of obliteration, pictures of the background—veritable pictures of the more or less distant landscape—have been painted on their canvases! Such in effect are the elaborate "markings of field and forest birds."

Again he writes: "Brilliantly changeable or metallic colours are usually supposed to make the birds that wear them conspicuous, but nothing could be further from the truth. Iridescence is, indeed, one of the strongest factors of concealment. The quicksilver-like intershifting of many lights and colours, which the slightest motion generates on an iridescent surface, like the back of a bird or the wing of a butterfly, destroys the visibility of that wing or back as such and causes it to blend inextricably with the gleaming and scintillating labyrinthine-shadowed world of wind-swayed leaves and flowers."

According to Thayer, the skunk, which for years has been an important item of the stock-in-trade of the advocates of the theory of warning colouration, is an excellent example of obliterative colouring, since its enemies are supposed to mistake for the sky-line the line of junction between [187] the white fur of the back and the dark fur of the sides. Similarly the crocodiles are supposed to mistake a flamingo for the sky at sunrise or at sunset!

There is doubtless something in this theory of obliterative colouration.

Any one can see, by paying a visit to the South Kensington Museum, that an animal which is of a lighter colour below than above, is less conspicuous in a poor light than it would be were it uniformly coloured. There is then no doubt that this scheme of colour, which is so common in nature, has some protective value.

To this extent has Mr Thayer made a valuable contribution to zoological science. But when he informs us that obliterative colouring is a "universal attribute of animal life," we feel sorely tempted to poke fun at him.

We would ask all those who believe in the universality of obliterative colouring to observe a flock of rooks wending their way to their dormitories at sunset.

Let us now pass on to the examination of the more orthodox theories of animal colouration.

Objections to the Theory of Cryptic Colouring

Before criticising the theory of cryptic colouring, we desire to state distinctly that we admit [188] that, where other things are equal, it is of advantage to all creatures which hunt or which are preyed upon to be inconspicuous. If difficult to distinguish amid their natural surroundings, the former are likely to secure their prey readily, and the latter have a chance of escaping from their enemies. Our quarrel is with the theory of cryptic colouring as it is enunciated by many Neo-Darwinians, with the theory that every hue, every marking, every device displayed by an organism is of utility to the organism and has been directly developed by natural selection.

The extreme advocates of the theory of cryptic colouring have greatly exaggerated the degree in which animals are assimilated to their natural environment.

Fauna of Polar Regions

We grant that a great many creatures, which when seen in a menagerie appear very conspicuous, are the reverse of conspicuous when standing motionless amid their natural surroundings. As Beddard has pointed out, it is often not easy to find a sixpenny piece which has been dropped on the carpet, but the reason for this is, not that the coin is protectively coloured, but that any small object, no matter how coloured, is difficult to distinguish amid a variegated environment. The assumption of a white winter coat by many organisms that live in northern latitudes has been cited, again and again, as showing how important it is for an [189] animal to be protectively coloured. If, it is urged, those creatures that live in lands which are covered in snow for half of the year have become white in winter by the action of natural selection in order to escape their foes, it is obviously of paramount importance to all creatures that they should be cryptically coloured. Popular books on natural history convey the impression that during winter the snow-clad, ice-bound Arctic regions are peopled by a fauna whose fur or hair rivals in whiteness the snowy mantle of the earth. The impression thus conveyed is misleading. It is true that an unusually large percentage of the animals that inhabit the polar regions are white in winter, but the majority of the creatures which dwell there do not assume the white garb of winter.

As the fauna of the polar regions is a small one, we are able to give lists of all the birds and mammals which dwell in the Arctic and the Antarctic regions. We have arranged these in in three columns. In the first are placed those creatures which are white throughout the year, in the third those that retain their colour through the winter, while the middle column contains those forms which change their colouring with the season.

[190]
ARCTIC FAUNA.
Mammals.
White.
Polar Bear.
Arctic Fox (some individuals).
White Whale or Beluga.
Changing with the Seasons.
Arctic Fox (most individuals).
Arctic Lemming.
Stoat.
Weasel.
Blue Hare.
Coloured.
Arctic Fox (sometimes).
Reindeer.
Musk-ox.
Glutton.
Moose.
Sable.
Seals.
Walrus.
Narhwal.
Greenland Whale.
Birds.
White.
Ivory Gull.
Snowy Owl.
Gyrfalcon.
Snow Goose.
Changing with the Seasons.
Black Guillemot.
Ptarmigans.
Snow Bunting (whitest in summer!)
Razorbill.
Little Auk (throat only becomes white).
Coloured.
Sea Eagle.
Greenland Redpoll (very pale).
All Arctic Geese and Ducks other than Snow Goose.
Raven.
Cormorant.
Brunnich's Guillemot.
Puffin.
Fulmar Petrel.
Ross's Gull.
Glaucous Gull (very pale).
Sandpipers.
[191]

ANTARCTIC FAUNA.
Mammals.
White.
Antarctic White Seal (Lobodon carcinophaga), in some cases.
Changing with the Seasons.
None.
Coloured.
Other Seals than Lobodon.
Whales.
Birds.
White.
Sheathbill.
Snowy Petrel.
Giant Petrel (some individuals).
Chick of Emperor Penguin.
Changing with the Seasons.
None.
Coloured.
Penguins.
Cormorant.
Skua Gull.
Giant Petrel (usually).
Other Petrels.

It will be observed that the third column contains the largest number of forms. It is thus evident that the whiteness of the Arctic and Antarctic faunas in winter has been greatly exaggerated.

The Arctic fox appears in all three columns, as the creature seems to fall into three races—a permanently white race, a permanently coloured race, and a seasonally dimorphic race.

Of the creatures set forth in the middle column of the above tables all are whiter in winter than in summer with the exception of the snow bunting, [192] who sets at naught the theory of cryptic colouring by turning darker in winter! The same may be said of the Alpine chamois.

The advocates of the theory of protective colouring assert that the creatures which do not turn white in winter are strong and active animals which have no enemies to fear.

This contention is met by F. C. Selous as follows (African Nature Notes and Reminiscences, p. 9): "According to the experience of Arctic travellers, large numbers of young musk oxen are annually killed by wolves. . . . Nothing, I think, is more certain than that a far smaller percentage of so-called protectively coloured giraffes are killed annually by lions in Africa than of musk oxen by wolves in Arctic America."

Another difficulty which confronts the Neo-Wallaceian school is that, ex hypothesi, the assumption of the white coat was gradual. Hence the change in the direction of whiteness cannot, in its first beginning, have been of perceptible utility to an organism. How then can natural selection have operated on it?

Pelagic Organisms

The transparency of pelagic organisms is frequently cited as exemplifying cryptic colouring. We all know that the common jelly-fish is as transparent as glass. Floating on the surface of the ocean are millions of tiny organisms, so transparent as to be invisible to the human eye. At first sight this certainly appears to be a [193] remarkable case of protective colouring. Unfortunately, nearly all the more highly developed forms display conspicuous pigment (as in most jelly-fish) in some part of the body.

"An animal floating about in the sea," writes Beddard, "perfectly transparent, but decked with dense black patches, of the size of saucers, would betray its whereabouts even to the least observant; if the observer were stimulated by hunger or fear, the conspicuousness would not be lessened. . . . Besides the internecine warfare which is continually going on amongst the smaller surface organisms, they are devoured wholesale by the larger pelagic fish, and by whales and other Cetacea. A whale, rushing through the water with open mouth and gulping down all before him, is not the least inconvenienced by the invisibility of the organisms devoured in such enormous quantities; nor do a solid phalanx of herring or mackerel stop to look carefully for their food: they take what comes in their way, and get plenty in spite of 'protective absence of colouration.'

"If the transparency of the pelagic organisms be due entirely to natural selection, it is remarkable that there is so little modification in this direction among the species inhabiting the bottom at such depths as are accessible to the sun's rays; the advantage gained by this transparency and consequent invisibility would be equally great. And [194] yet this is not the case; the bulk of the bottom fauna of the coasts are brilliantly coloured animals, and those that show any protective colouring at all appear to be coloured so as to resemble stones or sea-weeds."[7]

Before leaving the subject of marine animals, we may point out that the majority of the creatures that live in the everlasting blackness of the depths of the ocean display exceedingly conspicuous colouring, and this colouring seems to be constant. In such cases the colouring cannot be useful as such to its possessors. The same may be said of the colour of blood, or of the colouring of the internal tissues of all organisms. We must not lose sight of the fact that every organism, and every component part thereof, must of necessity be either of some colour or perfectly transparent. It seems to us that since the appearance of The Origin of Species zoologists have tended to exaggerate the importance of colouring to organisms; they frequently speak of it as though it were the one and only factor in the struggle for existence. It is on this account that they feel it incumbent upon them to find ingenious explanations for every piece of colouring displayed by every plant or animal.

Unimportance of Colour

The tendency to exaggerate the importance to an animal of its colouring is doubtless in large [195] part due to the fact that many zoologists are content to study nature in museums rather than in the open. Some of those who observe organisms in their natural surroundings, especially in such favourable localities as the tropics, seem to be of opinion that natural selection has but little influence on the colouration of organisms.

Thus D. Dewar writes (Albany Review, 1907): "Eight years of bird-watching in India have convinced me that, so far as the struggle for existence is concerned, it matters not to a bird whether it be conspicuously or inconspicuously coloured, that it is not the necessity for protection against raptorial foes which determines the colouring of a species; in short, that the theory of protective colouration has but little application to the fowls of the air."

Similarly, F. C. Selous writes, on page 13 of African Nature Notes and Reminiscences: "Having spent many years of my life in the constant pursuit of African game, I have certainly been afforded opportunities such as have been enjoyed by but few civilised men of becoming intimately acquainted with the habits and life-history of many species of animals living in that continent, and all that I have learned during my long experience as a hunter compels me to doubt the correctness of the now very generally accepted theories that all the wonderfully [196] diversified colours of animals—the stripes of the zebra, the blotched coat of the giraffe, the spots of the bushbuck, the white face and the rump of the bontebok, to mention only a few—have been coloured either as means of protection from enemies or for the purpose of mutual recognition by animals of the same species in times of sudden alarm."

So also G. A. B. Dewar—a very close observer of nature in England—writes, in The Faery Year: "Few theories in natural history have received more attention of late years than protective or aggressive colour, 'mimicry,' and harmony with environment. . . . To doubt this use of colour to animals seems like inviting back chaos in place of cosmos—for abandon the theory, and a world of colour is straightway void of purpose, a muddle of chance. So we all like the theory. Some, however, perceive plans to aid the wearer in every colour, tint, shade, and pattern. We may be sceptical of a good many of the cases they cite in support of colour aid, though attracted by the main idea."

Writing of the commoner British butterflies, he says: "After a little practice, any man furnished with good eyesight can easily distinguish these butterflies—blues, coppers, small heaths, and meadow browns—from their perches; and so we may be sure that the small beast, bird, or insect of prey, with sense of colour or form, [197] could also distinguish them. . . . Quite often, without even searching for them, I can see cabbage whites and other butterflies asleep on perches to which they by no means assimilate." Mr G. A. B. Dewar suggests that the safety of the resting butterfly lies in "the position, the couch on high, . . . not the mask of colour or marking."

Gadow on Coral Snakes

Two short visits to Southern Mexico sufficed to show Dr Hans Gadow that some of the commonly accepted explanations of colour phenomena are not the correct ones.

Thus writing of coral snakes, he says, on page 95 of Through Southern Mexico: "They are usually paraded as glaring instances of warning colouration, but I am not at all sure whether this is justifiable. Certainly these Elaps are most conspicuous and beautiful objects. Black and carmine or coral red, in alternate rings, are the favourite pattern; sometimes with narrow golden-yellow rings between them, as if to enhance the beautiful combination. But these snakes are inclined to be nocturnal in their habits, and, except when basking, spend most of their time under rotten stumps, in mouldy ground, or in ants' nests in search of their prey, which must be very small, to judge from the size of the mouth."

Dr Gadow goes on to show that although black and red are very strong contrasts in the [198] day-time, the combination ceases to be effective in the dark. He suggests that red and black is a self-effacing rather than a warning pattern. He further points out that several kinds of harmless snakes have the same colouring and pattern. "There seems," he says, "to be no reason why we should not call these cases of mimicry; and yet this is most likely a wrong interpretation, since such harmless snakes are also found in districts where the Elaps does not occur, not only in Mexico, but likewise in far-distant parts of the world, where neither elapines nor any other similarly coloured poisonous snakes exist. To interpret this as an instance of 'warning colours' in a perfectly harmless snake, which has no chance of mimicry, amounts in such cases to nonsense, and we have to look for a different explanation upon physiological and other grounds."

It is, to say the least of it, significant that all the opposition to the theory of protective colouration comes from those who observe nature first hand, while the warmest supporters of the theory are cabinet naturalists and museum zoologists.

In the case of nocturnal creatures, as Dr H. Robinson very sagely points out (Knowledge, January 1909), the value for protective purposes of any given colouration must depend very largely on the state of the moon. "It was," he writes, "a common experience in the South [199] African War that on overcast or moonless nights the nearly black army great-coat made a picquet sentry invisible at a distance of a few feet. In strong moonlight this

78

garb could be seen at a great distance, whereas a khaki pea jacket, useless on a dark night, answered the requirements of invisibility very well." It is thus evident that the dark colour of the buffalo and sable antelope cannot be protective on both dark and moonlight nights.

The theory of protective colouration is based on the tacit assumption that beasts of prey rely on eyesight for finding their quarry. Raptorial birds certainly do use their eyes as the means of discovering their victims; but the great majority of predaceous mammals trust almost entirely to their power of smell as a means for tracking down their prey.

F. C. Selous Quoted

"Nothing," writes F. C. Selous, on page 14 of African Nature Notes and Reminiscences, "is more certain than that all carnivorous animals hunt almost entirely by scent until they have closely approached their quarry, and usually by night, when all the animals on which they prey must look very much alike as far as colour is concerned."

The herbivora—the quarry for the beast of prey—too, have a keen sense of smell, so that they trust their noses rather than their eyes for safety.

[200]
No observer of nature can have failed to remark how the least movement on the part of an animal will betray its whereabouts, even though in colouring it assimilates very closely to the environment. So long as the hare squats motionless in the furrow, it may remain unobserved, even though the sportsman be searching for it; but the least movement on its part at once attracts his eye. Thus, in order that protective colouration can be of use to its possessor, the latter must remain perfectly motionless. But, in tropical countries, where flies, gnats, etc., are a perfect scourge, no large animal is, when awake, motionless for ten seconds at a time. The tail is in constant motion, flicking off the flies that attempt to settle on the quadruped. The ears are used in a similar manner. Thus the so-called protective colouring of herbivora cannot afford them much protection. It is further worthy of note that the brush-like tip to the tail of many mammals is not of the same colour as the skin or fur. It is very frequently black. Thus we have the spectacle of a protectively coloured creature continually moving, as if to attract attention, almost the only part of its body that is not protectively coloured!

Sexual Dimorphism

Many species of birds display what is known as seasonal dimorphism, still more display sexual dimorphism.

Seasonally dimorphic birds very often assume [201] a bright livery at the breeding season; this nuptial plumage is by no means invariably confined to the cock, so that we are brought face to face with the fact that some hen birds, that are normally inconspicuously coloured, become showy and easy to see at the nesting time, that is to say, precisely at the season when they would seem to be most in need of protection.

In the great majority of cases of sexual dimorphism among birds the cock is the more showily coloured. Now, if it be a matter of life-and-death importance to a bird to be protectively coloured, we should expect the showily coloured cock birds to be far less numerous than the dull-plumaged hens, since the former are, ex hypothesi, exposed to far greater danger than the inconspicuous hens. As a matter of fact, cock birds in practically all species appear to be at least as numerous as the hens. Nor can it be said that this is due to their more secretive habits. As a general rule, cock birds show themselves as readily as the hens; indeed, in the case of the familiar blackbird, the conspicuous cock is less retiring in his habits than the more sombre hen. It may, perhaps, be thought that the greater danger to which the sitting bird is exposed accounts for the fact that hens, notwithstanding their protective colouration, are not more numerous than the cocks. Unfortunately for the supposition, in many sexually dimorphic [202] hens, as, for example, the paradise fly-catcher (Terpsiphone paradisi), the showy cock shares the burden of incubation equally with the hen.

It frequently happens that allied species of birds are found in neighbouring countries. The Indian robins, for example, fall into two species. The brown-backed robin (Thamnobia cambayensis) occurs north of Bombay, while the black-backed species (T. fulicata) is found south of Bombay. The hens of these two species are almost indistinguishable, but the cocks differ, in that one has a brown back, while the other's back is glossy black. The Wallaceian theory of colouration seems quite unable to explain this phenomenon—the splitting up of a genus into local species—which is continually met with in nature. Equally inimical to the theory of protective colouration is the existence, side by side, of species which obtain their living in much the same manner. On every Indian lake three different species of kingfisher pursue their profession cheek by jowl; one of these—Ceryle rudis—is speckled black and white, like a Hamburg fowl; the second is the kingfisher we know in England; and the third is the magnificent white-breasted species—Halcyon smyrnensis—a bright-blue bird with a reddish head and a white wing bar. It is obvious that all three of these diversely plumaged species cannot be protectively coloured. It may perhaps be objected that the piscatorial methods [203] of these kingfishers differ in detail. We admit that this is the case, but would maintain, at the same time, that these comparatively slight differences in habit do not account for the very striking differences in plumage. We may also cite the yellow and pied wagtails of our own country, which may be seen feeding in the same meadows. Most familiar and striking of all is the everyday sight of a blackbird and thrush plying their respective avocations within a few yards of each other on the same lawn, differently coloured though they be.

Another weighty objection to the generally accepted theory of protective colouration is that some of the creatures which assimilate most closely to their environment are those which appear to be the least in need of such protection.

Precis Artexia

The butterfly Precis artexia, writes F. C. Selous, "is only found in shady forests, is seldom seen flying until disturbed, and always sits on the ground amongst dead leaves. Though handsomely coloured on the upper side, when its wings are closed it closely resembles a dead leaf. It has a little tail on the lower wing, which looks exactly like the stalk of a leaf, and from this tail a dark-brown line runs through both wings (which on the under side are light brown) to the apex of the upper wing. One would naturally be inclined to look upon this wonderful resemblance to a dead leaf in a butterfly sitting with closed wings [204] on the ground amongst real dead leaves as a remarkable instance of protective form and colouration. And of course it may be that this is the correct explanation. But what enemy is this butterfly protected against? Upon hundreds of different occasions I have ridden and walked through forests where Precis artexia was numerous, and I have caught and preserved many specimens of these butterflies, but never once did I see a bird attempting to catch one of them. Indeed, birds of all kinds were scarce in the forests where these insects were to be found."

Similarly D. Dewar writes (Albany Review, 1907): "If a naturalist be asked to cite a perfect example of protective colouring, he will, as likely as not, name the sand grouse (Pteroclurus exustus). This species dwells in open, dry, sandy country, and its dull brownish-buff plumage, with its soft dark bars, assimilates so closely to the sandy environment as to make the bird, when at rest, practically invisible, at any rate to the human eye. Unfortunately for the theory, this bird stands less in need of protective colouration than any other, for it has wonderful powers of flight. Even a trained falcon is unable to catch it, because it can fly upwards in a straight line as though it were ascending an inclined plane, with the result that the pursuing hawk is never able to get above it to strike."

[205]
Striped Caterpillars

Lord Avebury, who is a typical Wallaceian, points out the connection that exists between longitudinal stripes on caterpillars and the habit of feeding either on grass or low-growing plants among grass. The inference, of course, is that birds mistake these caterpillars for leaves, or, at any rate, fail to observe them when feeding, not only because they are green in colour, but because their longitudinal stripes look like the parallel veins on the blades of grass. But the butterflies of the family Satyridæ, as Beddard points out, all possess striped larvæ, and these feed chiefly by night, when neither their colouring nor marking is visible, while during the day many of them lie up under stones; other caterpillars of this family feed inside the stems of plants. "Now," writes Beddard (Animal Colouration, p. 101), "in these cases the colour obviously does not matter: if, therefore, the longitudinal striping is kept up by constant selection on account of its utility, and has no other signification, we might expect that in these two species (Hipparchia semele and Œnis), and in others with similar habits, the cessation of natural selection would have permitted the high standard required in the other cases to be lowered—perhaps, even, as has been suggested in the case of cave animals, the colours being useless to their possessors, might have disappeared altogether—but they have not."

[206]
Many exceedingly conspicuous birds—as, for example all the crow-tribe, the egrets, the kingfishers—flourish in spite of their showy plumage. Such creatures, while scarcely constituting a valid objection to the theory of protective colouration, serve to show that protective colouring is not a necessity. An animal otherwise able to take care of itself can afford to dispense with cryptic colouration. "An ounce of good solid pugnacity is a more effective weapon in the struggle for existence than many pounds of protective colouration."

There used to live in the gardens of the Zoological Society of London a black cat belonging to the manager of one of the restaurants. This animal used to catch birds on the lawn. We believe that not even Mr Thayer will maintain that a black cat is cryptically coloured when stalking on a well-watered lawn! Nevertheless the nigritude of that cat did not prevent it securing a meal.

Colours of Eggs

The case of birds' eggs furnish an excellent example of the lengths to which Wallace and his followers have pushed the theory of protective colouration.

D. Dewar maintains that it is possible to divide birds' eggs that are coloured, as opposed to those that are white, into two classes—those which are protectively coloured and those which are not. The former class includes all those [207] which are laid in shingle or on the bare ground, as, for example, the eggs of the ring-plover and the lap-wing.[8] He maintains that the variously coloured and speckled eggs that are laid in cup-shaped nests are not protectively coloured at all; he declares that they are usually very conspicuous when in the nest, and, moreover, it would be futile for them to be cryptically coloured, for a bird or lizard that habitually sucks eggs will examine carefully the interior of each nest it discovers.

Needless to say, this view does not appeal to the so-called Neo-Darwinians. Wallace writes, on page 215 of Darwinism: "The beautiful blue or greenish eggs of the hedge-sparrow, the song-thrush, the blackbird, and the lesser redpole seem at first sight especially calculated to attract attention, but it is very doubtful whether they are really so conspicuous when seen at a little distance among their usual surroundings. For the nests of these birds are either in evergreen, or holly, or ivy, or surrounded by the delicate green tints of early spring vegetation, and may thus harmonise very well with the colours around them. The great majority of the eggs of our smaller birds are so spotted or streaked with brown or black on variously tinted grounds that, [208] when lying in the shadow of the nest and surrounded by the many colours and tints of bark and moss, of purple buds and tender green or yellow foliage, with all the complex glittering lights and mottled shades produced among these by the spring sunshine and sparkling rain-drops, they must have quite a different aspect from that which they possess when we observe them torn from their natural surroundings."

The obvious comment on this is that it is very fine and poetic English, but it is not science. It is futile to deny what should be obvious to every field naturalist, namely, that the majority of eggs laid in open nests are most conspicuous.

D. Dewar thus summarises the main facts which show that eggs in nests (as opposed to those laid on the bare ground) are not protectively coloured:—

"1. Allied species of birds, even though their nesting habits are very different, as a rule lay similarly coloured eggs.

"2. Eggs laid in domed nests certainly do not need protective colouring, yet many of these are coloured.

"3. The same is true of many eggs laid in holes in trees or in buildings.

"4. The protective resemblances of eggs which are laid in the open are apparent to everyone, which certainly is not true of those deposited in nests.

[209]
"5. Many birds lay eggs which exhibit very great variations.

"6. Some birds lay eggs of different types, and these sometimes differ from one another so greatly that it is difficult to believe that they could have been laid by the same species."[9]

7. It not infrequently happens that one species lays in the disused nest of another, and the eggs of the latter are often very different in colouring from those of the former.

We have up to the present considered the theory of general cryptic colouration, which declares that the majority of creatures are so coloured as to be inconspicuous. We have still to deal with the hypothesis of special cryptic colouring.

Certain animals look, when resting, very like an inanimate object, such as a dead leaf or a twig. This resemblance is said to be the result of natural selection, since it enables its possessors to escape destruction; they are seen, but mistaken for something else.

The classical examples of this kind of protective colouring are furnished by the Kallimas or leaf-butterflies, which display an extraordinary resemblance to dead leaves.

Other examples are the stick-insects and the lappet moth, which looks like a bunch of dry leaves. It is needless to multiply instances. [210] In every work on animal colouration numbers of such cases are cited.

We may grant that in some cases, at any rate, the resemblance is of value to its possessor, in that it deceives predatory creatures. But it does not follow from this that the likeness has originated through the action of natural selection. In order that there can be selection there must be varying degrees of a tolerable resemblance to select from. How did the initial similarity arise? This is a matter upon which Wallaceians are silent. As Poulton truly says, in discussing the degree of protection afforded by such resemblances, we tacitly endow animals with senses exactly similar to our own. Are we justified in so doing? Most certainly not in the case of the invertebrate animals, especially as regards the arthropods, of which the eyes are constructed very differently from those of human beings.

D. Dewar has often seen a toad shoot out its tongue and touch a lighted cigarette end, apparently mistaking it for an insect. Similarly, he has again and again induced a gecko lizard to chase and try to swallow a piece of black cotton, one end of which was rolled up into a ball. It is only necessary to take hold of the unrolled end of the cotton and place the rolled-up end a few inches from the lizard, and gradually draw it away in order to induce the lizard to attempt to seize it.

[211]
Eyesight of Birds

It would therefore seem that all these elaborate "protective" devices are unnecessary refinements if regarded as a protection against invertebrate, reptilian, and amphibian foes. Birds, on the other hand, appear to have exceedingly sharp eyesight, so that in order to deceive them the resemblance requires to be very close. Indeed, as regards those birds which systematically hunt for their prey among leaves and grass, it seems doubtful whether the alleged "protective" resemblances of caterpillars to twigs, etc., are sufficient to be of much use to them. Thus Beddard writes (on page 91 of Animal Colouration): "Judging of birds by our own standard—which is the way in which nearly all the problems relating to colour have been approached—does it seem likely that we should fail to see a caterpillar, perhaps as long or longer than the arm, of an obviously different texture from the branches, and displaying in many cases through its semi-transparent skin the pulsation of the heart, for which we were particularly searching?"

Now, birds certainly feed very largely on caterpillars, while they are but rarely seen to eat butterflies. If, therefore, the aim and object of these special resemblances is the protection of the species, we should expect to see them in a nearly perfect state in caterpillars on which birds feed very largely, and poorly developed in butterflies, which do not appear to be greatly [212] preyed upon by birds, but have to fear chiefly the comparatively dull-eyed lizards and mammals, of which the latter hunt mainly by scent. As a matter of fact, the most striking cases of resemblance to inanimate objects are seen among butterflies, which seem to stand least in need of them.

We have already cited the case of the butterfly Precis artexia. Even more marked does the unnecessary elaboration of the likeness seem to be in the Kallima butterflies.

The Theory of Warning Colouration

All biologists admit that there exist some organisms which are not coloured so as to be inconspicuous. Indeed, the colouring of certain species is such as to render them particularly conspicuous. Such species are said to be warningly coloured. They are supposed to be inedible, or to have powerful stings or other weapons of defence, or to resemble in appearance organisms which are thus protected. In the first two cases they are said to be warningly coloured, and in the last they are cited as examples of protective mimicry. With the theory of mimicry we shall deal shortly. We must first discuss the hypothesis of warning colouration.

When animals are unpalatable, or when they possess a sting or poison-fangs, it is, to use the [213] words of Wallace, "important that they should not be mistaken for defenceless or eatable species of the same class or order, since in that case they might suffer injury, or even death, before their enemies discovered the danger or the uselessness of the attack. They require some signal or danger-flag which shall serve as a warning to would-be enemies not to attack them, and they have usually obtained this in the form of conspicuous or brilliant colouration, very distinct from the protective tints of the defenceless animals allied to them" (Darwinism, page 232).

Examples of Warning Colouration

For examples of so-called warningly coloured animals, we may refer the reader to Wallace's Darwinism, Poulton's Essays on Evolution, or Beddard's Animal Colouration. An instance familiar to all is our English ladybird. "Ladybirds," says Wallace, "are another uneatable group, and their conspicuous and singularly spotted bodies serve to distinguish them at a glance from all other beetles."

In order to establish the theory of warning colouration, it is necessary to prove that all, or the great majority of conspicuously-coloured organisms, are either unpalatable or mimic unpalatable forms. If this be so, we are able to understand that the possession of gaudy colouring may be of advantage to the individual. But even if this be satisfactorily proved, we [214] must bear in mind that it does not necessarily follow that these warning colours can be accounted for on the theory of natural selection. For, in order to explain the existence of any organ by the action of natural selection, we must be able to demonstrate the utility, not only of the perfected organ, but of the organ at its very beginning, and at each subsequent stage of development. This, as we shall show, is precisely what the Neo-Darwinians are unable to do. We shall have no difficulty in proving that it would be more advantageous even to a highly nauseous creature to have remained inconspicuously coloured rather than to have gradually become more and more conspicuous.

In the first place, let us briefly examine the evidence on which rests the assertion that all gaudily-coloured insects, etc., are unpalatable, or possess stings, or mimic forms which are thus armed.

In England wasps, bees, and ladybirds are familiar examples of conspicuous insects.

The banded black and yellow pattern of the common wasp and the humble bee are regarded as advertisements or danger signals of the powerful sting.

The red-coat with its black spots is similarly believed to be a warning that the ladybird is not fit to be eaten.

Caterpillars are usually coloured grey or brown, [215] so as to be inconspicuous; but numerous exceptions occur which are brightly coloured, and of these individuals many have been experimentally proved to be objectionable as food to most insect-eating animals, being either protected by an unpleasant taste, or covered with hairs or spines.

Familiar cases are those of the abundant and conspicuous black and yellow mottled caterpillars of the European Buff-tip Moth (Pygæra bucephala), which are much disliked by birds; and the gaily—coloured Vapourer Moth caterpillar (Orgyia antiqua), with its conspicuous tufts of hair. Readers will remember that a few years back these caterpillars were a perfect plague in London, in spite of the abundance of sparrows, which feed freely on smooth green and brown caterpillars.

Oft-cited examples of warning colouration, are the three great groups of mainly tropical butterflies—the Heliconidæ of America, the Acræidæ of Africa, and the Danainæ found all over the world. In all of these the sexes are alike. They are, every one, strikingly coloured, displaying patterns of black and red, chestnut, yellow, or white. In most butterflies the lower surface of the wings is of a quiet hue, in order to render the organism inconspicuous when at rest, but in these warningly coloured groups the under surface of the wings is as gaudy as the [216] upper surface. Their flight is slow. They are tough, and exhale a characteristic odour.

Belt showed that, in Nicaragua, birds, dragonflies, and lizards seem to avoid the Heliconine butterflies, as the wings of these last are not found lying about in places where insectivorous creatures feed, whereas wings of the edible forms are to be found. Moreover, a Capuchin monkey, kept by Belt, always refused to eat Heliconine butterflies.

Finn investigated the palatability of a number of Indian insects. He found that most of the birds with which he experimented objected to the Danaine butterflies; but they disliked still more intensely two butterflies belonging to groups not universally protected—a swallowtail (Papilio aristolochiæ) and a white (Delias eucharis).

Finn further experimented with the tree-shrew or Tupaia (Tupaia ellioti), which feeds largely on insects. He found that this creature refused most emphatically all these warningly-coloured butterflies. It would under no circumstances eat the Danainæ, whereas the birds would do so if no more palatable insects were offered to them at the time.

Colonel A. Alcock found that a tame Himalayan bear indignantly refused to eat a locust (Aularches militaris) gaily coloured with black, red, and yellow, and exhaling an unpleasant-smelling [217] froth; but this bear readily devoured ordinary brown or green species.

Among cold-blooded vertebrates the common European salamander, with its bright black and yellow markings, is a striking example of warning colouration; its skin exudes, on pressure, a very poisonous secretion.

Colonel A. Alcock has described a small siluroid sea-fish, brightly banded with black and yellow, and armed with poison spines.

A well-known Indian poisonous snake, the banded Krait (Bungarus cœruleus), is conspicuously barred with wide bands of black and yellow; and in South America there occur numerous species of coral snakes, in which red is added to these conspicuous colours.

The only known poisonous lizard—the Heloderm of Mexico—is conspicuously blotched with black and salmon-colour.

Among birds, no instances of warning colouration have been recorded, though Professor Poulton has suggested that possibly the striking and contrasted tints of many tropical species may be due to this cause. The suggestion is an ingenious one, but is at present totally unsupported by evidence.

The skunks are often cited as an excellent example of warning colouration among mammals. Skunks are most conspicuously arrayed in black and white—the latter above, not below, as is [218] usual—and have bushy tails, which they carry erect. Although less powerful and ferocious than other members of the weasel family, to which they belong, skunks are notoriously protected by their abundant secretion of a very fetid liquid.

For further examples of warning colouration we would refer the reader to Beddard's illuminating book, entitled Animal Colouration.

It should be noticed that in all the cases which we have cited the colouration is not only conspicuous, but is found in both sexes, whereas in many undefended animals the male may be just as strikingly coloured, but the female is not.

We may take it as proved that there is a very general relation between gaudy colouring and inedibility, or rather unpalatability, among insects. It may safely be said that any species of insect which lives, either as an adult or as a larva, in the open will perish in the struggle for existence if, being conspicuously coloured, it is neither inedible nor armed with a weapon such as sting, nor provided with a thick cuticle, nor resembles in appearance some creature which is protected.

Warning Colouring a Drawback

But from this it is not legitimate to conclude, as Neo-Darwinians do, that these brilliant colours have been slowly brought into being by natural selection.

Why should any creature, having by the "luck" of variation and heredity acquired some [219] quality—be it strength, pugnacity, sting, or unpleasant taste—which renders it comparatively immune from persecution, proceed to advertise the fact by assuming a gaudy or striking colour? It would surely be better for such an organism to remain inconspicuous. By becoming showy it is visible to every young bird who, not having yet learned that the creature in question is unfit for food, seizes and perhaps kills it. It is true that the young bird vows that never again will it touch another such organism. But of what avail to the dying example of warning colouration is the resolution of the young bird? Moreover, the organism in question, by being conspicuous, also advertises itself to those few enemies which will eat it. There are always, as Professor Poulton justly remarks, animals which are enterprising enough to take advantage of prey which has at least the advantage of being easily seen and caught.

Conspicuous Animals Attacked

It is possible to cite cases where animals, notwithstanding the fact that they possess natural defences, become the prey of others in some exceptional cases.

The salamander can be eaten with comparative impunity by the toad, a creature very likely to meet with it.

The toad itself may be eaten; Finn saw the Indian toad (Bufo melanostictus) eat another of its own kind. He further observed that the [220] Indian water-snake (Tropidonotus piscator) and the "Crow pheasant" cuckoo (Centropus sinensis), in the free state, and the Indian Roller (Coracias indica) and the Pied Hornbill (Anthracoceros), in captivity, eat the warningly-coloured toad. On the other hand, a captive Racket-tailed drongo rejected toads when offered to it. The common cuckoo is well known to feed on hairy and "warningly-coloured" caterpillars.

Finn has also seen the glossy cuckoo in Zanzibar devouring black-and-yellow caterpillars. Moreover, in America crows are found to select deliberately highly polished and strongly flavoured beetles. Yet again, wasps are preyed upon by bee-eaters, and also eaten by our common toad. In India, Finn found, by many experiments, that the common garden lizard, or "bloodsucker" (Calotes versicolor), would eat, both in captivity and in freedom, all "warningly-coloured" butterflies, not only the Danainæ, but even Delias eucharis and the pre-eminently nauseous Papilio aristolochiæ. That this reptile is a great enemy to butterflies is rendered probable by the frequent occurrence of specimens of these insects with its semicircular bites in their wings.

Further, Finn found that bulbuls, the commonest garden birds in India, ate the Danainæ readily in captivity, even when other butterflies could be had, which was not the case with most [221] other birds. Bulbuls did, however, usually refuse the Delias and Papilio mentioned above.

The Skunk is preyed upon in America by the Eagle-owl (Bubo virginianus) and the Puma.

Thus, animals provided with natural defences are not immune from attack.

Hence natural selection cannot have encouraged the survival of individuals which displayed a conspicuous colour, for the sake of the "warning."

We must not forget that many creatures armed with powerful weapons possess the unobtrusive drab, brown, or green colouration which is associated with concealment from foes.

There can be little doubt that, but for the fact that the hive-bee can inflict a sting more severe than that of the wasp, this useful insect would have been cited as a case of a protectively coloured creature. Notwithstanding its sober brown colouring, the hive-bee is recognised and avoided.

Professor Poulton records that the dull inconspicuous caterpillar of the moth (Mænia typica) is rejected by reptiles. It must be admitted, however, that these cases among insects are very rare.

The smooth newt (Molge vulgaris), a relation of the salamander, is protected by a poisonous skin; nevertheless the creature has a dark brown back and spends most of its time on land. Its [222] black-spotted, yellow under-surface may have some protective value in the water. Neither the pike nor the common European water-tortoise will eat this newt.

Toads are nearly all very inconspicuous; nevertheless they are well protected by the acrid secretion from the skin glands; moreover, they are both recognised and avoided by those predacious creatures to whom they are distasteful. Hawks, although as a rule plainly coloured, are certainly recognised by all other birds. It would seem, therefore, that "warning colours," like the similar striking hues of many domestic animals, are incidental attributes. It has been possible for their owners to develop them, because for the most part let alone.

Eisig, long ago, pointed out that the brightly coloured pigment in the skin of these warningly coloured insects is in certain cases of an excretory nature. Therefore the inference which should be drawn is, as Beddard points out on page 173 of his Animal Colouration, "that the brilliant colours (i.e. the abundant secretion of pigment) have caused the inedibility of the species, rather than that the inedibility has necessitated the production of bright colours as an advertisement." In other words, Neo-Darwinians put the cart before the horse!

BOURU FRIAR-BIRD
BOURU FRIAR-BIRD

Like most of the group to which it belongs, this honey-eater (Tropidorhynchus bouruensis) is a soberly coloured bird, but is noisy, active, and aggressive.

BOURU ORIOLE
BOURU ORIOLE

This "mimicking" oriole (Oriolus bouruensis) is of the same tone of colour as its supposed model the Friar-bird of the same island.

[223]
In some cases these brilliantly coloured insects may be survivals of an age in which there were no birds. When these came into being and began to prey upon insects, the conspicuously coloured species which were not inedible or very unpalatable would soon

become extinct, while those that were inedible would survive as warningly-coloured insects. In other cases it is not improbable that these warningly-coloured creatures have arisen by mutations from more soberly-hued insects. It is conceivable that every now and again a mutation occurs which renders its possessor conspicuous. This will result in the early destruction of these aberrant individuals unless their newly-acquired gaudiness is either correlated with, or the result of, distastefulness.

Aposematic Sounds

In the case of warning colouration, the Neo-Darwinians have, as usual, pursued their theory to absurd lengths. Professor Poulton, for example, extends it to sounds and attitudes. "Sound," he writes, on page 324 of Essays on Evolution, "may be employed as an Aposematic character, as in the hiss of some snakes and some lizards. Certain poisonous snakes when disturbed produce by an entirely different method a far-reaching sound not unlike the hiss. Thus the rattle-snake (Crotalus) of America rapidly vibrates the series of dry, horny, cuticular cells, movably articulated to each other and to the end of the tail. The stage through which the character probably arose is witnessed in [224] another genus which vibrates its tail among dry leaves, and thus produces a warning sound. The deadly little Indian snake (Echis carinata) ('the Kuppa') makes a penetrating swishing sound by writhing the coils of its body one over the other. Special rows of the lateral scales are provided with serrated keels which cause the sound when they are rubbed against each other. Large birds, when attacked, often adopt a threatening attitude, accompanied by an intimidating sound which usually suggests more or less closely the hiss of a serpent, and thus includes an element of mimicry. . . . The cobra warns an intruder chiefly by attitude and by the broadening of its flattened neck, the effect being heightened in some species by the 'spectacles.' In such cases we often witness a combination of cryptic and Aposematic methods, the animal being concealed until disturbed, when it instantly assumes a warning attitude.

"The benefit of such intimidating attitudes is clear: a venomous snake gains far more advantage by terrifying than by killing an animal it cannot eat. By striking, the serpent temporarily loses its poison, and with this a reserve of defence. Furthermore, the poison does not cause immediate death, and the enemy would have time to injure or destroy the snake."

Intimidating Attitudes

At first sight this reasoning may seem very convincing. But consider for a moment the [225] process by which the hiss originated and gradually increased by natural selection. We must suppose that the rattle-snake was formerly incapable of making any sound. One day a variety appeared in which the skin was slightly hardened, so that when the creature moved its body rapidly there issued a slight sound. This must have caused an enemy to refrain from attack; it thus lived to transmit this peculiarity to its offspring, and those which made more noise than their ancestors escaped, while those that made less succumbed to their enemies. For ourselves, we find it quite impossible to believe that the rattle was thus gradually evolved by means of natural selection. Indeed, we are inclined to think that neither the hiss of the cobra nor its "intimidating attitude" has any terrifying effect on its adversary. In the case of the cobra we are able to cite positive evidence that dogs and cattle show no alarm at the attitude.

"Dogs," writes D. Dewar of this display, "regard it as a huge joke. Of this I have satisfied myself again and again, for when out coursing at Muttra we frequently came across cobras, which the dogs used invariably to chase, and we sometimes had great difficulty in keeping the dogs off, since they seemed to be unaware that the creature was venomous."

Colonel Cunningham writes, on page 347 of Some Indian Friends and Acquaintances: "Sporting [226] dogs are very apt to come to grief where cobras abound, as there is something very alluring to them in the sight of a large snake when it sits up nodding and snarling; and it is often difficult to come up in time to prevent the occurrence of irreparable mischief."

Colonel Cunningham also states that many ruminants have a great animosity to snakes, and are prone to attack any that they may come across.

We may therefore well be sceptical as to the value of intimidating attitudes to those creatures which are in the habit of striking them.

Mimicry

In a work of this kind it is neither possible nor necessary to consider in great detail the mass of evidence which has been advanced in favour of the theory of mimetic resemblance.

Chapters vii. and viii. of Professor Poulton's Essays on Evolution contain an up-to-date statement of the facts in favour of the theory. Professor Poulton believes that in all cases mimetic resemblance is the result of the action of natural selection.

He admits that there is no direct evidence in its favour, but asserts that "the facts of the cosmos, so far as we know them, are consistent with the theory, and none of them inconsistent with it" (page 271).

[227]
Theory of Protective Mimicry

We are not at all sure that no facts are against the theory of protective mimicry. We shall presently set forth some which to us seem, if not actually inconsistent with the theory, at least to point to the conclusion that the phenomenon may be explained otherwise than as a product of natural selection.

Evidence for the Theory

Let us first briefly state the case for the theory of protective mimicry.

1. It is asserted that the mimicking species and that which is mimicked are often not nearly related. For example, the unpalatable larva of the Cinnabar Moth (Euchelia jacobaeæ) is said to mimic a wasp, because it has black and yellow rings round its body.

"The conclusion which emerges most clearly," writes Poulton (p. 232), "is the entire independence of zoological affinity exhibited by these resemblances." This is supposed to be proof that Darwin was wrong when he asserted that the original likeness was due to affinity. Says Poulton: "The preservation of an original likeness due to affinity undoubtedly explains certain cases of mimicry, but we cannot appeal to this principle in the most remarkable instances."

2. It is asserted that species which are mimicked are invariably either armed with a sting, well defended, or unpalatable, so that it is against the interest of insectivorous creatures to attack them. It is further asserted that the [228] species imitated are "even more unpalatable than the generality of their order."

3. It is pointed out that the most distasteful groups of butterflies—the Danaidæ, the Acræinæ, the Ithomiinæ, and the Heliconinæ—consist of large numbers of species which

89

closely resemble one another. This is said to be due to Müllerian mimicry. Mayer states that in South America there are 450 species of inedible Ithomiinæ which display only 15 distinct colours, while the 200 species of Papilio, which are edible, exhibit 36 distinct colours. Nevertheless, he says, there is no lack of individual variability among the former hence their conservatism as regards colour cannot be attributed to their having but little tendency to vary.

4. It is asserted that although in many cases the mimetic resemblances extend to the minutest detail, nevertheless they are not accompanied by any changes in the mimetic species except such as assist in the production or strengthening of a superficial likeness.

Pictures illustrating such cases of mimicry are figured on pp. 241, 247, and 251 of Wallace's Darwinism (1890 edition).

5. It is stated that mimetic resemblance is not confined to colour, but extends to pattern, form, attitude, and movement; that deep-seated organs are affected when the superficial resemblance is intensified, but not otherwise. Poulton cites [229] Clytus arietis, the "wasp-beetle," as an example of this.

6. It is asserted that mimetic resemblances are produced in the most diverse ways; that the modes whereby the similarity in appearance is brought about are varied, but the result is uniform.

"A lepidopterous insect," writes Poulton (p. 251), "requires above all to gain transparent wings, and this, in the most striking cases that have been studied, is produced by the loose attachment of the scales, so that they easily and rapidly fall off and leave the wing bare except for a marginal line and along the veins (Hemaris, Trochilium)."

7. It is alleged that the imitator and imitated are always found in the same locality. If they did not do so no advantage would be derived from the resemblance. It is further alleged that where the mimicking species is edible it is invariably less abundant where it occurs than the species it imitates.

8. It is pointed out that it sometimes happens that where in the mimic the sexes differ in appearance, the male copies one species, the female quite a different one. This is said to be because the deception would be liable to be detected if the mimicking species became common relatively to that which is imitated. "We therefore find that two or more models are mimicked [230] by the same species" (Essays on Evolution, p. 372).

Occasionally the female mimics two other species, i.e. she occurs in two forms, each like a different species.

It sometimes happens that the female alone mimics. This is said by Wallace to be due to her greater need of protection. When she is laden with eggs her flight is slow, and therefore she requires a special degree of protection.

9. It is said that in some species we find a non-mimetic ancestor preserved on islands where the struggle for existence is less severe, while on the adjacent continent mimicry has been developed.

10. It is alleged that in the cases where moths resemble butterflies the former are either as diurnal as the butterflies or are species which "readily fly by day when disturbed."

11. It is asserted that some seasonally dimorphic forms are examples of mimicry only in one state, in the form that comes into being at the time when the struggle for existence is

most severe; that is to say, in the dry season, in Africa, when insect life is far less abundant than in the rainy season.

In other cases the mimicry of the dry-weather form is said to be far more perfect.

Instances of this phenomenon are set forth in Professor Poulton's Essays on Evolution.

[231]
Alternative Theories

It will be observed that we have quoted very largely from Professor Poulton's work. Our reason for so doing is that he appears to be the most prominent advocate of the theory of protective mimicry, and his work, which was published in 1908, may be taken as the latest Neo-Darwinian pronouncement on the subject.

Hence if we can show, as we believe we can, that his arguments are not sound, we may take it that we have demonstrated that the theory in its present form is untenable.

It is worthy of notice that Professor Poulton sets forth three other suggestions which have been proposed as substitutes for natural selection as an explanation of the phenomena of mimicry.

The first is the theory of External Causes, namely, that the resemblance is due to some external cause, such as food or climate.

The second is the theory of Internal Causes, which states that mimetic resemblance is due to internal developmental causes.

The third is the suggestion that sexual selection has caused the origin of these resemblances.

He then proceeds to demolish these to his own satisfaction, and adds triumphantly, "The conclusion appears inevitable that under no theory, except natural selection, do the various resemblances of animals to their organic and [232] inorganic environments fall together into a natural arrangement and receive a common explanation" (p. 228).

To reasoning of this description there is an obvious reply. Even if it be granted that the alternatives to the theory of natural selection as set forth by Professor Poulton are untenable, it does not follow that natural selection affords an adequate explanation. If A, B, C and D are charged with theft and the prosecutor proves that neither A nor B nor C committed the theft, this will not suffice to secure the conviction of D. It is quite possible that a fifth person, E, may be the culprit.

Much of the popularity of the theory of natural selection is due to the fact that biologists have not yet been able to discover a substitute for it.

It seems to us that the proper method of making progress in science is not to bolster up natural selection by ingenious speculations, but to look around for other hitherto undiscovered causes.

KING-CROW OR DRONGO
KING-CROW OR DRONGO

This very conspicuous black bird (Dicrurus ater), ranging from Africa to China, is a striking feature of the landscape wherever it occurs.

DRONGO-CUCKOO

The fork of the tail in this bird is unique among cuckoos, but is nevertheless much less developed than in the supposed model, and may be an adaptation for evolution in flight, as such tails usually appear to be.

Objections to the Theory that the so-called Cases of Mimicry owe their Origin to Natural Selection

It is obvious that for one creature to resemble another can be of little or no benefit to either until the resemblance is tolerably close. It is, [233] therefore, insufficient to prove the utility of the perfected resemblance. We may readily grant this and yet maintain that the origin of the resemblance cannot be due to the action of natural selection.

The Drongo-cuckoo (Surniculus lugubris) displays so great a likeness to the King Crow (Dicrurus ater) that it is frequently held up by Neo-Darwinians as an excellent example of mimicry among birds. But D. Dewar writes, on page 204 of Birds of the Plains: "I do not pretend to know the colour of the last common ancestor of all the cuckoos, but I do not believe that the colour was black. What then caused Surniculus lugubris to become black and assume a king-crow-like tail?

"A black feather or two, even if coupled with some lengthening of the tail, would in no way assist the cuckoo in placing its egg in the drongo's nest. Suppose an ass were to borrow the caudal appendage of the king of the forest, pin it on behind him, and then advance among his fellows with loud brays, would any donkey of average intelligence be misled by the feeble attempt at disguise? I think not. Much less would a king-crow be deceived by a few black feathers in the plumage of a cuckoo. I do not believe that natural selection has any direct connection with the nigritude of the drongo-cuckoo."

Darwin was fully alive to this difficulty when [234] he wrote: "As some writers have felt much difficulty in understanding how the first step in the process of mimicry could have been effected through natural selection, it may be well to remark that the process probably commenced long ago between forms not widely dissimilar in colour" (Descent of Man, 10th Ed., p. 324). Such a statement is of course quite inconsistent with the Neo-Darwinian position. "The conclusion which emerges most clearly," writes Poulton (Essays on Evolution, p. 232), "is the entire independence of zoological affinity exhibited by these resemblances; and one of the rare cases in which Darwin's insight into a biological problem did not lead him right was when he suggested that a former closer relationship may help us to a general understanding of the origin of mimicry. The preservation of an original likeness due to affinity undoubtedly explains certain cases of mimicry, but we cannot appeal to this principle in the most remarkable instances."

It is unnecessary to labour this point. It is surely evident to everyone with average intelligence that, until the resemblance between two forms has advanced a considerable way, the likeness cannot be of utility to either, or at any rate of sufficient utility to give its possessor a survival advantage in the struggle for existence. Until it reaches this stage, natural selection cannot [235] operate on it. It is therefore absurd to look upon natural selection as the direct cause of the origin of the likeness. When once a certain degree of resemblance has risen, it is quite likely that in some cases natural selection has strengthened the likeness.

The second great objection to the Neo-Darwinian explanation of the phenomenon known as mimicry is that in many cases the resemblance is unnecessarily exact. Even as we saw how the Kallimas, or dead-leaf butterflies, carried their resemblance to dead leaves to such an extent as to make it appear probable that factors other than natural selection have had a share in its production, so do we see in certain cases of mimetic resemblance an unnecessarily faithful likeness.

The Brain-fever Bird

The common Hawk Cuckoo of India (Hierococcyx varius) furnishes an example of this: "The brain-fever bird," writes Finn, on page 58 of Ornithological and Other Oddities, "is the most wonderful feather copy of the Indian Sparrow-hawk or Shikra (Astur badius). All the markings in the hawk are reproduced in the cuckoo, which is also of about the same size, and of similar proportions in the matter of tail and wing; and both hawk and cuckoo having a first plumage quite different from the one they assume when adult, the resemblance extends to that too. Moreover, their flight is so much the same that [236] unless one is near enough to see the beak, or can watch the bird settle and note the difference between the horizontal pose of the cuckoo and the erect bearing of the hawk, it is impossible to tell them apart on a casual view." Moreover, the tail of the cuckoo sometimes hangs down vertically, thus intensifying the likeness to the hawk.

It is quite possible that the brain-fever bird derives some benefit from the resemblance; indeed, it has been seen to alarm small birds, even as the hawk-like common cuckoo frightens its dupes, but, as D. Dewar pointed out, on page 105 of vol. 57 of the Journal of the Society of Arts, "this is not sufficient to explain a likeness which is so faithful as to extend to the marking of each individual feather. When a babbler espies a hawk-like bird, it does not wait to inspect each feather before fleeing in terror; hence all that is necessary to the cuckoo is that it should bear a general resemblance to the shikra. The fact that the likeness extends to minute details in feather marking, points to the fact that in each case identical causes have operated to produce this type of plumage." This conclusion is still further strengthened by the fact that the likeness extends to the immature plumage, that is to say, exists at a time when it cannot assist the cuckoo in its parasitical work.

Poulton meets this objection as follows:

SHIKRA HAWK
SHIKRA HAWK

The upper surface of the tail, not shown in this drawing, exactly corresponds with that of the cuckoo "mimic."

HAWK-CUCKOO
HAWK-CUCKOO

This species (Hierococcyx varius) is commonly known in India as the "Brain-fever bird."

[237]
Hypertely

"All such criticism is founded on our imperfect knowledge of the struggle for existence. The impressions and judgments of man are immensely influenced by the 'corroborative detail,' giving 'artistic verisimilitude to a bold and unconvincing narrative.' Indeed, the laughter which is invariably raised by this passage from The Mikado is, I have always thought, not only or chiefly due to the humour of the application, but to the way in which a great and familiar truth breaks in upon the listener with all the pleasing surprise which belongs to epigram. Birds, the chief enemies of insects, are known to have powers of sight far superior to those of man, and, from our experience of them in captivity, it may be safely asserted that their attention is attracted by excessively minute detail. Until our knowledge of the struggle for life is far more extensive than at present, the argument founded on Hypertely may be left to contend with another argument often employed against the explanation of cryptic and mimetic resemblance by natural selection. Hypertely assumes that there are unnecessary details in the resemblance, that the resemblance is perfect beyond the requirements of the insect; the second argument maintains that birds are so supremely sharp-sighted that no resemblance, however perfect, is of any avail against them. In the meantime the majority of naturalists will probably reject both extremes, and believe that [238] the enemies are certainly sharp-sighted and successful in pursuit, but that perfection in detail makes their task a harder one, and gives to the individuals possessing it in a higher degree than others, increased chances of escape, and of becoming the parents of future generations." (Essays on Evolution, p. 302.)

This long quotation requires careful consideration, since to us it appears to be typical of the kind of reasoning resorted to by Neo-Darwinians.

Note the reference to our "imperfect knowledge of the struggle for existence." This is almost invariably the last refuge of the Neo-Darwinian when worsted in argument. We fully admit that there is still much to be learned of the nature of the struggle for existence, but such a statement sounds very curious when uttered to those who pin their faith to the theory which sees in the principle of natural selection an explanation of all the phenomena of the organic world. Natural selection, be it remembered, is but a name for the struggle for existence.

Birds capturing Butterflies

"Birds," says Professor Poulton, "are the chief enemies of insects." This may be so. But we greatly doubt whether they are the chief enemies of butterflies and moths, among which the most perfect examples of mimicry are supposed to occur.

We have watched birds closely for some years, but believe that we could almost count on our [239] fingers the cases in which we have seen a bird chase a butterfly.

Professor Poulton, being aware of this objection, sets forth, on pp. 283-292 of Essays on Evolution, the evidence he has gathered in favour of the view that birds are the chief enemies of butterflies and other lepidoptera.

As the result of five years' observation in S. Africa, Mr G. A. K. Marshall was able to record some eight cases of birds capturing butterflies. In three cases the butterfly seized was warningly coloured, or, at any rate, conspicuous! In two of these eight cases the bird failed to capture its quarry!

Says Mr Marshall, "the fact that birds refrain from pursuing butterflies may be due rather to the difficulty in catching them than to any widespread distastefulness on the part of these insects."

During six years' observation in India and Ceylon, Colonel Yerbury records some half dozen cases of birds capturing, or attempting to capture, insects. He writes: "In my opinion an all-sufficient reason for the rarity of the occurrence exists in the fact that in butterflies the edible matter is a minimum, while the inedible wings, etc., are a maximum."

Colonel C. T. Bingham in Burma states that between 1878 and 1891 he on two occasions witnessed the systematic hawking of butterflies [240] by birds, although he observed on other occasions some isolated cases.

This appears to be the sum total of the evidence adduced by Professor Poulton as regards the capture of butterflies by birds. This seems to us an altogether insufficient foundation upon which to build the theory that the cases of resemblance between unrelated species have been effected by natural selection.

It is, however, to be noted that probably among birds the most dangerous enemies of butterflies are not those that habitually catch insect prey on the wing. Such are experts in the art of fly-catching, and would despise the comparatively meatless butterfly. One often comes across butterflies with an identical notch in each wing, which leaves little room for doubt that those particular butterflies had been snapped at, while resting, by a bird. Among birds the chief enemies of butterflies and moths are probably to be found in those that hunt for their food in bushes and trees.

Thus, what we do know of the nature of the struggle for existence offers but poor support to the Neo-Darwinian explanations of the cases of so-called mimicry in nature.

Observing-powers of Birds

Professor Poulton's idea of pitting the argument of Hypertely against that of the alleged supreme sharp-sightedness of birds is ingenious, but is not likely to satisfy very many people save [241] those content to live in a fools' paradise. If birds are supremely sharp-sighted, and pay attention to excessively minute detail, the difficulty of accounting for the origin of protective mimicry on the natural selection hypothesis becomes all the greater.

The question whether or not birds are good observers is a most interesting one. Unfortunately, hitherto, but little attention has been paid to the subject. The evidence available seems to point to the fact that birds, like savages, have sharp eyes only for certain objects—that is to say, for the things they are accustomed to look out for. All observers of nature must have noticed how quick a butcher-bird is to catch sight of a tiny insect upon the ground at a distance of some yards from his perch.

On the other hand, it is said that when there is snow upon the ground wood pigeons will approach quite close to a man wearing white clothes and a white hat, provided he keep perfectly still. Finn once witnessed in Calcutta a sparrow pick up a very young toad, obviously by mistake, for it dropped it at once with evident distaste. Birds of prey are supposed to have remarkably good eyesight; yet they can readily be caught by a net stretched out before their quarry. They are not trained to be on the watch for such things as nets, and so do not appear to notice one when erected.

[242]
It is thus our belief that the very perfection and detail of some so-called mimetic resemblances are a very serious objection to the theory of protective mimicry as enunciated by Professor Poulton and other Neo-Darwinians.

There is yet a further objection to this theory, one which, in our opinion, is fatal to the hypothesis in its generally accepted form.

A number of cases occur where two species, in no way related, show close resemblance to one another under such circumstances that neither can possibly derive any benefit from the likeness. The theory of protective mimicry is quite unable to explain these cases. This fact leads to a suspicion that, in the instances where the theory does at first sight appear to offer an explanation, the resemblance may also be due to mere coincidence.

We may perhaps call the cases which the theory of mimicry is unable to account for "false mimicry," but in so doing we must bear in mind the possibility that some, at any rate, of the examples of so-called mimicry may, on further investigation, prove to be nothing of the kind.

95

"False" Mimicry among Mammals

The Cacomistle of Mexico (Bassaris astuta), one of the raccoon family, has a grey body and long black-and-white ringed tail, just like the ring-tailed Lemur of Madagascar (Lemur catta); [243] both are arboreal and about the same size, and this lemur's colouration is exceptional in its family.

The banded Duiker-buck of West Africa (Cephalophus doriae), has the same very unusual colouration as the thylacine or marsupial wolf of Tasmania, light brown, with bold black bands across the hinder part of the back, and the animals are about the same size.

The dormouse of Europe closely resembles a small American Opossum (Didelphys murina), and a larger opossum (D. crassicaudata) is very like the Siberian Mink (Mustela sibirica).

The Flying Squirrel of North America (Sciuropterus volucella) is closely copied by the Flying Phalanger (Petaurus breviceps) of Australia.

It will be readily seen that in no one of these cases can the likeness be of utility to either the "model" or the "copy."

False Batesian Mimicry among Birds

There are many instances of this phenomenon among birds. The New Zealand Cuckoo (Urodynamis tritensis) shows a far closer resemblance to the American Sparrow-hawk (Accipiter cooperi) than to any New Zealand hawk, and in fact closely mimics this quite alien bird.

The stormy petrel, a purely oceanic bird, closely resembles in size, colour, and style of flight the Indian Swift (Cypselus affinis), a purely [244] inland creature; both are sooty black, with a conspicuous white patch on the lower back.

The Pied Babbling Thrush (Crateropus bicolor) of Africa is singularly like the Pied Myna (Græulipica melanoptera) of Java, both being of about the same size, with white body and black wings and tail quills. This, we may add, is a very unusual colouration among small birds.

The black-headed Oriole (Oriolus melanocephalus) of India is very similar in appearance to the common Troupial (Icterus vulgaris) of Brazil; indeed, the troupials, a purely American group, are so like the old world orioles in colour that they usurp their name in America.

The little insectivorous Iora (Ægithina tiphia) of India strongly resembles in size and colour a Siskin (Chrysomitris colambiana) from South America, the males in both being black above and yellow below, while in the females the black is replaced by olive-green.

Another Indian babbler (Cephalopyrus flammiceps), yellowish-green, with orange forehead, is closely copied by, or copies, the well-known Brazilian Saffron-finch (Sycalis flaveola).

In Fergusson Island, near New Guinea, there is a ground pigeon (Otidiphaps insularis) which is black with chestnut wings, like several of the powerful ground cuckoos of the genus Centropus, but no species of these cuckoos so coloured appears to inhabit the island.

[245]

In Africa there is a tit (Parus leucopterus) which has the same very unusual colouration as an East-Indian bulbul (Micropus melanoleucus), both being black with a white patch on the wing-coverts. These two birds are about the same size. As showing the purely coincidental character of such resemblances, we may mention that this same rare pattern occurs again in our Black Guillemot (Uria grylle) and in the Muscovy Duck (Cairina moschata).

We have already quoted Gadow (p. 198) on "false mimicry" among snakes. He also gives, on p. 110 of Through Southern Mexico, an example of this phenomenon among amphibia. It is, he writes, "impossible to distinguish certain green tree-frogs of the African genus Rappia from a Hyla, unless we cut them open. If they lived side by side, which they do not, this close resemblance would be extolled as an example of mimicry."

We should be very greatly surprised if abundant examples of "false mimicry" are not found among insects. We trust that this remark will stimulate some entomologist to pay attention to the subject.

It is the essence of Müllerian mimicry that both model and copy are immune from attack from enemies. Unfortunately for the theory, similar resemblances occur among birds of prey, [246] where neither party can benefit from the association. This gives rise to what we may perhaps call false Müllerian mimicry. Thus the goshawk and peregrine falcon resemble each other in being brown above and streaked below in immature plumage, and having barred underparts and a grey upper plumage when adult.

Theory of Mimicry Criticised

Having stated the more important objections to the theory of protective mimicry, it now remains for us to deal specifically with each head of evidence offered in its favour.

1. With regard to the assertion that the model and its copy are often not nearly related, we have shown that among mammals and birds instances of resemblance between widely-separated groups occur under such circumstances that neither party can derive any benefit therefrom.

2. As regards the assertion that species which are mimicked are either well-defended or unpalatable, this certainly does not hold good with regard to some at any rate of the coincidental resemblances among birds which we have pointed out; even if these pairs of similar species lived in the same country it would require considerable ingenuity to say why one should mimic the other.

3. As regards the argument that the inedible species of Ithomiinæ, etc., display only fifteen colours, while the less numerous edible Papilios [247] display more than double this number of colours, we may draw attention to the fact that those birds which are most immune from attack are precisely those which display the smallest range as regards colour, e.g., hawks, owls, crows, gulls, storks, and cranes. As we have already submitted, no question of Müllerian association comes in here.

On the other hand, the eminently edible families of game-birds and ducks display great variety of colour, in the males at all events.

4. As regards the statement that although in many cases the mimetic resemblances extend to the minutest detail, they are not accompanied by any structural changes except such as assist in the production of a superficial likeness, we may refer to the case we have already cited of the New Zealand cuckoo, which, though it so closely copies an American hawk, is typically cuculine in structure. Here, of course, there can be no question of advantage to the "mimicking" cuckoo in the resemblances.

5. In answer to the argument that mimetic resemblance extends to form, attitude, and movement, as well as colour, and that deep-seated organs are affected only when the superficial resemblance is thereby intensified, we may draw attention to such cases as the following:—

(a) The harmless Indian Snake (Lycodon aulicus) is closely similar to the well-known Krait (Bungarus cœruleus), [248] also Indian; but the resemblance extends to a structural detail which can hardly have mimetic value—namely, the harmless snake has long, fang-like front teeth, though these are unconnected with poison-glands. Animals which come into contact with the krait and its mimic are hardly likely to inspect their teeth.

(b) A considerable number of birds of the shrike group—known as Cuckoo-Shrikes (Campophaga)—closely resemble cuckoos in plumage; but even if they derive any benefit from mimicking birds which are credited with being mimics already, they cannot profit by the fact that the shafts of the rump-feathers in both groups are stiffened; this being a peculiarity which would not be perceptible until the bird was in the grasp of an aggressor.

(c) As a third case of coincidence we may refer to the tubercle in the nostril of the Brain-fever-bird (Hierococcyx varius), as a minute detail of hawk-like appearance, though not present in the particular species imitated.

6. The argument that mimetic resemblances are produced in the most diverse ways, but the result is uniform, loses much of its force when we consider the various methods by which short-tailed birds appear to have long caudal appendages.

In the peacock it is the upper tail coverts which are elongated; in the Stanley Crane [249] (Tetrapteryx paradisea) it is the innermost or tertiary quills of wing; in one of the egrets some of the feathers of the upper back grow to a great length and form a train; in the Bird of Paradise (Paradisea apoda) the long flank plumes are commonly mistaken for the tail.

In these cases there can be no question of mimicry.

7. We have shown that the idea that imitator and imitated are always found in the same area is absolutely fallacious. In birds, for example, the most striking resemblances appear to occur between species that dwell far apart.

8. We can cite, as parallel to the case of a mimicking species of which the male copies one model and the female another, the strange similarity between the barred brown plumage of the female blackcock and that of the female eider-duck. The males of these species, although both black and white, differ greatly in appearance; but the male blackcock is admittedly very like the male of another species of sea-duck—the scoter.

9. Against the supposed ancestral non-mimetic forms existing on islands we can pit the "mimetic" orioles in small islands and their non-mimetic cousins on the mainland. In Australia an oriole of what appears to be an ancestral style lives beside, but declines to mimic, a friar bird of a very pronounced type.

[250]
10. The case of certain diurnal moths mimicking butterflies appears to be explicable without the aid of the theory of protective mimicry. When two species adopt the same method of obtaining food, it not infrequently happens that a professional likeness springs up between them. Of this the swifts and swallows afford a striking illustration.

11. As a set-off to the cases where the alleged mimicry is confined to certain seasons of the year, we may cite the case of the pheasant-tailed Jaçana (Hydrophasianus chirurgus),

98

which in its winter plumage might easily be mistaken, when on the wing, for the paddy bird or Pond Heron (Ardeola grayii), both being of like size and having a brown back, long green legs, and white wings. Moreover, they are to be found in the same localities in India. At the breeding season, however, they are absolutely different in plumage.

Yet another argument commonly adduced in favour of the theory of protective mimicry is that local variations of the imitated species are sometimes followed by the imitator; thus the butterfly Danais chrysippus shows a white patch on the hind wings in Africa, and this is followed by its mimic.

But the same thing occurs, quite irrationally, so to speak, among birds. The peregrine falcon and hobby of Europe are only winter migrants [251] to India, where they are replaced as residents by the Shaheen (Falco peregrinator) and Indian Hobby (F. severus). Both these differ from the migratory forms by being blacker above and chestnut below, instead of cream colour. Thus the resemblance occurs in each race. A similar distinction, as noted by Blyth, exists between the Common Swallow (Hirundo rustica) and the Swallow (H. tytleri) of Eastern Asia, the latter having the whole ventral surface rufous instead of only the throat. Yet no one will suggest that swallows mimic falcons, or that there is mimicry between the peregrine and hobby. It is obvious that such parallel changes occur independently of mimicry.

The Water-rail (Rallus aquaticus) and Baillon's Crake (Porzana bailloni) of Europe are distinguished from their allies of Eastern Asia by having the sides of the head plain grey, whereas the Eastern Asiatic forms (R. indicus and P. pusilla) have a brown streak along each side of the face. Here, again, we have an instance of birds of the same family varying together with geographical distribution.

"Recognition" Colours

One of the prettiest conceits of the Wallaceian school of zoologists is the theory of recognition markings.

"If," writes Wallace, on page 217 of Darwinism, [252] "we consider the habits and life-histories of those animals which are more or less gregarious, comprising a large proportion of the herbivora, some carnivora, and a considerable number of all orders of birds, we shall see that a means of ready recognition of its own kind, at a distance or during rapid motion, in the dusk of twilight or in partial cover, must be of the greatest advantage and often lead to the preservation of life. Animals of this kind will not usually receive a stranger in their midst. While they keep together they are generally safe from attack, but a solitary straggler becomes an easy prey to the enemy; it is therefore of the highest importance that, in such a case, the wanderer should have every facility for discovering its companions with certainty at any distance within the range of vision.

"Some means of easy recognition must be of vital importance to the young and inexperienced of each flock, and it also enables the sexes to recognise their kind and thus avoid the evils of infertile crosses; and I am inclined to believe that its necessity has had a more widespread influence in determining the diversities of animal colouration than any other cause whatever. To it may probably be imputed the singular fact that whereas bilateral symmetry of colouration is very frequently lost among domesticated animals, it almost universally prevails in a state of nature; [253] for if the two sides of an animal were unlike, and the diversity of colouration among domestic animals occurred in a wild state, easy recognition would be impossible among numerous closely allied forms."

As examples of recognition colouration, Wallace cites, among others, the white upturned tail of the rabbit—a "signal flag of danger," the conspicuous white patch displayed by many antelopes, the white marks on the wing- and tail-feathers of the British species of butcher-birds, the stone-chat, the whin-chat, and the wheat-ear.

Wallace therefore asserts, firstly, that recognition marks not only help herbivorous animals to keep together, but act as a danger signal; the member of a flock which first catches sight of the enemy takes to its heels, displaying its white flag, which is the signal of danger to the other members of the flock. Secondly, that recognition marks prevent the evils of infertile crosses. Thirdly, that the necessity of being able to recognise one another has rigidly preserved bilateral symmetry among animals in a state of nature.

As regards assertion number one, we would point out that where a flock of herbivora is being stalked by a beast of prey, the member of the flock nearest to the enemy—that is to say, the hindmost member—will probably be the first to observe him. As that creature will be more unfavourably situated for escape than the rest of [254] the herd, it will not be to their advantage to follow the line it has taken. Moreover, being at the rear of the flock, it is not in a good position to take the lead, and its pursuer is likely to see the danger signal before its friends do. It would thus seem that "danger signals," while possibly sometimes of service to their possessors, are on the whole ornaments which might profitably be dispensed with. Natural selection can scarcely be charged with the production of a character of such doubtful utility to the organism.

Moreover, flourishing species of many gregarious animals do not possess any "signal flag of danger," while, on the other hand, a great many solitary species display markings that render them very conspicuous when in motion. Take the case of the famous Indian Paddy Bird (Ardeola grayii). This, when at rest, is coloured so as to be very difficult to distinguish from its surroundings, but flight transforms it, for it then displays its milk-white pinions, which would make a perfect danger signal, if only it were not peculiarly solitary in its habits. Its gregarious brethren, the Cattle Egrets (Bubulcus coromandus), on the other hand, display no danger signal.

Interbreeding of Allied Species

That these recognition marks prevent the intercrossing of allied species and the production of infertile hybrids appears to be pure fiction. As we have already shown, hybrids between allied species are by no means always infertile. [255] Moreover, species which differ only in colour seem usually to interbreed in those parts where they meet.

"This interbreeding," writes Finn, on page 14 of Ornithological and Other Oddities, "occurs where the carrion crow (Corvus corone) meets the hooded crow (Corvus cornix), where the European and Himalayan goldfinches (Carduelis carduelis and C. caniceps) encounter each other, and where the blue rollers of India and Burma (Coracias indicus and C. affinis) come into contact, to say nothing of other cases."

Of these other cases, the Indian bulbuls of the genus Molpastes form a very remarkable one. In all places where two of the so-called species meet they appear to interbreed, and so freely do they interbreed that at the points where the allied species run into one another it is not possible to refer the bulbuls to either species. Thus William Jesse writes of the Madras Red-vented Bulbul (Molpastes hæmorrhous) (page 487 of The Ibis for July 1902): "This bird, although I have given it the above designation, is not the true M. hæmorrhous. I have examined numbers of skins and taken nests and eggs time after time, and have come to the conclusion that our type is very constant, and at the same time differs from all the red-vented bulbuls hitherto described. The dimensions tally with those given by Oates for M. hæmorrhous, while the black of the crown [256] terminates rather abruptly on the hind neck, and is not extended along the back, as is the case with M. intermedius and M. bengalensis. On the other hand, as in the two last species, the ear coverts are chocolate. Furthermore, I may add—although I attach little importance to this—that the eggs of the

Lucknow bird which I have seen are, without exception, far smaller than my eggs of genuine M. intermedius from the Punjab. My own opinion is that the Lucknow race is the result of a hybridisation between the other three species."

Further, in Bannu, Mr D. Donald saw M. intermedius and M. leucogenys paired at the same nest. That gentleman could not possibly be mistaken on the point, as the latter species has white cheeks and yellow under tail-coverts, while the cheeks of the former species are dark-coloured and the patch of feathers under the tail is red. Similarly, Whitehead and Magrath, writing of the birds of the Kurram Valley (Ibis, January 1909), record that the former shot no fewer than twelve bulbuls, which undoubtedly appear to be hybrids between these two species. As these hybrids differ considerably inter se, there seems no room for doubt that they breed with one another and with the parent species.

Symmetry in Nature

Wallace's third statement, that if the two sides of animals in a state of nature were alike, easy recognition would be impossible among numerous [257] closely allied forms, reminds us forcibly of the sad case of the boy whose tailor was his mother. Humanum est errare: she made her son one pair of trousers that fastened up behind, so that the poor boy when wearing them never knew whether he was going to or coming home from school! If animals are able to recognise their mates, their bilateral symmetry does not seem necessary to enable them to distinguish their fellows from allied species.

It is, indeed, true that asymmetrically marked animals are very rarely seen in the wild state, while they are the rule rather than the exception among domesticated species. But this appears to be due, not to the necessity of recognition markings in nature, but to the fact that those animals that display a tendency to massed pigment perish in the struggle for existence, since this massing of pigment appears to be correlated with weakness of constitution. In other words, this massing of pigment is an unfavourable variation, which under natural conditions dooms its possessor. In the easier circumstances of domestication, animals which are irregularly pigmented are able to survive, so that, among them, the almost universal tendency to the massing of pigment can be followed without let or hindrance.

It is unnecessary to say more upon this subject. The few facts we have set forth suffice to destroy this particular excrescence on the Darwinian theory.

[258]
The Colouring of Flowers and Fruits

Extremely interesting though the subject be, we are unable to consider at length the generally accepted theory that the colour markings and perfumes of wild flowers are the result of the unconscious selection exercised by insects.

While not denying that many flowers profit by their colouring, that these colours may sometimes serve to attract the insects, by means of which cross-fertilisation is effected, we are not prepared to go to the length of admitting that all the colours, etc., displayed by flowers and floral structures are due to the unconscious selection exercised by insects. It is one thing to admit that the colour of its flowers is of direct utility to a plant; it is quite another to assert that the colour in question owes its origin and development to natural selection. Our attitude towards the generally accepted explanation of the colours of flowers is similar to that which we adopt towards the theory of protective mimicry among animals. In certain cases we are prepared to admit that the mimicking organism derives benefit from the likeness; but this, we assert, is no proof that natural selection has originated the likeness.

Cross- versus Self-fertilisation

101

The theory that flowers have developed their colours in order to attract insects to them, and thus secure cross-fertilisation, is based on the [259] assumption that cross-fertilisation is advantageous to plants. It is questionable whether this assumption is justified. True it is that numbers of experiments have been performed, which show that, in many cases, flowers which are artificially self-fertilised yield comparatively few seeds. But experiments of this kind do not prove very much.

To place on the stigma pollen from the anthers of the same flower, in case of a plant which for many generations has been cross-fertilised, is to subject the plant in question to a novel experience—an experience which may be compared to transplanting it to another soil. The immediate effect may appear to be unfavourable, although, if the experiment be persisted in, the ultimate results may prove beneficial to the plant.

That this is the case with some flowers that are artificially fertilised is asserted by the Rev. G. Henslow. This observer states, that had Darwin pursued his investigations further, he would probably have modified his views regarding the benefits of self-fertilisation. Darwin's statement that "Nature abhors perpetual self-fertilisation" seems to be as far from the truth as that which declares "Nature abhors a vacuum."

From the mere fact that cross-fertilised flowers yield a greater quantity of seed than they do when self-fertilised, it does not necessarily follow [260] that cross-fertilisation is advantageous. The amount of seed produced is probably not always a criterion as to the advantages of the crossing to the plant. Some flowers yield most seed when fertilised by the pollen from flowers belonging to a different species!

It is significant that some plants produce cleistogamous flowers, that is to say, flowers which invariably fertilise themselves. Such flowers never open; so that the visits of insects are precluded.

According to Bentham, the Pansy (Viola tricolor) is the only British species of Viola in which the showy flowers produce seeds. The other species are all propagated by their cleistogamous flowers. The genus Viola is an advanced species: it would therefore seem that the production of cleistogamous flowers is an advance on the production of entomophilous flowers. Cleistogamous blossoms are obviously more economical.

Insects and Flowers

In the case of the malvas, epilobias and geraniums, where we see, side by side, races of which the individuals produce insect-fertilised flowers and those that are characterised by self-fertilised flowers, the latter are quite as thriving as the former.

The common groundsel, which, according to Lord Avebury, is "rarely visited by insects," flourishes like the green bay tree, as many [261] gardeners know to their cost. The same may be said of the pimpernels. In this connection it is important to bear in mind that the anemophilous, or wind-fertilised, angiosperms, as, for example, the grasses, are believed to be descendants of insect-fertilised or entomophilous forms.

A weighty objection to the theory that the colours of flowers have been developed because they attract insects has been urged by Mr E. Kay Robinson, namely, that among wild flowers the most highly coloured ones are the least attractive to insects.

"Show me," writes he, on page 222 of The Country-Side for March 20, 1909, "the insect-collector who will seek for specimens among the brilliant scarlet poppies. Of what use is the dog rose, with its large discs of pinky-white, to him? On the other hand, does he not find that by far the most attractive flowers are the almost invisible spurge laurel blossoms in February and March, the fuzzy sallow catkins in March and April, the bramble blossom in midsummer, and the ivy's small green flowers in autumn? Of these only the bramble has any pretensions to colour, and if you try, as I have tried, the experiment of picking off every petal from sprays of bramble blossoms you will find that its attraction to moths does not appear diminished.

[262]
"The fact that insects do visit many conspicuously coloured flowers does not show that the colour attracts them, when the fact is borne in mind that they neglect others which are equally coloured, while the flowers which they particularly haunt are inconspicuous. Conspicuous flowers which have abundance of nectar attract insects, of course, but so do inconspicuous flowers which have nectar. If they have no nectar, neither the conspicuous nor the inconspicuous flowers attract insects other than pollen or petal eaters, whose visits are not good for the plant. This shows that the nectar attracts the insects and that the colour of the flowers makes no difference."

In autumn many leaves assume bright and beautiful tints. These are not believed to be in any way useful to the plant. The autumnal hues and shades are regarded, and rightly regarded, as the garb of death and decay. Such colours are the result of the oxidation of the chlorophyll or green colouring matter of the leaves. Why should not the colours of the petals of the flowers, which wither and fade long before the green leaves do, be due to a similar cause? The bright colours of fruits are supposed to have been effected by natural selection in order to attract fruit-eating animals. Surely a hungry animal does not require that its food be brightly coloured in order to find it! We [263] must remember that during the greater part of the year most animals have no occupation save that of finding their food. Inconspicuously coloured fruits, like those of the ivy, are frequently eaten by birds. The bright colours of some ripening fruits are undoubtedly the colours of decay. Many fungi and seaweeds have bright colours. It is never hinted that these are of any direct utility to their possessor.

Every flower, every plant, every organism must be of some colour.

Honey

Many flowering plants produce honey. This is said by some botanists to have been directly caused by natural selection, because the honey attracts insects. Possibly those who take up this attitude are putting the cart before the horse. It is probable that honey, like oxygen, is an ordinary product of the metabolism of the plant, and that the visits of bees and other insects to such plants are the result rather than the cause of the honey being there. Boisier found that some plants, for example, Potentilla tormentilla and Geum urbanum, gave honey in Norway, but very little near Paris.

He further discovered that by supplying certain plants copiously with water he could induce them to produce more than their normal output of honey.

As is their habit, Neo-Darwinians have pushed their pet theory to absurd lengths in its [264] application to flowers. They assert that the visits of insects are responsible for not merely the general colour of every flower, but also the various lines, spots, and other markings of flowers. The lines that frequently occur on the petals are supposed to guide the insects to the honey! This particular refinement of Neo-Darwinism, to quote Kay Robinson, "needs little discussion. Insects have very poor sight. You can see this when a bee or a butterfly flies bang against a whitewashed wall; when a wasp pounces upon a black spot on a sunlit floor, mistaking it for a fly; or when a settled dragon-fly will allow you to poke it in the face with the end of a walking-stick, although it will be off like a flash if you raise your arm. There is, therefore, large reason to doubt whether insects can even see the fine lines in the throats of flowers which are supposed to guide them to the nectar. It is rather absurd, too, to suppose that such lines can be needed, since insects come in swarms to inconspicuous and apparently scentless flowers or to 'sugared' tree-trunks in the dark. Where there is nectar, insects which have come to the feast from a distance need no pencilled lines to guide them over the last quarter of an inch of their journey."

Scents of Flowers

Neo-Darwinians further assert that the scents of flowers have been developed by natural selection because they serve to attract insect visitors [265] to the flowers. In support of this contention it is urged that the most highly scented flowers are not usually the most conspicuous ones, since it is not necessary for a flower to be both highly coloured and strongly scented. Again, those flowers which open at night are usually very highly scented.

Plausible though this view seems, there are weighty objections to it. These are so admirably summarised by Kay Robinson in the issue of The Country-Side for March 27, 1909, that we feel we cannot do better than reproduce his words:—

"It is true that many flowers which are strongly scented are visited by insects, but these flowers have abundance of nectar, and the insects come in spite of the scent, and not on account of it. They visit unscented flowers, provided that they have nectar, equally freely; and they do not visit flowers which have scent without nectar.

"Moreover, fruits are more generally scented even than flowers; but what explanation have those, who attribute the scents of flowers to the tastes of insects, for the scents of fruits? Insects which visit fruits are only robbers. Therefore, if we say that plants have scents for the purpose of attracting insects, we accuse all plants which have scented fruits of attempted suicide.

"There are hosts of plants, again, with scented leaves. Here also the insects are only robbers, [266] and it is quite clear that the scent is not useful in attracting insects. If, therefore, you adopt the insect theory to explain the scents of flowers, you must invent entirely new theories to explain the scents of fruits and leaves."

It is thus evident that the ordinarily accepted explanation of the colours, scents, and markings of flowers is far from satisfactory.

Kay Robinson's Theory

Mr E. Kay Robinson has put forth in recent issues of The Country-Side (March 20, 27, and April 3, 1909) quite a new explanation of the phenomena, and one which deserves careful consideration. He maintains that "the real, primary, and original meaning of the colours, markings, nectar and scents of flowers is not to attract insects, but to deter grazing and browsing animals."

"I say," he writes, "that grazing and browsing animals avoid eating conspicuous flowers. I have watched a flock of five hundred sheep pass across a yard-wide strip of close-nibbled turf on the Norfolk coast, grazing as they passed, and the number of open daisy blossoms after they had passed seemed the same as before they came. Every one of five hundred sheep had eaten something from that yard of grass, and not one had eaten any of the hundred and thirty odd daisies.

"Every summer the farm horses are turned into the same old pasture, and as the summer wanes the field always presents the same appearance—the [267] green grass close-grazed, the tall buttercups left standing high.

"Once, leaning over a gate with friends, I pointed out that a flock of sheep grazing in a sainfoin field were nibbling the greenstuff close, but were not eating the flowery stalks, when one sheep near us accidentally pulled up a whole sainfoin plant by the roots and proceeded to munch it upwards. Inch by inch the stem passed into its jaws, and I began to be afraid that it was going to establish an 'exception' to my rule. But, just when the bright cluster of pink sainfoin blossom was within two inches of its teeth, it gave an extra nip, and the flower head fell to the ground, and the sheep resumed its search for greenstuff.

"I do not say that this would always happen—I should be sorry for any theory which depended upon the intelligence of a sheep—but it was a very striking object-lesson to my two companions; and any one who looks around during this summer with an inquiring mind will find plenty of evidence that grazing, browsing, and nibbling animals avoid flowers, and stick to greenstuff when they can get it.

"I do not say that all animals avoid the same flowers. Horses, for instance, may dislike large flowers like roses and conspicuous yellow flowers like buttercups, but they will bite off flat clusters of minute white or pale yellow flowers, such as [268] yarrow or wild parsnip. These distinctions made by certain kinds of beasts will probably in the future be found to afford valuable evidence as to the regions of origin of our flowers and animals. Such plants as the yarrow and the wild parsnip, for instance, probably did not originate in the home of the wild horse, because they are not protected against it.

"As a general rule, however, there is abundance of evidence that plants with conspicuous flowers gain a large advantage in the struggle for existence, because grazing and browsing animals avoid them; while there is no real evidence at all that conspicuous flowers attract insects."

Kay Robinson extends this explanation to the shape, the scent, and the nectar of flowers. He admits that many flowers are adapted to the visits of insects, but this is, he asserts, but a secondary result. The "real, primary meaning" of the shapes of flowers of curious configuration is, he insists, "a deterrent to grazing or browsing animals."

According to him plants, like the snap-dragon, which have "blossoms in the semblance of a mouth," are avoided by grazing animals, because they mistake such flowers for mouths, and have no wish to be bitten! Orchids, he asserts, "are strongly deterrent to grazing and browsing animals, which are looking for greenstuff, and regard these gaudy, spidery, winged blossoms as [269] live creatures." "If this is not the truth," he asks, "will any adherent of the theory that we owe the shapes of flowers to insects explain why some of our common British orchids are so like bees, spiders, etc.? Some which have no particular resemblance to any insect still exhibit weird shapes, suggestive to the human mind of living things, such as lizards, etc. The reason why they look like bees, spiders, lizards, and various unclassed creatures is quite simple. Grazing animals are looking for greenstuff, and do not wish to eat living creatures which may bite or sting or taste nasty. Thus the orchids have acquired the power of looking like creatures.

"Every one," he continues, "who is familiar with the blossom of the wild carrot—a flat head of minute, dull-white blossoms—must have noticed how very often the centre blossom in each head is purplish or reddish-black. This makes it very conspicuous in the middle of the flat white flower head. Now what conceivable use can this barren little blackish blossom—scarcely bigger than a pin's head—be to the wild carrot plant if we regard the flat head of white flowers as an attraction to the sight of insects? If, on the other hand, we rightly regard the flat head of white blossoms as an advertisement to grazing animals that it is not wholesome greenstuff, but innutritious blossoms liable to be infested with ants and other stinging insects, we [270] see at once the great use of this small blackish flower in the middle. It looks like an insect, and possibly in the home of the wild carrot there is some minute blackish insect with a peculiarly villainous smell or taste—or perhaps a potent sting—which grazing animals carefully avoid whenever they can see it. Thus the wild carrot flourishes; though here in Britain—where the wild carrot has established itself now—we may fail at first to see the exact meaning of the trick. I think, however, that, when we understand it, it fits admirably into the theory that the shapes and colours of flowers are primarily useful as deterrents to grazing and browsing animals and not as attractions to insects.

"Thus we see," he concludes, "that the queer shapes of these orchids, which are a great stumbling-block in the way of those who preach that we owe the shapes of flowers to the tastes of insects, become a strong confirmation of my theory that we owe the shapes of flowers to grazing and browsing animals."

Of the nectar of flowers, Kay Robinson writes: "Since this is eagerly sought for by hosts of insects, whose visits are in most cases useful to the flowers, it seems only natural to suppose that we see cause and effect in this connection.

"Here, however, I will outline my theory of the origin of nectar and of flowers in general.

[271]
"I think there is no doubt whatever that all the parts of a flower are modified leaves. The original type of flowering plant—I think we may safely assume—had a single stem and produced its seed at the summit, as the crown of its year's endeavour. The flower, before it became what we would recognise as a flower, was a cluster of protecting leaves round the seed-making parts of the plant. To the production of the seed the whole energies of the plant were devoted, and into the cluster of leaves at the top of the stem all the essences of the plant were concentrated. If during the coming spring you handle and examine the leaves at the end of the strong shoots of thorns or fruit bushes, you will find that the surface of the young leaves is quite sticky. If you observe browsing animals also, you will discover that—contrary to expectation—they do not like strong-growing, juicy shoots, evidently preferring mature leaves lower down the branch. This shows, I think, that plants have the power of protecting their new shoots by crowding into them the volatile oils and essences which they produce as a protection against animals. Now nectar appears always to be distasteful to grazing and browsing animals; and they also dislike scented flowers. I think, therefore, that it is reasonable to suppose that the nectar and scents which now distinguish so many flowers were first produced as an exudation of concentrated sap [272] upon the surfaces of the protecting leaves round the seed-making parts of the original flowers. As these leaves became more efficiently protective by assuming colours, shapes, and markings which warned animals of their character, so their apparatus for producing scent and honey became specialised; and at this point the insect appeared upon the scene as a factor in the life's success of the plant."

Such, then, is Kay Robinson's bold and original theory. In some respects it seems far-fetched. The natural inclination is to ask, "Is it possible that cattle can be so stupid, so blind, as to really believe that a snap-dragon is the mouth of an animal, or that an orchid is a spider?"

At present we know so little of animal psychology that we are not yet in a position to give an answer to this question. Horses, we know, are apt to be frightened by the most harmless things, such as a piece of brown paper lying on the road. Mr Robinson's theory should give a stimulus to the study of the mind of animals—a study which, if properly undertaken, will probably throw a flood of light upon some of the problems of evolution. Mr Robinson's theory equally with the ordinarily-accepted hypothesis, utterly fails to explain the first origins of colours, scents, etc. When once a flower has acquired a certain amount of colour, it is easy to understand how that flower may attract insects or repel [273] grazing animals. But how can the origin of the colour or other characteristic be explained?

We asked Mr Kay Robinson how he would account for the great success in the struggle for existence of some species of grasses on which herbivorous animals feed so largely. He replied, in the issue of The Country-Side, dated April 3, 1909:—

"The grass has a manner of growth which defies the grazing animal. Its long, thin leaves are constantly pushing upwards from the ground, and, if they are grazed down one day, they will have pushed up again the next. Moreover, when the outside blade of grass has exhausted its power of growing, there is another blade inside it with many inches still to grow, and another inside that which has scarcely begun to grow, and yet another further in which has not yet seen daylight; and so on. In a state of nature grazing animals are nowhere so numerous on any given patch of ground from day to day as to keep down the grass. If they were, carnivorous animals would stay there to eat the grazing animals, and grow fat and multiply. Thus the grazing herds are scattered and wandering, followed wherever they go by the beasts of prey; and in their absence the grass pushes ahead, so that when the grazing animals return its clump is larger and its roots are stronger, and it is better able to survive attack than before.

[274]
"The method of the clovers and trefoils is quite different. When circumstances are favourable and enemies few, they will form large-leaved luxuriant clumps, with fine heads of blossom; but where grazing animals abound they have the power of adapting themselves to altered circumstances. They creep so closely along the ground that the teeth of the grazing animal cannot pick them up between the surrounding grass, and they produce leaves so small and short-stalked that to eat them would be like nibbling the pile off velvet. Any clover or trefoil thus growing in self-defence is accepted as the 'shamrock' of Ireland; and it is certainly a fine emblem for a race which regards itself as surviving in spite of incessant oppression.

"These are the reasons, however, why the grasses and clovers or trefoils continue to enrich old pastures when most of the other plants disappear, with the exception of daisies and buttercups, and the acid sorrels."

We should be glad to hear how Mr Robinson accounts for the conspicuous flowers in the species of "prickly pear" (Euphorbia), which is so abundant in India, and which is not browsed upon by animals.

We regret that we are not able to devote more space to this most interesting theory. We can only add that, even if it fail to become widely accepted, it is of great value as showing that it [275] is possible to offer a plausible explanation of a large number of phenomena, which nine out of ten botanists explain in a very different way.

So satisfied are the majority of naturalists with the "insect theory," that they seem of late years to have paid but little attention to the subject of floral colouration. This affords a striking instance of the pernicious influence which Neo-Darwinism is exercising on the minds of men to-day. It tends to stifle research instead of stimulating it.

Accepted Theories Unsatisfactory

We have now dealt with the theory of protective colouration, the theory of warning colouration, the theory of mimicry, and the theory of recognition markings. We have shown that although many organisms undoubtedly derive profit from the fact that they are difficult to see in their natural surroundings or from their resemblance to other organisms, the hypothesis that this inconspicuousness or the mimicry of these animals has been caused by the natural selection of small variations is untenable.

Warning colours, we have shown, although a disadvantage to their possessors, are sometimes seen in nature because they are accompanied by unpalatability. The theory of recognition markings must, we fear, be laid to rest in the burial ground of exploded hypotheses.

The extreme popularity of the existing theories regarding animal colouration and their very [276] general acceptance are to be attributed, firstly, to their simplicity; secondly, to the fact that they have thrown light on many phenomena which previously had seemed inexplicable; thirdly, that if we assume, as the great majority of biologists do, that evolution has been effected by the accumulation of numerous variations, small in degree and indefinite in direction, we seemed forced either to accept Neo-Darwinism or admit that the whole subject of animal colouration baffles us, in other words, to reject what appears like cosmos and substitute for it chaos.

With a few exceptions, books that deal with the colours of organisms, while emphasising the evidence in favour of the generally-accepted theories, seem almost entirely to ignore the host of facts that do not appear to fit in with them.

This is largely due to the almost unavoidable bias of the human mind when obsessed by a pet theory. There are none so blind as those who will not see. It is also, in part, the consequence of the prevalent neglect of the scientific method of comparison which leads men to theorise on insufficient evidence. This, of course, is a natural result of specialisation in biology. Naturalists are in the habit of confining their study to the habits of the animals of one particular country and then making far-reaching generalisations therefrom.

As an example of the kind of theorising to [277] which this method leads, we may cite the often-quoted theory which ascribes the green colouring of some arboreal fruit-eating pigeons to adaptation to an existence among tropical foliage, and ignores the fact that in America tree-haunting pigeons are never of this colour, and that it is not by any means universal even among the old-world pigeons.

White Down of Nestlings

Similarly, a theory has been advanced (W. P. Pycraft, Knowledge, 1904, p. 275) that the white down of some nestling birds, is an adaptation to resisting the heat of the sun in open nests. This is at once negatived by the fact that young owls, usually hatched in shaded places, are also generally white, while young cormorants, living in open nests, are black; yet the allied darters, with the same breeding haunts in some cases, have white young. Lest it should be thought that black has some especial value in a nestling living exposed, we may mention that young petrels, which are born in holes, have black or dark down.

As we have already pointed out, naturalists in too readily accepting the theory that variation is minute in degree and indefinite in direction, have raised quite unnecessary difficulties, even for the selection hypothesis. We have cited certain facts, which seem to show that variations, as a rule, are not indefinite in direction; of these the most striking is furnished by [278] birds in which the tail feathers are greatly elongated. Were variations indeterminate, we might reasonably expect to find that the elongation occurred in one particular feather or pair of feathers in one species, in another pair in a second species, in a third pair in a third species, and so on. But this is not the case; no bird has one single long feather in its tail, and when two are elongated, as is so commonly the case, these are almost invariably the middle or outside pair; e.g., in the European bee-eater and pheasant it is the former, in the swallow and blackcock, the latter.

Exceptions are so rare that they may almost be said to prove the rule; e.g., although most terns have the outer-tail feathers elongated, in some of the Noddy Terns (Anous, Gygis) the third pair, in others the fourth pair, of tail feathers are the longest. This must mean one of two things, either that the variation, as regards length in tail feathers, other than middle or outer, does not ordinarily occur, or that it occurs, but is, in some way, inimical to the welfare of the species. The latter hypothesis does not seem probable, as the Noddies are particularly abundant birds where they occur, that is to say, in the tropical seas; therefore, we can only conclude that that particular variation has not occurred in birds as a whole.

We have adduced abundant evidence to show [279] that mutations or discontinuous variations occur in nature; and as these afford much more favourable material on which natural selection can act, it is reasonable to suppose that they have played a considerable part in evolution.

When discussing the phenomena of inheritance, we attempted to show that, not improbably, these discontinuous variations are due to some re-arrangement in the constituent parts of the unit characters, or biological molecules, as we have called them.

Cranes

In this connection we may mention the apparently singular phenomenon of different species in the same natural group, exhibiting either a definite excess or deficiency of plumage on the head. Among cranes, most species are more or less bald; but the Demoiselle (Anthropoides virgo) has a fully-feathered head with long side-plumes, while the head of the Stanley Crane (A. paradisea) appears to be swollen, so abundantly is it feathered. The crowned cranes, although bare-cheeked, have double crests, the two parts of which have been respectively compared to a pen-wiper and a bunch of toothpicks!

Among the guinea-fowls, several species are crested, while others, as, for example, the domestic one, are bare-headed. Now, on the theory of evolution, by accumulation of minute variations, phenomena such as these are difficult [280] of explanation; but, on the assumption that a slight rearrangement of the biological atoms in the molecule may produce very diverse results, as we see in the case of chemical molecules, and of seasonally dimorphic butterflies, there is no particular ground for surprise at such a phenomenon.

In this connection we may cite the significant fact, so well known to canary breeders, that two crested birds when mated tend to produce a bald-headed one.

If the colour of any part of an organism be due to the internal arrangement of the constituent parts of the biological molecule from which it is derived, we should expect any rearrangement of the component parts to produce quite a different colour. In other words, we should expect occasionally to see colour-mutations. These are precisely what we do see. Similarly, if the scheme of colouring of an organism be due to a certain grouping of biological molecules, we should expect the same scheme of colouring to occur in organisms which are not nearly related. This, too, we observe in nature.

Many of the phenomena of mimicry, and all the cases which we have cited as pseudo-mimicry, seem to us to be referable to this.

Magpie Colouring

Take, for example, the magpie colouration in birds—that is to say, a scheme of colouring in which the body is white, and head, wings, and [281] tail black. This occurs in the following birds belonging to the most diverse groups:—

The Magpie.

The Magpie Tanager (Cissopis leveriana).

The Magpie Robin (Copsychus saularis), cock only; in the hen the black is replaced by brownish grey.

The Pied Honeyeater (Entomophila picata).

The Chaplain Crow (white-bodied form of the hoodie crow).

The New Ireland Swallow Shrike (Artamus insignis).

The Magpie Goose (Anseranas melanoleucus).

Combinations of this kind, in which the black is replaced by brown or grey, are excessively rare.

On the other hand, we see in several birds the combination in which the white is replaced by yellow:—

The Common Troupial (Icterus vulgaris).

The Black-headed Oriole (Oriolus melano cephalus).

The Black-and-yellow Grosbeak, male only.

What we may call imperfect magpie colouration, i.e. where the head becomes white, occurs in several species of birds. The head of a black species sometimes becomes white as a mutation; in the domestic Muscovy duck, for example, an individual is sometimes produced having a white head, although the black of the remainder of the plumage remains unchanged.

[282]
As examples of this scheme of colouration we may cite—

Black-and-white Fruit Pigeons (Myristicivoræ).

Several Gannets (Sula capensis, S. serrator, etc.)

Swallow-tailed Kite (Elanoides furcatus).

Several Storks (Euxenura maguari, Anastomus oscitans, Pseudotantalus cinereus).

Moreover, a common variety of the barn-door fowl has also a white body and black primaries and tail, showing that this scheme of colour may arise as a mutation.

A further elimination of black in the tail and body leads us to white birds with more or less black wings:—

White Storks (Ciconia alba, C. boyciana, and Euxenura maguari).

The White Crane (Grus leucogeranus).

The Snow Geese (Chen nivalis, C. rossi).

The Common Gannet (Sula bassana).

The White Buzzard (Leucopternis).

The Scavenger Vultures (Neophron).

A recurring combination in mammals is black, with a white marking on the breast.

Most of the bears, even young brown bears, show a tendency to this. It is also found in the Tasmanian devil, and in varieties of our domestic cats, rats, and dogs; also in the domestic duck.

The white-spotted pelage, not uncommon in deer, especially fawns, is curiously repeated in [283] the Australian carnivorous marsupials, known as Native Cats (Dasyurus).

In domestic animals we frequently find the following localisation of white—white socks, collar, breast, and muzzle. The arrangement occurs in cats, dogs, rabbits, guinea-pigs and mice, also in the horse and pig, but without the collar. The arrangement is not seen in goats, cattle, or sheep, nor in wild animals of any kind. This would lead to the conclusion that the combination is correlated with some character unfavourable to survival under natural conditions.

Many variations which frequently occur among both wild and domestic animals do not persist in nature.

Albinos

As instances of such variations we may mention pure albino forms, that is to say those in which pigment does not occur in the eyes.

It is easy to see why this variation is not allowed to persist in nature. Its possessors are handicapped by bad eyesight, and so have no chance of surviving in the struggle for existence. It is thus that natural selection acts. On the other hand, white species with pigmented eyes are fairly numerous. These enjoy normal eyesight, but labour under the disadvantage of being easily seen by their foes. Hence we find that white species generally either occur in a snowy habitat, or are powerful and both able and ready to [284] defend themselves. In this connection it is interesting to notice that in New Zealand all birds, whether introduced or indigenous, are particularly liable to albinism. Owing to the fewness of their enemies these albinistic forms are able to persist.

A variation, or rather a mutation, that frequently occurs among domesticated birds, but which is seen in very few wild species, is that which takes the form of white primary feathers on the wing. This variation must often occur in nature, but it rarely establishes itself, apparently because white feathers do not resist wear so well as coloured ones do.

Biological Molecules and Colour

Black-and-yellow colouration occurs in several widely separated species of birds. The arrangement of the two colours follows to some extent the same rules as the black-and-white combination.

Several birds have a yellow body with black head, wings, and tail, such as—

The Black-headed Oriole (Oriolus melanocephalus).

The Black-and-Yellow Grosbeaks (Pycnorhamphus icteroides, P. affinis) (cock).

The Common Troupial (Icterus vulgaris).

In others the black on the head is nearly or quite suppressed, that on the tail remaining to a greater or less extent; such are—

The Golden Orioles (Oriolus galbula, O. kundoo, etc.).

Several species of Icterus.

Several fly-catchers of the genus Piezorhynchus (males only).

BRAZILIAN TROUPIAL
BRAZILIAN TROUPIAL

This species (Icterus vulgaris) is that most frequently seen in captivity; the pattern of colour is found in several other allied forms.

INDIAN BLACK-HEADED ORIOLE
INDIAN BLACK-HEADED ORIOLE

Several other orioles besides this (O. melanocephalus) have the black head.

[285]
We have said sufficient to show that certain combinations of colours recur in nature in species which are neither nearly related to one another nor subjected to similar environment. For such phenomena it is difficult, if not impossible, to account on the theory that natural selection, acting on minute variations, is responsible for all the varied colouring of the animal kingdom. The facts, however, are in accordance with the supposition that the organism is the result of the growth and development of a number of units or biological molecules which exist in the fertilised egg.

If there be any truth in the supposition, the colouration of every animal must be due to the development of one or more of these molecules. Colouration may be expression of the arrangement of all the molecules in the fertilised egg, or it may be due to the development of a number of molecules whose function is to determine the colouring of an organism, or it may be the result of the development of one such molecule, which perhaps splits up in such a way that a portion attaches itself to each of the other molecules.

But it is idle to speculate on this point. As we have already insisted, the tendency to build [286] up elaborate theories on very slender foundations is a too frequent failing of zoologists. We desire merely to emphasise the fact that the phenomena of animal colouration almost force us to the conclusion that the colouring of each organism is the result of the development of a number of units.

It may be objected that, if this be the case, the number of the units which contribute to the colour of any organism must be exceedingly large, since we see in nature an almost limitless number of different schemes of colouring. If the colour of each animal be the result of the development of a few units, it might be thought, firstly, that the diversity of schemes of colouration which we observe in nature could not possibly occur; and secondly, that, under such circumstances, the colour pattern of a bird or beast should be of the nature of a mosaic, each colour being sharply defined and separated from every other colour, instead of the colours shading one into the other, as is so frequently the case.

Such objections would be based on a misconception as to the nature of the units which combine to produce the colouration of an organism. These units show themselves as centres of development of colour, as points from which the colour or colouring they represent spreads, until it meets and mingles with other patches of colour which are being developed from other centres. The colour produced at one centre may spread [287] more rapidly than that which forms at another; this, of course, will result in a preponderance in the organism of the colour which is produced at the former centre.

112

Further, we must bear in mind that the development of each colour-producing unit is largely affected by conditions external to it, as we shall see when dealing with Sexual Dimorphism.

More than one naturalist, who has paid careful attention to the subject of animal colouration, has perceived that through the apparently endless diversity of the colouring of organisms something like order runs.

Mr Tylor Quoted

Over thirty years ago Mr Alfred Tylor called attention to this important fact. That observer, whose views met with the approval of Wallace, was of opinion that colour follows structure, and that in a many-hued animal it changes at points where the function changes.

"If," writes Mr Tylor, "we take highly decorated species—that is, animals marked by alternate dark or light bands or spots, such as the zebra, some deer, or the carnivora, we find, first, that the region of the spinal column is marked by a dark stripe; secondly, that the regions of the appendages, or limbs, are differently marked; thirdly, that the flanks are striped or spotted, along or between the regions of the lines of the ribs; fourthly, that the shoulder and hip regions are marked by curved lines; fifthly, [288] that the pattern changes, and the direction of the lines, or spots, at the head, neck, and every joint of the limbs; and, lastly, that the tips of the ears, nose, tail, and feet, and the eyes are emphasised in colour."

More recently Mr J. Lewis Bonhote has devoted much attention to this important subject. The results of his researches are summarised on page 185 of vol. xxix. of the Proceedings of the Linnæan Society, and on page 258 of the Proceedings of the Fourth International Ornithological Congress, 1905. Mr Bonhote states that the presence or absence of colour tends almost invariably to make its appearance, first of all, on certain definite tracts, common to mammals and birds alike, which he calls pœcilomeres.

Pœcilomeres

"Pœcilomeres," he writes, "are situated on the following parts, viz., chin, malar stripe, maxillary stripe, a spot above and slightly in front of the eye, a spot below or slightly behind the eye, the ear, crown of the head, occiput, fore-end of sternum, vent, rump, thighs, wrist, shoulders (above and below).

"Now, there is hardly any species of bird on which one or more of these pœcilomeres is not 'picked out' (to use a painter's expression) in some colour different from that of the surrounding parts, and, in fact, most of the so-called recognition or protective markings will be found on these patches.

[289]
"On the other hand, among many species the differentiation of colour on the pœcilomeres is not so conspicuous as to attract the eye or to serve in any way for protection or mimicry, yet we still find them marked by differences of colour so slight that, unless especially looked for, they would never be noticed.

"Or, again, some species occasionally, but not invariably, show a few white feathers on certain parts of their body, and, when such is the case, it will be found that these white feathers appear on the pœcilomeres. . . . There is hardly a species in which examples of these pœcilomeres may not be found. . . . The Kingfisher (Alcedo ispida) shows the various head pœcilomeres very clearly, and as examples of inconspicuous differences on these tracts, the rump of the hen sparrow (Passer domesticus) and hen chaffinch (Fringilla cœlebs), the malar stripe and dark ear-patch of the hen Yellow Bunting (Emberiza citrinella), and the dark ante-orbital patch of the Barn Owl (Strix flammea) are familiar examples. And, lastly, as an instance of the class where a few white feathers frequently, but not invariably, appear, the young of the cuckoo (Cuculus canorus) forms a good example.

"These spots may, however, appear in a transitory manner, as, for instance, where a change of plumage (not necessarily moult) is occurring."

As an instance of this, Bonhote cites the case [290] of a young male Shoveler (Spatula clypeata), "in which the metallic colour on the head first showed itself on the post-orbital and auricular pœcilomeres, gradually meeting and joining up across the head with the crown and occipital pœcilomeres, and then finally spreading forwards. And it may be well to note that the joining up of the auricular and post-orbital pœcilomeres formed a metallic patch similar in size and position to that found in the male Teal (Querquedula crecca), and, further, in the last stage, when the whole head, except the portion round the beak, was metallic, the markings are similar to those found permanently in the hen Scaup (Fuligula marila).

"Now, these resemblances taking place in the normal pure-bred wild shoveler, the question of reversion does not come in, and no one would suppose these resemblances due to anything more than transitional variation, and it is the object of this portion of the paper to show that variation in colour follows along definite lines."

Biological Molecules

Mr Bonhote continues: "As a further illustration of how widely spread these lines are throughout the mammalian and avian kingdoms, we may note the assumption of the brown head in the case of the Black-headed Gull (Larus ridibundus), which invariably follows each year on lines similar to those related in the case of the shoveler, and . . . the method by which, on the approach of winter, the stoat assumes his [291] white dress, is (although the change is from brown to white) again conducted along precisely similar lines." Mr Bonhote argues with great force that, as the process occurs in two animals so widely separated, the fundamental cause must be a deep-seated one. There can be no doubt that these pœcilomeres of Bonhote are connected with our biological molecules. Each of these pœcilomeres is the result of the development of one of these unit characters; each is to be regarded as the centre of activity, the sphere of influence of a biological molecule, or the portion of one, which controls the colouring of a definite region of the organism. In the case of creatures which display the same colour throughout, these molecules all give rise to the same kind of colouring; in the case of animals which display a variety of colours and markings the various molecules give origin to various colours. But we must bear in mind that the final colour to which each colour-producing molecule gives rise depends to some extent on circumstances other than the constitution of the molecule. Thus it is that the young in most organisms differ in colour and marking from the adults. On this also depends the phenomena of seasonal and sexual dimorphism. The same colour-producing molecule may give rise to one colour under one set of conditions and to a totally different colour under another set of conditions.

[292]
It is a significant fact that under abnormal conditions the feathers of birds tend to disappear precisely on those spots where the pœcilomeres of Bonhote occur.

Thus in a sickly cage bird the feathers frequently show a tendency to fall off on the following spots: crown of head, lores, jaws, head generally, rump, vent and thighs.

Many wild birds—as, for example, the cranes—display patches of naked skin on the head, and these are usually situated on pœcilomeres. Similarly, natural excessive developments of plumage tend to occur on the pœcilomeres, or, rather, the spots characterised by pœcilomeres—for example, the train of the peacock. Loral plumage, it is true, is seldom long, but is often of a peculiar nature.

114

Colour mutations tend to occur on the pœcilomeres. Thus it is that these pœcilomeres often form the distinctive characters and markings of allied species. This is precisely what we should expect if the pœcilomeres correspond to biological molecules and mutations are the result of the rearrangement of the constituent parts of these molecules.

Still more significant is the fact that the colour-markings in hybrids tend to follow pœcilomeres.

Bonhote has performed a large number of experiments in hybridising ducks. Some of his hybrids were produced from three pure ancestors, [293] as, for example, the pintail, the spotbill, and the mallard; others from two ancestors. Some of these hybrids were crossed with other hybrids, and others with the parent forms, hence Bonhote secured a number of hybrids, each of which had a distinctive appearance; but all the variations appearing among the hybrids were found to start on one or more of the pœcilomeres.

Certain of the hybrids showed a resemblance to one or other of the parent species, others were unlike either parent, and resembled either no known species or species other than their parents.

When a hybrid shows a resemblance to a species other than that to which either parent belongs, it is said to exhibit the phenomenon of atavism or reversion,—the individual is supposed to have been "thrown back" to an ancestral form.

The true explanation of the phenomenon would seem to be that, as the result of the crossing, biological molecules in the fertilised egg have been formed which, on development, give rise to combinations of colour like those seen in other species.

Thus the phenomena of "mimicry" and "reversion" are, we believe, due to the fact that in the fertilised egg of both the pattern and its copy a similar arrangement of biological molecules obtains. If we regard the sexual act as resembling in many respects a chemical synthesis, the phenomenon need not surprise us.

[294]
To sum up, the observed facts of animal colouration seem to indicate that there are in each organism some twelve or thirteen centres of colouring, which we suggest may correspond with portions of the fertilised egg. From each of these centres the colour develops and spreads, so that every part of the organism is eventually coloured. These centres of colouring are not altogether independent of one another. Sometimes they all give rise to the same hue, in which case we have a uniformly-coloured organism, such as the raven. More often from some one colour develops, and from others another colour; if these two colours happen to be black and white, the result is a pied organism, which displays a definite pattern due to the correlation of the various colour-producing biological molecules.

Thus it occasionally happens that two widely different organisms exhibit very similar markings, and therefore resemble one another. When this resemblance is believed to be of advantage to one or other of the similarly-coloured species, naturalists call it mimicry, and assert that the likeness is due to the action of natural selection; but where neither organism can profit by the resemblance, zoologists make no attempt to explain it. What we suggest is that the colouration of an animal depends upon the structure, or, at any rate, the nature, of the parts of the egg which produce these centres of colour. But this [295] is not by any means the only cause that determines the colouration of the organism. If it were, young creatures in their first plumage would invariably resemble the parents, the two sexes would always be alike, and there would be no such phenomenon as seasonal dimorphism.

As a matter of fact, the portions of the egg (we call them, for the sake of clearness, colour-producing biological molecules) which give rise to the pœcilomeres exhibit themselves merely in the shape of tendencies; the ultimate form the colouring will take depends to a large extent upon other and extraneous circumstances, such as the secretion of hormones.

Thus it is that organisms seem to display an almost endless diversity of colouration. But beneath all this diversity we see something like order. It occasionally happens (why, we do not know) that one, or more, of the biological molecules which make up the nucleus of the fertilised ovum becomes altered in the sexual act, with the result that a discontinuous variation or mutation appears in the resulting organism. The mutation may be a favourable one, or one which does not affect in any way the chances of an organism in the struggle for existence, or an unfavourable one. In the last of the three cases the organism will perish early and not leave behind any offspring exhibiting its peculiarity.

It is thus that natural selection acts. Natural [296] selection weeds out relentlessly all organisms which display unfavourable variations. It is thus obvious that many species may, and we believe do, exist which possess characters of no direct utility to them, or even slightly harmful ones. For this reason Wallace and his followers fail in their attempts to prove that every patch of colour in every organism is of direct utility. Natural selection has to take an animal as it finds it—the good with the bad. If an organism as a whole is not wanting—that is to say, if it is able to hold its own against other organisms, and is fitted to fill any place in nature—that organism will probably survive, although it may be defective in many respects. As its name implies, natural selection is a mere selecting agency. It has to choose from what is presented to it. It is not, as many seem to think, a manufacturer or inducer of variations. Natural selection can no more make an animal vary in any given direction than the human breeder can. Its power is limited to the destroying of all variations which do not pass the test prescribed by it.

[297]

CHAPTER VII
SEXUAL DIMORPHISM

Meaning of the term—Fatal to Wallaceism—Sexual Selection—The law of battle—Female preference—Mutual Selection—Finn's experiments—Objections to the theory of Sexual Selection—Wallace's explanation of sexual dimorphism stated and shown to be unsatisfactory—The explanation of Thomson and Geddes shown to be inadequate—Stolzmann's theory stated and criticised—Neo-Lamarckian explanation of sexual dimorphism stated and criticised—Some features of sexual dimorphism—Dissimilarity of the sexes probably arises as a sudden mutation—The four kinds of mutations—Sexual dimorphism having shown itself, Natural Selection determines whether or not the organisms which display it shall survive.

In some species the sexes are so similar in appearance that it is not possible to tell by mere outward inspection to which sex a given individual belongs.

In other species the sexes differ so widely in external appearance that it is difficult to believe that the male and the female belong to the same species. Between these two extremes are a great number of species in which the sexes are more or less dissimilar. Those species in which the sexes differ in appearance are said to be sexually dimorphic. The phenomena of sexual dimorphism are fatal to that form of Neo-Darwinism which sees in natural selection an [298] explanation of all the peculiarities of animal structure and colouration.

It is not easy to understand how natural selection can have caused marked sexual dimorphism in a species where the habits of the sexes are the same, in the Paradise

Flycatcher (Terpsiphone paradisi), for example, where the cock and the hen obtain their food in the same way, and share equally the duties of nest-building, incubation, and feeding the young.

Of course, in all species where each individual carries only one of the two kinds of sexual organs, there must of necessity be some slight difference between the individuals that carry the male organ, which performs one function, and those that carry the female organ, which performs another function.

But in many species the sexes display differences which have no direct connection with the generative organs—for example, the deer, where the stag alone has horns.

Those characters which differ with the sex, but are not directly connected with the organs of reproduction, are known as secondary sexual characters.

QUEEN WHYDAH
QUEEN WHYDAH

This species (Tetraenura regia) is a typical example of seasonal sexual dimorphism, the male being long-tailed and conspicuously coloured only during the breeding season, and at other times resembling the sparrow-like female.

Theory of Sexual Selection

In nearly all species where the male and female differ in beauty, it is the male who surpasses the female. Natural selection is, in many cases, not able to explain the origin of these differences, or why, when they occur, the male should be more beautiful than the [299] female. This Darwin saw. In order to account for the phenomena of sexual dimorphism, he formulated the theory of sexual selection. This hypothesis is based on the assumption that there is, in all species of animals, a competition among the males to secure females as mates. It is not difficult to understand how this competition arises in polygamous species. Assuming that approximately equal numbers of males and females are born (an assumption which appears to be justified as regards the majority of species), it is clear that for every male who secures more than one wife, at least one male will be obliged to live in a state of single blessedness.

But how can there be competition in the case of monogamous species? The sexes being approximately equal in number, there are sufficient females to allow of a mate for every male.

The Law of Battle

Such is the nature of things, said Darwin, that, even under these circumstances, there is competition among the males for females.

"Let us take any species," he writes, on page 329 of The Descent of Man (Ed. 1901), "a bird for instance, and divide the females inhabiting a district into two equal bodies, the one consisting of the more vigorous and better-nourished individuals, and the other of the less vigorous and healthy. The former, there can be little doubt, would be ready to breed in the spring before the others; and this is the opinion of Mr Jenner [300] Weir, who has carefully attended to the habits of birds during many years. There can also be no doubt that the most vigorous, best nourished, and earliest breeders would on an average succeed in rearing the largest number of fine offspring. The males, as we have seen, are generally ready to breed before the females; the strongest, and with some species best armed of the males, drive away the weaker; and the former would then unite with the more vigorous and better-nourished females, because they are the first to breed. Such vigorous pairs would surely rear a larger number of offspring than the retarded females, which would be compelled to unite with the conquered and less powerful males, supposing the sexes to be numerically equal; and this is all that is wanted to add, in the course of successive generations, to the size, strength, and courage of the males, or to improve their weapons."

From this competition among the males there arise, firstly, contests between the males for mates; secondly, the preference of the females for favoured males.

It is a matter of common knowledge that at the breeding season the males of nearly all, if not all, species are very pugnacious. Two males often engage in desperate fights for one or more females; the victor drives away his foe and secures the harem. In such contests the [301] stronger male wins, and thus emerges that particular form of sexual selection which Darwin termed "the law of battle."

"There are," writes Darwin, on page 324 of The Descent of Man, "many other structures and instincts which must have developed through sexual selection—such as the weapons of offence and the means of defence of the males for fighting with and driving away their rivals—their courage and pugnacity—their various ornaments—their contrivances for producing vocal or instrumental music—and their glands for emitting odours." The former characters have, according to Darwin, been developed by the law of battle, and the latter, since they serve only to allure or excite the female, by the preference of the female.

"It is clear," continues Darwin, "that these characters are the result of sexual and not of ordinary selection, since unarmed, unornamented, or unattractive males would succeed equally well in the battle for life and in leaving a numerous progeny, but for the presence of better-endowed males. We may infer that this would be the case, because the females, which are unarmed and unornamented, are able to survive and procreate their kind. . . . Just as man can improve the breed of his game-cocks by the selection of those birds which are victorious in the cockpit, so it appears that the strongest and most vigorous [302] males, or those provided with the best weapons, have prevailed under nature, and have led to the improvement of the natural breed or species."

Selection by Females

"With mammals," says Darwin (loc. cit., p. 763), "the male appears to win the female much more through the law of battle than through the display of his charms."

In the case of birds, however, feminine preference comes more into play. It is well known that cocks display their charms to the hens at the breeding season, and Darwin believed that the hen selected the most beautiful of her rival suitors.

"Just as man," he writes (p. 326 of The Descent of Man, new edition, 1901), "can give beauty, according to his standard of taste, to his male poultry, or, more strictly, can modify the beauty originally acquired by the parent species, can give to the Sebright bantam a new and elegant plumage, an erect and peculiar carriage, so it appears that female birds in a state of nature have, by a long selection of the more attractive males, added to their beauty or other attractive qualities."

Thus the theory of sexual selection is based on three assumptions. Firstly, that there is in all species competition among the males for females with which to mate. Secondly, that this results in either "the law of battle" among [303] the males, or selection by the female of one among several admirers. Thirdly, that the female selects, as a rule, the most attractive of her suitors.

The evidence upon which Darwin founds this theory may be thus summarised:—

1. In cases where the sexes differ in appearance, or power of song, it is almost invariably the cock who is the more beautiful or the better singer, as the case may be.

2. All male birds that possess accessory plumes or other attractions, make a most elaborate display of these before the females at the mating season, hence "it is obviously probable that these appreciate the beauty of their suitors."

3. Darwin was able to cite specific instances in which the hens showed preference.

In the case of polygamous species there can be no doubt that there is considerable competition among males for their wives. It cannot be said that the contention is so well established in the case of monogamous species. D. Dewar suggests that circumstances may occur in which the hens have to fight for the cock, or in which the male is in the happy position of being able to select his mate. He states his belief that in many cases the selection is mutual, as in the case of human beings.

"I have seen," he writes, on page 13 of Birds of the Plains, "one hen Paradise Flycatcher [304] (Terpsiphone paradisi) drive away another and then go and make up to a cock bird. Similarly, I have seen two hen orioles behave in a very unladylike manner to one another all because they both had designs on the same cock. He sat and looked on from a distance at the contest."

Darwin quotes, on page 500 of The Descent of Man, a case of a male exercising selection: "It appears to be rare when the male refuses any particular female, but Mr Wright of Geldersley House, a great breeder of dogs, informs me that he has known some instances: he cites the case of one of his own deerhounds who would not take any notice of a particular female mastiff, so that another deerhound had to be employed."

Similarly, Finn records, in The Country-Side for August 29th, 1908, that the male Globose Curassow (Crax globicera) in the London Zoological Gardens, which bred with the female Heck's Curassow (C. hecki), as related on p. 104, selected the hen of this very distinctly coloured form or species in preference to any of the typical hens of his own kind.

Male Attractiveness

The cases on record of cocks being in a position to select their mates are comparatively rare, while instances of selection on the part of the hens are far more numerous.

Hence it would seem that the sex, which is in a minority, and so has the opportunity of selecting [305] a mate, does exert a choice and prefer one particular individual; and that, for the reasons pointed out by Darwin, it is in most cases the female who is in the position of being able to pick and choose her mate. It is, as Darwin truly said, far more difficult to decide what qualities determine the choice of the female. He believed that it is "to a large extent the external attractions of the male, though no doubt his vigour, courage, and other mental qualities come into play."

Darwin argued that it is the love of hen birds for "external attractions" in cock birds that has brought into being all the wonderful plumes that characterise such birds as the peacock. "Many female progenitors of the peacock," he writes, on page 661 of The Descent of Man (ed. 1901), "during a long line of descent, have appreciated this superiority, for they have unconsciously, by the continued preference of the most beautiful males, rendered the peacock the most splendid of living birds."

This conclusion has been vigorously attacked. It is argued, with some show of reason, that it is absurd to credit birds with æsthetic tastes equal, if not superior, to those of the most refined and civilised of human beings.

Is it likely, it is asked, that a bird, which will nest in an old shoe cast off by a tramp, can appreciate beauty of plumage?

[306]

As Geddes and Thomson say (page 29 of The Evolution of Sex), "When we consider the complexity of the markings of the male bird or insect, and the slow gradations from one step of perfection to another, it seems difficult to credit birds or butterflies with a degree of æsthetic development exhibited by no human being without special æsthetic acuteness and special training. Moreover, the butterfly, which is supposed to possess this extraordinary development of psychological subtlety, will fly naively to a piece of white paper on the ground, and is attracted by the primary æsthetic stimulus of an old-fashioned wall-paper, not to speak of the gaudy and monotonous brightness of some of our garden flowers. Thus we have the further difficulty, that we must suppose the female butterfly to have a double standard of taste, one for the flowers which she and her mate both visit, the other for the far more complex colourings and markings of the males. And even among birds, if we take those unmistakable hints of real awakening of the æsthetic sense which are exhibited by the Australian bower-bird or by the common jackdaw in its fondness for bright objects, how very rude is his taste compared with the critical examination of infinitesimal variations of plumage on which Darwin relies. Is not, therefore, his essential supposition too glaringly anthropomorphic?

[307]

"Again, the most beautiful males are often extremely combative; and on the conventional view this is a mere coincidence, yet a most unfortunate one for Mr Darwin's view. Battle thus constantly decides the question of pairing, and in cases where, by hypothesis, the female should have most choice, she has simply to yield to the victor."

Darwin, with characteristic fairness, quotes some instances which appear to be opposed to the theory that the hen selects the most beautiful of her suitors. He informs us that Messrs Hewitt, Tegetmeier, and Brent, who have all had a long experience of domesticated birds, "do not believe that the females prefer certain males on account of the beauty of their plumage. . . . Mr Tegetmeier is convinced that a game-cock, though disfigured by being dubbed and with his hackles trimmed, would be accepted as readily as a male retaining all his natural ornaments. Mr Brent, however, admits that the beauty of the male probably aids in exciting the female; and her acquiescence is necessary. Mr Hewitt is convinced that the union is by no means left to mere chance, for the female almost invariably prefers the most vigorous, defiant, and mettlesome male"; and, in consequence, when there is a game-cock in the farmyard, the hens will all resort to him in preference to the cock of their own breed. Darwin thinks that "some [308] allowance must be made for the artificial state in which these birds have long been kept," and cites in his favour the case of Mr Cupples' female deerhound that thrice produced puppies, and on each occasion showed a marked preference for one of the largest and handsomest, but not the most eager, of four deerhounds living with her, all in the prime of life.

The question what is it that determines the choice of the female is obviously one of considerable importance, and it was to be expected that many zoologists would have conducted experiments with a view to deciding it. This legitimate expectation has not been realised.

The matter of sexual selection remains to-day practically where Darwin left it. Wallace rejects the whole theory, and believes that natural selection alone can explain all the phenomena of sexual dimorphism. To such an extent does the enticing idea of the all-puissance of natural selection dominate the minds of scientific men that but few of them have paid any attention to the question of sexual selection. This neglect of the subject affords an example of the baneful results of the too-ready acceptance of an enticing theory, "Natural selection explains everything, why then investigate further?" seems to be the general attitude of our present-day naturalists.

Edmund Selous and D. Dewar have made some observations on birds, and the Peckhams [309] on spiders, in a state of nature. Such observations demonstrate that selective mating occurs in nature, but, for the most part, fail to show what it is that determines the choice.

D. Dewar, however, states (Birds of the Plains, p. 42) that the coloured peahens in the Zoological Gardens at Lahore show a decided preference for the white cocks, which are kept in the aviary along with normally coloured cocks. He gives it as his opinion that "the hens select the white cocks, not because they are white, but because of the strength of the sexual instincts of these latter. The white cocks continually show off before the hens; the sexual desire is developed more highly in them than in the ordinary cocks, and it is this that attracts the hens."

Pearson's Investigations

The only zoologists who have investigated experimentally the question of sexual selection appear to be Karl Pearson and Frank Finn. The former tried to determine, by actual measurements, whether there is any preferential mating among human beings as regards physical characteristics. "Our statistics," he writes, on page 427 of The Grammar of Science, "run to only a few hundreds, and were not collected ad hoc. Still, as far as they go, they show no evidence of preferential mating in mankind on the basis of stature, or of any character very closely correlated with stature. Men do not appear, for example, to select tall women for [310] their wives, nor do they refuse to mate with very tall or very short women." As regards eye-colour, Pearson seems to have arrived at somewhat more definite results. "We conclude," he writes (p. 428), "that in mankind there certainly exists a preferential mating in the matter of eye-colour, or of some closely allied character in the male; in the case of the female there also appears to be some change of type due to preferential mating. . . . The general tendency is for lighter-eyed to mate, the darker-eyed being relatively less frequently mated."

But Pearson's experiments seem to show that as regards stature and eye-colour there is "a quite sensible tendency of like to mate with like." "In fact," writes Pearson, "husband and wife for one of these characters are more alike than uncle and niece, and for the other more alike than first cousins." He adds, "Such a degree of resemblance in two mates, which we reasonably assume to be not peculiar to man, could not fail to be of weight if all the stages between like and unlike were destroyed by differential selection."

Two obvious criticisms of the results obtained by Prof. Pearson occur to us. The first is that his conclusions do not seem to be in accordance with the popular notion that fair-haired men prefer dark hair in a woman, while dark-haired men prefer fair-haired women, and vice versa. [311] The second is that the human animal is not a typical one. Husbands and wives are selected for mental and moral qualities rather than physical ones. The same may, of course, be to some extent true of animals, but in these there must of necessity be far less variation as regards mental attributes. Moreover, the question of income is much bound up with human matrimonial alliances; a rich man or woman has the same advantage in selection as is possessed by an animal endowed with more than the average physical strength of its species.

Finn's Experiments

Finn adopted the plan of experiment suggested by Prof. Moseley. His apparatus consisted of a cage divided into three compartments by wire partitions, so that a bird living in one of them could see its neighbour in the next compartment. In the middle compartment he placed a hen Amadavat (Sporæginthus amandava), and in each of the other compartments he put a cock bird. Under such circumstances, the hen in the middle compartment will sit and roost beside the cock she prefers. The male amadavat, he writes, in The Country-Side, vol. i. p. 142, "is in breeding plumage red with white spots, and the hen brown. The red varies in intensity even in full-plumaged birds, and I submitted to the hen first of all two male birds, one of a coppery and the other of a rich scarlet tint. In no long time she had made her choice of the latter bird; the other, I am sorry [312] to say, very soon died; and, as he had appeared perfectly healthy, I fear grief was accountable for his end—a warning to future experimenters to remove the rejected suitor as early as possible. In the present case I took away the favoured bird, and put in the side compartments he and his rival had occupied two other cocks, which differed in a similar way, though not to the same extent. Again the hen kept at the side of the rich red specimen, so, deeming I knew her views about the correct colour for an amadavat, I took her away too, and tried a second hen with these two males. This was an unusually big bird, and a very independent one, for she would not make up her mind at all, and ultimately I released all three without having gained any result.

"Subsequently I made another experiment with linnets. In this case all three were allowed to fly in a big aviary-cage together, a method which I do not recommend.

"In this case, however, the handsomest cock, which showed much richer red on the breast, had a crippled foot, and proved, as I had expected, to be in fear of the other; nevertheless, the hen mated with him. It must be said, in justice to the duller bird, that he did not press the advantage his soundness gave him, but with a less gentle bird than the linnet this would have happened."

[313]
It is obvious that there is a wide field for observation on these lines. In the case of large birds the experiment could be made still more conclusive by confining the three birds to be experimented on in a single enclosure, divided into three compartments by fences. The males should be placed each in a separate compartment, and have a wing clipped so as to prevent them leaving their respective compartments, while the hen should be allowed the power of flight so that she can visit at will any compartment.

Finn has also recorded (loc. cit.) some other observations bearing on the question of sexual selection. He writes:—

"One cannot observe or read about the habits of birds very much without finding out that, whatever may be the value of beauty, strength counts for a great deal. Male birds constantly fight for their mates, and the beaten individual, if not killed, is at any rate kept at a distance by his successful rival, so that, if he be really more beautiful, his beauty is not necessarily of much service to him. I was particularly impressed by this about a couple of years ago, when I frequently watched the semi-domesticated mallards in Regent's Park in the pairing season. These birds varied a good deal in colour; in some the rich claret breast was wanting, and others had even a slate-coloured head instead of the normal brilliant green. Yet I found these [314] 'off-coloured' birds could succeed in getting and keeping mates when correctly-dressed drakes pined in lonely bachelorhood; one grey-breasted bird had even been able to indulge in bigamy. That strength ruled here was obvious from the way in which the wedded birds drove away their unmated rivals, a proceeding in which their wives most thoroughly sympathised.

"Evidently, beauty does not count for much with the park duck, and the same seems to be the case with the fowl. As a boy, I often used to visit a yard wherein was a very varied assortment of fowls. Among these was one very handsome cock, of the typical black and red colouring of the wild bird, and very fully 'furnished' in the matter of hackle and sickle feathers. Yet the hens held him in no great account, while the master of the yard, a big black bird, with much Spanish blood, provided with a huge pair of spurs, was so admired that he was always attended by some little bantam hens, although they might have had diminutive husbands of their own class.

"It must be remembered, however, that these ducks and fowls had an unnaturally wide choice. In nature, varieties are rare, and the competing suitors are likely to be all very much alike; this makes matters very difficult for the observer, who may easily pass over small differences which are plain enough to the eyes of the hen birds."

COURTSHIP OF SKYLARK
COURTSHIP OF SKYLARK

Illustrating display by a species with no decorative colouring or sex difference.

[315]
Display of Undecorated Cocks

Finn observed that a young hen Bird of Paradise (Paradisea apoda) in the London Zoological Gardens, mated with a fully adult cock in the next compartment although a young cock in female plumage in her own compartment did his best to show off.

It would thus seem that the very limited evidence at present available is not sufficient to sustain the theory that the hens select the most attractive of their suitors. It is significant that plainly-coloured species of birds show off with as much care as their gaily-plumaged brethren; and, if they be nearly allied, assume similar courting attitudes. Thus the homely-attired males of the Spotted-bill (Anas poecilorhyncha), Gadwall, and Black Duck (Anas superciliosa), show off in precisely the same way as does the handsome mallard.

Howard describes and figures in his excellent and beautifully illustrated monograph the elaborate display at the pairing season of some of our plain-coloured little warblers. The skylark has also a notable display.

The common partridge assumes a nuptial attitude similar to that of the pheasant, and, although the cock of the former species has nothing brilliant to show off, the hen partridge pays far more attention to the display of her suitor than does the hen pheasant.

The fact that some cock birds show off after the [316] act of pairing seems to tell against the theory of sexual selection, or at any rate to indicate the purely mechanical nature of the performance. Finn has witnessed this post-nuptial display at the Zoological Gardens (London) in the pied wagtail, the peacock, the Andaman Teal (Nettium albigulare), the Avocet, the Egyptian Goose (Chenatopex ægyptiaca), and the Maned Goose (Chenonetta jubata).

Another objection to the theory that the bright colours of cock birds are due to feminine selection is presented by those birds which breed in immature plumage. Darwin admits that this objection would be a valid one "if the younger and less ornamental males were as successful in winning females and propagating their kind as the older and more beautiful males. But," he continues, "we have no reason to suppose that this is the case."

Unfortunately for the theory of sexual selection, there is evidence to show that the cock Paradise Fly-catcher (Terpsiphone paradisi) in immature plumage is quite as successful in obtaining a mate as is the cock in his final plumage. The cock of this beautiful species has a chestnut plumage in his second year, and a white one in the third and subsequent years of his life. Nevertheless, a considerable proportion of the nests found belong to chestnut cocks.

Plumage of Herons

Darwin was of opinion that any novelty in [317] colouring in the male is admired by the female; and in this manner he sought to overcome some difficulties to his theory which certain birds presented.

Writing of the heron family, he says:—

"The young of the Ardea asha are white, the adults being slate-coloured; and not only the young, but the adults of the allied Buphus coromandus in their winter plumage are white, their colour changing into a rich golden buff during the breeding season. It is incredible that the young of these two species, as well as of some other members of the same family, should have been specially rendered pure white, and thus made conspicuous to their enemies; or that the adults of one of these two species should have been specially rendered white during the winter in a country which is never covered with snow. On the other hand, we have reason to believe that whiteness has been gained by many birds as a sexual ornament. We may therefore conclude that an early progenitor of the Ardea asha and the Buphus acquired a white plumage for nuptial purposes, and transmitted this colour to their young; so that the young and the old became white like certain existing egrets, the whiteness having afterwards been retained by the young whilst exchanged by the adults for more strongly pronounced tints. But if we could look still further backwards in time to [318] the still earlier progenitors of these two species, we should probably see the adults dark-coloured. I infer that this would be the case, from the analogy of many other birds, which are dark whilst young, and when adult are white; and more especially from the adult of the Ardea gularis, the colours of which are the reverse of those of A. asha, for the young are dark-coloured and the adults white, the young having retained a former state of plumage. It appears, therefore, that the progenitors in their adult condition of the A. asha, the Buphus, and of some allies have undergone, during a long line of descent, the following changes of colour: firstly a dark shade, secondly pure white, and thirdly, owing to another change of fashion (if I may so express myself), their present slaty, reddish or golden-buff tints. These successive changes are intelligible only on the principle of novelty having been admired by the birds for the sake of novelty."

This reasoning may appear far-fetched and unconvincing. It seems, however, quite likely that the hen may select as her mate the suitor who is conspicuously different from the others, not because she admires novelty, but because his conspicuousness attracts her attention and enables her to make up her mind quickly to take him and thus rid herself of the other troublesome admirers, who are all very much alike.

[319]
Sexual Dissimilarity

It is perhaps worthy of note that, after the most successful of her suitors has succeeded in securing the hen, it may happen that a disappointed rival makes love to her in the absence of her lord and master and thereby nullifies the effect of her previous selection.

It is to be observed that, even if we take it as proved, as Darwin believed, that the hens alone exercise a choice of mates, and that they select the most beautiful of their suitors, we are still far from arriving at an explanation of the fact that the males alone have acquired beauty. Admitting that the hens always mate with the most beautiful cocks, we should expect the offspring of each union to be all more or less alike in beauty—that is to say, more beautiful than the mother and less so than the cock. How are we to explain the one-sided inheritance of this beauty? Why is it confined to the cocks?

In order to meet this objection Darwin had to call to his aid unknown laws of inheritance. "The laws of inheritance," he writes (Descent of Man, p. 759), "irrespectively of selection, appear to have determined whether the characters acquired by males for the sake of ornament, for producing various sounds, and for fighting together, have been transmitted to the males alone or to both sexes, either permanently or periodically, during certain seasons of the year. Why various characters should have been transmitted [320] sometimes in one way and sometimes in another is not in most cases known; but the period of variability seems often to have been the determining cause. When the two sexes have inherited all characters in common, they necessarily resemble each other; but, as the successive variations may be differently transmitted, every possible gradation may be found, even within the same genus, from the closest similarity to the widest dissimilarity between the sexes."

This statement, although it does not throw any light upon the problem, is somewhat damaging to the theory of sexual selection. If it be admitted that dissimilarity between the sexes is due to the fact that the males have varied in one way and the females in another way, there seems no necessity for invoking the aid of feminine preference.

Even greater is the difficulty presented by those species in which the males alone are provided with horns or antlers. "When," writes Darwin (Descent of Man, p. 767), "the males are provided with weapons which in the females are absent, there can hardly be a doubt that these serve for fighting with other males; and that they were acquired through sexual selection, and were transmitted to the male sex alone. It is not probable, at least in most cases, that the females have been prevented from acquiring [321] such weapons on account of their being useless, superfluous, or in some way injurious. On the contrary, as they are often used by the males for various purposes, more especially as a defence against their enemies, it is a surprising fact that they are so poorly developed, or quite absent, in the females of so many animals."

We have, we believe, demonstrated that Darwin's theory of sexual selection is unable to account satisfactorily for all the phenomena of sexual dimorphism. But, as we have seen, it is quite possible that sexual selection is a real factor of evolution.

We trust that what we have said will stimulate some leisured naturalist to study the question of male and female preference.

We now pass on to consider briefly some of the other attempts that have been made to explain the phenomena of sexual dimorphism.

Wallace's Explanation of Sexual Dissimilarity

Wallace does not accept the theory of sexual selection. He admits that the form of male rivalry, which Darwin calls "the law of battle," is "a real power in nature," and believes that "to it we must impute the development of the exceptional strength, size, and activity of the male, together with the possession of special offensive and defensive weapons, and of all [322] other characters which arise from the development of these, or are correlated with them" (Darwinism, p. 283). But the view that the female selects the most beautiful of her suitors has always seemed to Wallace "to be unsupported by evidence, while it is also quite inadequate to account for the facts." For example, the accessory plumes of birds "usually appear in a few definite parts of the body. We require some cause to initiate the development in one part rather than in another."

Wallace considers that natural selection is able to explain all the phenomena of sexual dimorphism. He points out that, when the sexes are dissimilar among birds, it is almost invariably the female which is duller coloured. The reason for this is, he believes, that the hen birds, while sitting, "are exposed to observation and attack by the numerous devourers of eggs and birds, and it is of vital importance that they should be protectively coloured in all those parts of the body which are exposed during incubation. To secure this, all the bright colours and showy ornaments which decorate the male have not been acquired by the female, who often remains clothed in the sober hues which were probably once common to the whole order to which she belongs. The different amounts of colour acquired by the females have no doubt depended on peculiarities of habits and environment, and on [323] the powers of defence and concealment possessed by the species."

In support of his contention, Wallace asserts that all species of birds, of which the hens are as conspicuously coloured as the cocks, nest in holes or build domed nests. The plumes and other ornaments, which the cocks of certain species display, Wallace would attribute to a surplus of strength, vitality, and growth power, which is able to expend itself in this way without injury.

"If," he writes, "we have found a vera causa for the origin of ornamental appendages of birds and other animals in a surplus of vital energy, leading to abnormal growths in those parts of the integument where muscular and nervous action are greatest, the continuous development of these appendages will result from the ordinary action of natural selection in preserving the most healthy and vigorous individuals, and the still further selective agency of sexual struggle in giving to the very strongest and most energetic the parentage of the next generation." (Darwinism, p. 293.) "Why," he says, "in allied species the development of accessory plumes has taken different forms we are unable to say, except that it may be due to that individual variability which has served as the starting point for so much of what seems to us strange in form, or fantastic in colour, both in the animal and vegetable world."

[324]
Wallace's Theory Criticised

Wallace's view that the dull plumage of the hen bird is due to her greater need of protection is based on the assumption that the hen bird alone takes part in incubation.

Is this assumption a correct one?

It certainly is not in all cases. As D. Dewar has stated in Birds of the Plains, the showy white cock Paradise Fly-catcher (Terpsiphone paradisi) sits in broad daylight on the open nest quite as much as the hen does. And this may prove to be true of many other species of birds. Again, the cocks of the various species of Indian sunbirds are brightly coloured while the hens are dull brown. In these species the hen alone sits on the eggs, but, as the nest is well covered-in, the hen might display all the colours of the rainbow without being visible to passing birds. Moreover, as D. Dewar pointed out in a paper read before the Royal Society of Arts (Journal, vol. lvii., p. 104), although, in most species of Indian dove, the sexes show little or no dissimilarity, there is one species (Œnopopelia tranquebarica) which exhibits considerable sexual dimorphism. But the nesting habits of this peculiar species are in all respects similar to those of the other species of dove. Why then the marked dissimilarity of the sexes?

Another objection to the theory of Wallace is that urged by J. T. Cunningham (Archiv für [325] Entwicklungsmechanik der Organismen, vol. xxvi., p. 378), namely, that the secondary sexual characters in those species which possess them show an entire absence of uniformity in nature and position. "Why," asks Cunningham, "should the male constitution of the stag show itself in bony excrescences of the skull, in the peacock in excessive growth of the other end of the body? Why should the larynx be modified in one mammal, the teeth in another, the nose in another? Why is the male newt distinguished by a dorsal fin, the male frog by a swelling on the fore foot?"

Another objection to the explanation of sexual dimorphism suggested by Wallace, is that in many species of bird, as, for example, the house sparrow and the green paroquets of India, the external differences between the sexes are so slight that it is unreasonable to believe that they are the result of natural selection. It seems impossible to hold that the Rose-ringed Paroquet (Palæornis torquatus)—a species which nests in holes—would have become extinct if the hens had developed the narrow rose-coloured collar that characterises the cocks.

Darwin pointed out that while Wallace's hypothesis might appear plausible if applied to colour, it can scarcely be said to explain the origin of such structures as the musical apparatus of certain male insects, or the larger size of the [326] larynx in some birds and mammals. We thus see that suggestions offered by Wallace, although they contain a modicum of truth, fail to explain the phenomena of sexual dimorphism.

The fairest possible criticism of these views is that of Darwin:—

"It will have been seen that I cannot follow Mr Wallace in the belief that dull colours, when confined to the females, have been in most cases specially gained for the sake of protection. There can, however, be no doubt, as formerly remarked, that both sexes of many birds have had their colours modified, so as to escape the notice of their enemies; or in some instances, so as to approach their prey unobserved, just as owls have had their plumage rendered soft, that their flight may not be overheard" (The Descent of Man, p. 745).

The Theory of Thomson and Geddes

Thomson and Geddes have attempted to explain sexual dimorphism on the hypothesis that males are essentially dissipators of energy, while females tend to conserve energy. They point out that the spermatozoon is a small intensely active body, which dissipates its energy in motion, while the ovum is a large inert body—the result of the female tendency to conserve energy and to build up material. The various ornaments and excrescences which appear in [327] male organisms are the result of this male tendency to dissipate energy. In the spermatozoon the dissipated energy appears in the form of active movement; in the adult organism it takes the shape of plumes and other ornaments, of song and contests for the females.

This theory, however, does not explain what we might call the haphazard nature of sexual dimorphism. If sexual dissimilarity is due to the tendency of the male to dissipate energy, why do we see very marked dimorphism in one species, and no dimorphism in a very nearly allied species? Why are the males larger than the females in some species, and smaller in other species? Again, how is it that in certain species of birds—the quails of the genus Turnix, the Painted Snipe (Rhynchæa), and the Phalaropes—it is the female who possesses the more showy plumage? Moreover, this theory, equally with that of Wallace, does not explain why the excrescences which characterise the male appear in various parts of the body in different species.

Stolzmann's Theory

Stolzmann has made an ingenious attempt to explain why in birds the cock is so frequently more conspicuously coloured than the hen. He asserts that among birds the males are more numerous than the females, and that this preponderance is not advantageous to the species. [328] Those males which have not managed to secure a mate are apt to persecute the females while sitting on the eggs, to the detriment of these latter. Natural selection, says Stolzmann, is concerned with the well-being of the species rather than of the individual. Hence anything that would tend to lessen the number of males would be a good thing for the species, so that a peculiarity, such as bright plumage, which renders the males conspicuous, or ornamental plumes, which cause their flight to be slow, and so leads to their destruction, will be seized upon and perpetuated by natural selection. He points out that the cock of one species of hummingbird—Loddigesia mirabilis—has not only longer tail feathers, but a shorter wing than the female, and must, in consequence, find it comparatively difficult to obtain food, and be more liable to fall a victim to birds of prey than the hen. Stolzmann further suggests that the excessive pugnacity of male birds at the breeding season may lead to the destruction of some individuals, and so prove of advantage to the species.

Several objections seem to present themselves to this most ingenious theory.

In the first place, there does not appear to be any satisfactory evidence to show that more cocks than hens are born.

We may grant that a superfluity of cocks is injurious to any species, since the unmated ones [329] are likely to persecute the hens; we may also grant that many cocks are handicapped in the struggle for existence by the excessive growth of certain of their feathers, but we fail to see how this excessive development has been caused by natural selection in the manner suggested by Stolzmann. Although it may be advantageous to the species for the cocks to be showy, natural selection can perpetuate this only by weeding out the least conspicuous of the cocks. But it is the more gaudy ones, those, according to Stolzmann, whose presence is beneficial to the species, which will be eliminated by natural selection. So that, in this case, that force will act in a manner contrary to the interests of the species, if Stolzmann's idea is a correct one.

The theory in question would therefore seem to be untenable. Nevertheless there is doubtless some truth in the notion that too many males spoil the species. Thus, excessive showiness and high mortality among the males may be beneficial to the species. But we must not forget that the more beneficial it is, the stronger must be the tendency of natural selection to eliminate the males that possess the desired peculiarity.

Neo-Lamarckian Explanation

Cunningham's Theory

J. T. Cunningham makes an attempt to explain the phenomena of sexual dimorphism on [330] Neo-Lamarckian principles. His theory is set forth in a paper entitled The Heredity of Secondary Sexual Characters in relation to Hormones, which was read before the Zoological Society of London, and published in full in the Archiv für Entwicklungsmechanik der Organismen. "The significant correlation of male sexual characters," he writes, "is not with any general or essential property of the male sex, such as katabolism (or the tendency to dissipate energy, as we have called it), but with certain habits and functions confined to one sex, but differing in different animals. . . . In those animals which possess such (i.e. secondary sexual) characters, the parts of the soma (i.e. the body) affected differ as much as they can differ; any part of the soma may show a sexual difference: teeth in one mammal, skull in another; feathers of the tail in one bird, those of the neck in another, and so on. But in all cases such unisexual characters correspond to their functions or use in habits and instincts which are associated, but only indirectly, with sexual production. These habits are as diverse and as irregular in their distribution as the characters. The cocks of common fowls and of the Phasianidæ generally are polygamous, fight with each other for the possession of the females, and take no part in incubation or care of the young, and they differ from the hens in their enlarged [331] brilliant plumage, spurs on the legs, and combs, wattles, or other excrescences on the head. In the Columbidæ per contra the males are not polygamous, but pair for life, the males do not fight, and share equally with the females in parental duties.

"Corresponding with this contrast of sexual habits is the contrast of sexual dimorphism, which is virtually absent in the Columbidæ.

"I think, then, the only scientific explanation is that the difference of habits is the cause of the sexual dimorphism, and that the special sexual habits which occur in some

128

species but not in others are the causes of the sexual characters. . . . The habits in question always involve certain definite stimulations applied to those parts of the body whose modification constitutes the somatic sexual characters. The stimulations are confined, as the characters are confined, to one sex, to one period of life, to one season of the year, to those animals which have the characters, to those parts of the body which are modified." Mr Cunningham believes that these stimulations cause hypertrophy or excessive growth of the part affected, and that this peculiarity is transmitted to the offspring. And thus he supposes all the ornaments and excrescences of the males of various species to have arisen.

As evidence in favour of his view, he points out that these excrescences are, in many species, [332] not only functionless but absolutely injurious, as in the case of the comb and wattles of the jungle cock and his domestic descendants, which merely serve as a handle for enemies to seize.

Cunningham asserts that the only objection to his theory is the dogma that acquired characters cannot be inherited. This assertion is, however, not correct. It is, indeed, a very serious objection that all the evidence available seems to show that acquired characters are not inherited, but this is by no means the only difficulty.

Before mentioning these further objections, let us say a word on the subject of the inheritance of acquired characters. Mr Cunningham himself compares the formation of a splint or spavin in a horse as the result of special strain, to the acquisition of secondary sexual characters. Unfortunately for Cunningham's theory, but fortunately for mankind in general, spavined horses and mares do not beget spavined offspring. If, then, spavin is not inherited, is it not unreasonable to assert that the thickening of the bone that develops on the head of a butting animal is inherited?

Another objection to Cunningham's theory is that many birds which show off their plumage most vigorously possess no ornamental plumes. As Howard has recorded, many of our dull-coloured British warblers show off in the same manner as bright-coloured birds do. If the [333] exercise has caused the development and inheritance of plumes in some species, why not in the others?

Again, Cunningham is not correct in saying that sexual dimorphism is "virtually absent" in the Columbidæ. Few birds display so striking a sexual dimorphism as the Orange Dove (Chryscena victor) of Fiji, in which the male is bright orange and the hen green. We have already cited the case of the curious sexually dimorphic red turtle-dove. Now, the courting attitudes and actions of this species are precisely the same as those of other allied turtle-doves; why, then, have these exercises caused only one species to become sexually dimorphic?

Existing Theories not Satisfactory

Our survey of the more important attempts which have been made to explain the phenomena of sexual dimorphism leads to the conclusion that these still require elucidation. We have weighed each theory in the balance and found it wanting.

The outstanding feature of sexual dissimilarity is the apparently haphazard manner of its occurrence.

We have already alluded to the case of the doves in India. In that country four species are widely distributed—namely, the Spotted Dove (Turtur suratensis), the Ring or Collared Dove (Turtur risorius), the Little Brown Dove (Turtur cambayensis), and the Red Turtle-dove (Œnopopelia [334] tranqebarica). The habits of all these four species appear to be identical, nevertheless in the first three the sexes show little or no dissimilarity in outward appearance, while in the last the sexual dimorphism is so great that the cock and hen were formerly thought to belong to different species.

Another very curious case is that of the South American geese of the genus Chloëphaga, in which some species, as the familiar Upland or Magellan Goose of our parks (C. magellanica), have the sexes utterly unlike, while in others, as the Ruddy-headed Goose (C. rubidiceps), they are quite similar to each other.

The ducks furnish us with another very good example of the apparently haphazard nature of sexual dimorphism. In the Common Mallard or Wild Duck (Anas boscas) the cock is far more showily coloured than the hen, but in all the species most nearly allied to it the males are as inconspicuous as the females, e.g. in the Indian Spotted-bill (Anas pœcilorhyncha), the Australian Grey Duck (A. superciliosa), the African Yellow Bill (Anas undulata), and the American Dusky Duck (A. obscura). As the dusky duck inhabits North America, where the mallard is also found, the case is particularly striking.

Among mammals the lion and the tiger and the sable and roan antelopes (Hippotragus niger and H. equinus) furnish familiar examples of nearly-related [335] species, in one of which the sexes are alike and in the other dissimilar in appearance.

Hormones

Another important point to be borne in mind is the intimate correlation that exists between the reproductive organs and the general appearance of the organism, more especially of the secondary sexual characters. These last, in most cases, do not show themselves until the maturity of the sexual organs. The well-known effects of castration illustrate this connection. Again, females in which the reproductive organs have ceased to be functional often assume male characters.

It has lately been proved by experiment that, in many cases at any rate, the development of the ornaments, etc., characteristic of the sexes is due to the secretion by the sexual cells of what are known as hormones—that is to say, secretions which excite development of the secondary sexual characters. The tendency to produce the external characteristics of the sex to which an organism belongs is inherited, but the actual development thereof is in many cases dependent on the secretion of these hormones. Accordingly, if a male individual be completely castrated it ceases to develop the external characters of its sex. The evidence upon which the doctrine of hormones is based is admirably summarised in the above-quoted paper by Cunningham. Into this evidence we cannot go. It must suffice that the doctrine is quite [336] in accordance with all the observed results of castration.

It is worthy of notice that the various features which characterise the sexes in sexually dimorphic animals are not associated with any particular organ or parts of the body, nor do they necessarily affect the same part in allied species. "We cannot say," writes J. T. Cunningham, "that any part of the soma (i.e. the body tissue) is specially sexual more than another part, except that such differences between the sexes are usually external. They usually affect the skin, and especially epidermic appendages, and the superficial parts of the skeleton, or whole limbs and appendages; or the difference may be one of size of the whole soma. In mammals and birds the male is often the larger, sometimes very much so, but there are cases in which the female is larger. There is no general rule."

Another important point is, that females, although they themselves show no trace of the male character, are capable of transmitting it to their progeny. This can be proved by crossing a hen pheasant with a cock barn-door-fowl; the male offspring of the union display the plumes so characteristic of the cock pheasant. These cannot have been derived from the barn-door-fowl father; they must have come from the dull-coloured hen pheasant.

In this connection we may mention the curious [337] fact recorded by Bonhote, on page 245 of the Proceedings of the Fourth International Ornithological Congress, that in the case of ducks descended from crosses between the pintail, the mallard, and the spotbill, the drakes in full breeding plumage showed a mixture of pintail and mallard characteristics, while, in their non-breeding plumage, the colouring of the spotbill is predominant.

Eye-colour, Comb, and Spurs

An important point, and one which does not seem to have been pointed out by any zoologist, is that eye-colour, comb, and spurs in birds and horns in mammals do not stand in the same relation to the sexual organs as do the other external characteristics. For example, the castrated Nilgai (Boselaphus tragocamelus) acquires horns, but not the characteristic male colour. In the common Indian Francolin Partridge (Francolinus pondicerianius), the cock differs from the hen only in the possession of spurs. The same applies to the various species of Snow Cock (Tetraogallus). There is a breed of game-cocks which display plumage like that of the hen, but such birds have the comb and spurs developed as in normally feathered cocks.

The white eye of the white-eyed Pochard Drake (Nyroca africana), and the yellow eye of the cock Golden Pheasant (Chrysolophus pictus), which are purely male characters, show themselves earlier than the male plumage. Occasionally [338] a hen golden pheasant assumes the plumage of the cock, but she never acquires the yellow eye.

Many birds when kept in captivity lose some of the beauty of their plumage, and this is usually attributed to the sexual organs becoming impaired and reacting on the somatic tissue. But this explanation cannot in all cases be the correct one, because the linnet, although losing the male plumage in captivity, lives long and well in a cage and breeds readily with hen canaries.

Another curious fact is that the male plumage sometimes appears pathologically in hen birds, more especially in those which have become sterile from age or disease. This phenomenon occurs comparatively frequently in the gold pheasant, and more rarely in the common pheasant, the fowl, and the duck.

Phenomena such as these seem to suggest that in some cases the bright colours of the male may be pathological, that the hormones which the male sexual cells secrete may exercise an injurious effect on the somatic or body tissues. Decay is known to be accompanied by the production of brightly coloured pigment in the case of leaves. Finn suggests that the white plumage which the cock paradise fly-catcher assumes in the fourth year of his existence may be a livery of decay, a sign of senility.

[339]
The Four Kinds of Mutations

It is our belief that sexual dimorphism arises frequently, if not invariably, as a mutation. Mutations may be of four different kinds.

Those which appear only, or especially, in conjunction with the male organs, for example, whiteness in domesticated geese allowed to breed indiscriminately.

Those which appear only, or especially, in conjunction with the female organs; mutations of this description appear to be very rare, but it may be noted that in fowls allowed to breed indiscriminately, as in India, completely black hens are common, but completely black cocks are rarely, if ever, seen. This indicates an association between blackness and femininity.

Those which appear in the same manner in both sexes. The great majority of mutations appear to be of this kind.

Lastly, those that appear in both sexes but take a different form in the case of the two sexes; thus in cats a mutation has given rise to sandy males and tortoise-shell females. The mutation which has produced the black-winged peacock shows itself in the form of a black wing in the cock, while it causes the plumage of the hen to be grizzly white.

We shall deal with the phenomenon of correlation at some length in the next chapter. It is a subject to which sufficient attention has not been paid. Even as certain characters are correlated [340] in certain species, so in some cases are certain characters correlated with sex.

Why this should be so we are not in a position to say; this, however, does not affect the indisputable fact that such correlation does exist.

Physicians in the course of their practice sometimes come across very curious cases of correlation in human beings.

Unilateral Transmission

"It is," writes Thomson (Heredity, p. 290), "an interesting fact that an abnormal element in the inheritance may find expression in the males only or in the females only. If we could understand this we should be nearer understanding what sex really means.

"Hæmophilia, or a tendency to bleeding, is a heritable abnormality, partly associated with weakness in the blood-vessels, which do not contract as they should and are apt to break, and partly connected with a lack of coagulating power in the blood. It is usually confined to males. But as it passes from a father through a daughter to a grandson, and so on, it must be a latent part of the germinal inheritance of the females, though for some obscure physiological reason it fails to find expression in them, or has its expression quite disguised. Colour-blindness or Daltonism has been recorded (Horner) through the males only of seven generations. Dejerine cites another case (fide Appenzeller) in which all the males in a family history had cataract through [341] four generations. There are other instances of what is sometimes awkwardly called the unilateral transmission of abnormal qualities. Edward Lambert, born in 1717, is said to have been covered with 'spines.' His children showed the same peculiarity, which began to be manifest from the sixth to the ninth month after birth. One of his children grew up and handed on the peculiarity to another generation. Indeed, it is said to have persisted for five generations, and in the males only—unilateral transmission."

In our view, these abnormalities are of such a kind that they are only possible in connection with the male organ; in other words, they are mutations of the first of the four kinds cited above—those which appear only in connection with the male organ.

It is a curious fact that the general rule in nature seems to be that the male is ahead of the female in the course of evolution. The sexes may be alike at a given period in the life-history of the species. Presently a mutation appears which is confined to the male alone; thus arises the phenomenon of sexual dimorphism. The next step in the evolution of the species is frequently a mutation on the part of the female which brings her once again into line with the male, and so the sexual dimorphism disappears, for a time at any rate. A good example of this is furnished by the sparrows; in the common [342] sparrow of a large part of Africa (Passer swainsoni) both sexes are very plain, like the hen of the house-sparrow; in this species (P. domesticus) as every one knows, the cock, though by no means brilliant, is noticeably handsomer than his mate; while in the Tree-sparrow (P. montanus) both sexes have a plumage of masculine type, much like that of the cock house-sparrow.

132

If we consider in conjunction with one another the various facts we have cited above, we begin to grasp the nature of the phenomena of sexual dimorphism.

Let us consider an imaginary case of a defenceless little bird which builds an open nest. Let us suppose that it is inconspicuously plumaged. Now suppose that a mutation of the first kind shows itself, a mutation which affects the cock only and makes him more conspicuous. Let us further suppose that the cock does not share in the duties of incubation. It is quite possible that, in spite of this apparently unfavourable mutation, the species may survive, for, as we have seen, it does not affect the hen, and she, since she alone incubates, stands the most in need of protective colouring. Moreover, as Stolzmann has suggested, the species can possibly afford to lose a few males. But suppose that both cock and hen share in the duties of incubation, it is then quite likely that the mutation [343] will cause the species to become extinct, by the elimination of all the males. Or, let us suppose that the mutation in the direction of showy plumage affects both sexes, then in such a case the species will almost certainly become extinct. If, however, the hypothetical species nested in holes in trees, it is quite possible that it might survive notwithstanding its showy plumage.

Greater Value of Females

Whether, as Wallace suggests, the hen does most of the incubating, and is exposed to special danger when sitting on her eggs in an open nest, or, as Stolzmann urges, it is of advantage to the species that there should not be too many males, the result is the same, that the species can afford to allow the cock to be more gaily attired than the hen. In either case the colouration of the cock becomes a matter of comparatively little importance to the species, and this, coupled with the fact that the male tends to mutate more readily than the female, will explain why, in most species which exhibit sexual dimorphism, it is the cocks that are the more conspicuous. In certain species the cocks alone incubate, and these then become more important than the females to the race, so that they have not been permitted to become showy, while the hens have been allowed more freedom in this respect. The extreme variability of the Ruff (Pavoncella pugnax) in breeding plumage points to the [344] fact that his colour is a matter of comparative indifference to the species; in consequence plenty of latitude is allowed to his tendency to vary.

Our view, then, is that evolution proceeds by mutations, which may be large or small.

The mutation is the result of a rearrangement in part or parts of the fertilised egg, and this rearrangement shows itself in the adult organism as a change in one or more of its characteristics. The mutation may be correlated with only one of the sexual organs, and when this is the case, it gives rise to the phenomenon of sexual dimorphism. The appearance in the adult of certain, if not of all, characteristics is affected by causes other than the nature of the biological molecules from which they are derived. The tendency to develop in a certain direction is there, but something else, such as the secretion of hormones from the sexual cells, is frequently necessary to enable a given tendency to fully develop itself. Thus it is that castration often affects the bodily appearance of those animals operated on. When a mutation appears, natural selection decides whether or not it shall persist.

[345]

CHAPTER VIII
THE FACTORS OF EVOLUTION

Variation along definite lines and Natural Selection are undoubtedly important factors of evolution—Whether or not sexual selection is a factor we are not yet in a position to decide—Modus operandi of Natural Selection—Correlation an important factor—Examples of correlation—Correlation is a subject that requires close study—Isolation a factor in

evolution—Discriminate isolation—Indiscriminate isolation—Is the latter a factor?—
Romanes' views—Criticism of these—Indiscriminate isolation shown to be a factor—
Summary of the methods in which new species arise—Natural Selection does not make
species—It merely decides which of certain ready-made forms shall survive—Natural
Selection compared to a competitive examination and to a medical board—We are yet in
darkness as to the fundamental causes of the Origin of Species—In experiment and
observation rather than speculation lies the hope of discovering the nature of these causes.

We have so far considered three factors of evolution. The first of these is the
tendency of organisms to vary along definite lines. This is a most important factor, because,
unless variation occurs in any given direction, there can be no evolution in that direction.
Variations are the materials upon which the other factors, or causes, of evolution work. The
second great factor is natural selection. Natural selection may be compared [346] to a
builder, and variations to his materials. The kind of building that a builder can construct
depends very largely on the material supplied to him. The Forth Bridge could not have been
built had those who constructed it had no material given them but bricks and mortar.
Wallaceians regard natural selection as a builder who is supplied with every kind of building
material—stone, bricks, wood, iron, aluminium, in any quantities he may desire. They
therefore regard natural selection as the one and only cause which determines evolution.
This, however, is a wrong idea. Natural selection should rather be likened to a builder who is
supplied with a limited variety of building materials, so that considerable restrictions are
imposed on his building operations. The doors, windows, fireplaces, etc., are supplied to him
ready-made. He merely selects which of these he will use for each building.

The third factor of evolution which we have considered is sexual selection. As we
have seen, sufficient attention has not been paid to this subject, so that we are not yet in a
position to say how much, if any, influence it has exercised on the course of evolution.

The Struggle for Existence

In addition to these three factors, there are, we believe, some others. Before
proceeding to a consideration of these, it is important to study carefully the modus operandi
of natural selection, or, in other words, the nature of the struggle for [347] existence, as
many of the statements contained in recent books on evolution seem to us to be based upon
a mistaken conception of this important factor.

As usual, Darwin's disciples have failed to improve upon the account he gave of the
nature of the struggle for existence. This is set forth in Chapter III. of the Origin of Species.

"The causes," writes Darwin (new edition, p. 83), "which check the natural tendency
of each species to increase in number are most obscure. Look at the most vigorous species;
by as much as it swarms in numbers, by so much will it tend to increase still further. We
know not exactly what the checks are even in a single instance." This is perfectly true.
Nevertheless elaborate theories of protective and warning colouration and mimicry have
been built up on the tacit assumption that the checks to the multiplication of all, or nearly
all, species are the creatures which prey upon them. Possibly no Wallaceian asserts this in so
many words, but it is a logical deduction from the excessive prominence each one gives to
the various theories of animal colouration; for, if the chief foes of an organism are not the
creatures which prey upon it, how can the particular shade and pattern of its coat be of such
paramount importance to it?

Checks on Increase

We shall endeavour to show that there are checks on the increase of a species far
more [348] potent than the devastation caused by those creatures which feed upon it. Let us,

however, first briefly set forth some of the checks on the multiplication of organisms which Darwin mentions in the Origin of Species.

"Eggs, or very young animals," he says, "seem generally to suffer the most, but this is not invariably the case." This is, as we have already insisted, a most important point to be borne in mind, especially when considering the various current theories of animal colouration. When once the average animal has become adult its chances of survival are enormously increased.

A second check mentioned by Darwin is the limitation of food supply. "The amount of food for each species," he writes (p. 84), "of course gives the extreme limit to which each can increase; but very frequently it is not the obtaining food, but the serving as prey to other animals, which determines the average numbers of a species. Thus there seems to be little doubt that the stock of partridges, grouse, and hares on any large estate depends chiefly on the destruction of vermin. . . . On the other hand, in some cases, as with the elephant and rhinoceros, none are destroyed by beasts of prey."

We are inclined to think that neither the food limit nor the beasts of prey are a very important check on the multiplication of organisms. The [349] lion, for example, was never so numerous as to reach the limit of its food supply. Before the white man obtained a foothold in Africa vast herds of herbivores were to be seen in those districts where lions were most plentiful. This is a most important fact, for, if the numbers of a species are not determined by those of the animals that prey upon it, the particular colour of an organism is probably not of any direct importance to it. This cuts away the foundation of some of the generally accepted theories of animal colouration.

"Climate," writes Darwin (p. 84), "plays an important part in determining the average numbers of a species, and periodical seasons of extreme cold or drought seem to be the most effective of all checks. I estimated (chiefly from the greatly reduced numbers of nests in the spring) that the winter of 1854-55 destroyed four-fifths of the birds in my own grounds, and this is a tremendous destruction when we remember that 10 per cent. is an extraordinarily severe mortality from epidemics with man."

In our opinion, Darwin did not lay nearly enough stress upon the importance of climate as a check on the increase of species. We have seen that he stated his belief that it is the most effective of all checks. But even this is not a sufficiently strong statement of the case. It [350] seems to us that before this check all other checks pale into insignificance.

Darwin failed to notice the potent effects of damp. Damp is more injurious to most species than even cold or drought, as every one who has tried to keep birds in England knows. All entomologists are aware how harmful damp is to insects. Caterpillars seem to take cover under leaves to avoid damp rather than to hide themselves from birds, since these make a point, when searching for insects, of invariably looking carefully under leaves.

It is a well-known fact that a wet winter in England causes much mortality among rabbits. The increase of the rabbit in Australia is usually attributed to the fact that the little rodent has not so many predatory creatures to contend with there as it has in Europe. This is not so. In Australia the rabbit has to fight against eagles, other large birds of prey, carnivorous marsupials, feral cats, monitor lizards and large snakes, to say nothing of the well-organised and persistent attacks of man.

Were predacious creatures the most important foes of the rabbit it would never have obtained a firm foothold in Australia. Damp appears to be its chief enemy. In Australia this does not exist. Hence the remarkable increase of the species. Stronger evidence it would not be possible to advance of the potency of damp as a check on [351] the increase of a species and of the comparative powerlessness of the attacks of raptorial creatures.

135

The failure of the sandgrouse to establish a footing in England is, we believe, due to the fact that it is constitutionally unfitted to withstand our damp climate.

The camel is an animal that revels in dry habitats, hence the difficulty of keeping camels in damp Bengal, although they seem to thrive well enough in the drier parts of India.

"When a species," writes Darwin (p. 86), "owing to highly favourable circumstances, increases inordinately in numbers in a small tract, epidemics—at least, this seems generally to occur with our game animals—often ensue; and here we have a limiting check independent of the struggle for life. But even some of these so-called epidemics appear to be due to parasitic worms, which have from some cause, possibly in part through facility of diffusion amongst the crowded animals, been disproportionately favoured: and here comes in a sort of struggle between the parasite and its prey."

Thus inadequately does Darwin deal with that bar to the increase of organisms, which is only second in importance to the effect of climate. The check occasioned by disease and parasites is one to which naturalists have as yet paid but little attention. The result is a very general misunderstanding of the true nature of the [352] struggle for existence, in other words, of the modus operandi of natural selection.

The tsetse-fly in Africa is a far more important check on the increase of some animals than the lions and other beasts of prey. There are in that continent large tracts of country, known as tsetse-fly belts, in which neither horse, nor ox, nor dog can exist. If races of these animals were to arise which could withstand the bite of the tsetse-fly, these species might increase more rapidly than the rabbit in Australia has done, nor would it matter if the creatures in question were bright crimson, or any other conspicuous colour.

Take the case of the lion in Africa. The chief bar to the increase in numbers of this species appears to be the teething troubles to which the whelps are liable. Now suppose that a mutation were to occur in the lion. Suppose that several members of a litter were all bright blue, and that these suffered from no teething troubles. They would probably all grow up, and although at some disadvantage as hunters on account of their conspicuous colouring, they would nevertheless probably increase at the expense of the normally coloured lions, because of the immunity of their offspring from death from teething troubles. Zoologists would then be at a loss to explain their bright colouring. We should have all manner of ingenious suggestions raised, namely, that in the [353] moonlight these creatures were really not at all conspicuous, indeed that they were obliteratively coloured. In other words, a totally wrong explanation of their colouring would be given and accepted. It is our belief that many of the explanations put forward and accepted of the colouration of existing species are wide of the mark.

As all bee-keepers are aware, the disease known as foul-brood works more havoc among their bees than all the insectivorous creatures put together.

Similarly throat disease among wood-pigeons does more towards keeping their numbers down than all the efforts of predacious birds.

A check on multiplication not mentioned by Darwin is that which is sometimes imposed by the individuals of the species on one another. Thus, in some animals, as, for example, the hyæna, the male occasionally devours his own young ones.

A check of a similar nature results from the habit which the Indian House Crow (Corvus splendens) has of interrupting the pairing operations of its neighbours.

Attributes of Successful Species

We are now in a position to sum up briefly the more important requisites for success in the struggle for existence.

These are not so much specialised structure as courage, a good constitution, mental capacity and prolificacy.

[354]
Few animals possess all these characteristics in a pre-eminent degree, for, to use the words of Mr Thompson Seton, "Every animal has some strong point or it could not live, and some weak point or the other animals could not live." Courage may be of two kinds— active courage, like that of the Englishman, or passive courage, like that of the Jew.

As D. Dewar has said: In the struggle for existence, "An ounce of good solid pugnacity is worth many pounds of protective colouration."

It is of course possible for an animal to possess too much courage. An excessive amount of courage will often cause a creature to fight unnecessary battles, which may lead to its premature death. This is perhaps the reason why the pugnacious black form of the leopard is not more numerous.

Under a good constitution we must include the power of resisting the rigours of climate, more especially damp, the ability to resist disease, and the enjoyment of a good digestion. When from any cause the normal food of a species becomes scarce, the members of that species will have to starve or supplement the normal diet with food of an unusual nature; and those that are endowed with a good digestion will be able to digest the new food and thus survive, while those which cannot assimilate food [355] to which they are unaccustomed will become emaciated and perish. We see this in every hard winter in England, when the redwing, which, unlike other thrushes, cannot thrive on berries, is the first to die. Most of the more successful birds—the crows and gulls, for example—are omnivorous—that is to say, they are able to digest all manner of food.

Under mental capacity, we would include cunning and sufficient intelligence to adapt oneself to changed conditions. It is largely through man's superior mental capacity that he has become the dominant species. It is true that he displays also courage and a good constitution, being able to adapt himself to life under the most diverse conditions; but this is, of course, in part due to his mental capacity, which enables him to some extent to adapt his environment to himself.

The advantages of prolificacy are so apparent that it is unnecessary to dilate upon them. Nearly as important as excessive fertility is the ability on the part of the parents to look after their young ones.

Every successful species possesses in a special degree at least one of the above attributes. It is interesting to take in turn the various species which are most widely distributed and consider to what extent they possess these several qualities.

[356]
Let us now consider a factor in evolution which is nearly as important as natural selection itself—we allude to the phenomenon of correlation.

Correlation

We may define correlation as the interdependence of two or more characters. This phenomenon is far more common than the majority of naturalists seem to think. It very frequently happens that one particular character never appears in an organism without being accompanied by some other character which we should not expect to be in any way related to it.

Darwin called attention to this phenomenon. "In monstrosities," he writes, on page 13 of the Origin of Species (new edition), "the correlations between quite different parts are very curious, and many interesting instances are given in Isidore Geoffroy St Hilaire's great work on this subject. Breeders believe that long limbs are almost always accompanied by an elongated head. Some instances of correlation are quite whimsical: thus cats which are entirely white and have blue eyes are generally deaf; but it has been lately stated by Mr Tait that this is confined to the males.

"Colour and constitutional peculiarities go together, of which many remarkable cases could be given among animals and plants. From the [357] facts collected by Heusinger, it appears that white sheep and pigs are injured by certain plants, whilst dark-coloured individuals escape. Professor Wyman has recently communicated to me a good illustration of this fact: on asking some farmers in Virginia how it was that all their pigs were black, they informed him that the pigs ate the paint-root (Lachnanthes), which coloured their bones pink, and which caused the hoofs of all but the black varieties to drop off; and one of the 'crackers' (i.e. Virginia squatters) added, "we select the black members of a litter for raising, as they alone have a good chance of living.'

"Hairless dogs have imperfect teeth; long-haired and coarse-haired animals are apt to have, as is asserted, long or many horns; pigeons with feathered feet have skin between their outer toes; pigeons with short beaks have small feet, and those with long beaks large feet.

"Hence, if man goes on selecting, and thus augmenting, any peculiarity, he will almost certainly modify unintentionally other parts of the structure, owing to the mysterious laws of the correlation of growth."

The great importance of the principle of the correlation of organs is, that natural selection may indirectly cause the survival of unfavourable variations, or of variations which are of no utility to the organism, because they happen to [358] be correlated with organs or structures that are useful.

Physiologists insist more and more upon the close interdependence of the various parts of the organism. All recent researches tend to show that each of the organs has, besides its primary function, a number of subordinate duties to perform, and that the removal of one organ reacts on all the others.

In face of these facts we should have expected those zoologists who have followed Darwin to have paid very close attention to the subject of correlation. As a matter of fact, the phenomenon seems to have been almost completely neglected. This is an example of the manner in which the superficial theories which to-day command wide acceptance have tended to bar the way to research.

There seems to be, in the case of some organisms, at any rate, a distinct correlation between their colouring and their constitution or mental characters. For example, the black forms of the cobra, the leopard, and the jaguar are notoriously bad-tempered.

"There is," writes Col. Cunningham, on p. 344 of Some Indian Friends and Acquaintances, "much variation in the temper of different varieties of cobras, and, as is often so noticeable among other sorts of animals, there would seem to be a distinct correlation between darkness of [359] colour and badness of temper. It is probably in part owing to a recognition of this that the cobras ordinarily seen in the hands of the so-called snake charmers are of a very light colour, although the choice may also be to some extent of æsthetic origin, seeing that the paler varieties are specially ornamental, due to the brilliancy of their markings and the great development of their hoods." It would thus appear that there is also a correlation between the colour of the cobra and the size of its hood.

Hesketh Pritchard informs us, in Through the Heart of Patagonia, that the Gauchos assert that a "picaso" colt—that is to say, a black one with white points—is the reverse of docile. Similarly, black mice are said to be very hard to tame.

We have already called attention to the importance of courage and the power of resisting the rigours of climate in the struggle for existence. It is apparently because black is so frequently correlated with courage that it is seen comparatively often in nature, in spite of the fact that it is a very bad colour as regards protection from enemies. Those birds and beasts which are black are usually thriving species. The dominance of the crow tribe is a case in point. Crows, it is true, are not really courageous, but they are dangerous owing to their gregarious habits, and are dreaded by other creatures on account of their power of combination. In Birds of the [360] Plains, D. Dewar records an instance of a number of crows killing in revenge so powerful a bird as the kite.

Since very many species seem to throw off melanistic variations, it may perhaps be asked, How is it that more black species do not exist?

The reply is twofold. In the first place, it is quite likely that in some organisms black variations are not correlated with courage or extreme pugnacity, and when such is the case the melanistic varieties will be more likely to be exterminated by foes, on account of their conspicuousness. It must be remembered that, other things being equal, the inconspicuously coloured organism has a better chance of survival than the showily coloured one. This is, of course, a very different attitude from that which insists on the all-importance to animals of protective colouration. Secondly, it is not difficult to see how too much courage may be fatal to an animal in leading it to take risks which a more timid creature would refrain from doing. This, as we have already suggested, is probably the reason why the black panther is so scarce. The black colour is readily inherited, so there must be some cause which tends to kill off the black varieties of the panther.

Lest it be thought the idea that excessive courage and pugnacity are harmful is mere fancy, let us quote from the account of the nesting [361] habits of the White-rumped Swallow (Tachycineta leucorrhoa) given by Mr W. H. Hudson on p. 32 of Argentine Ornithology. He says that no matter how many nesting sites are available, there is always much fighting amongst these birds for the best places. "Most vindictively," he writes, "do the little things clutch each other, and fall to the earth twenty times an hour, where they often remain struggling for a long time, heedless of the screams of alarm their fellows set up above them; for often, while they thus lie on the ground punishing each other, they fall an easy prey to some wily pussy who has made herself acquainted with their habits."

We have already emphasised the importance to many species of possessing the power of resisting the effects of damp. In the case of some organisms favourable variations in this direction may possess a greater survival value than those in the shape of greater speed or physical strength.

Now, if there be any correlation between the power of resisting damp and the colour an animal bears, it is quite probable that animals of this colour, whether or no it be conspicuous, are likely to survive in preference to those who are more protectively coloured. There is some evidence that in certain cases, at any rate, resistance to climate is correlated with colour peculiarities. For example, some fanciers assert that yellow-legged poultry resist cold and damp better than [362] those whose legs are not yellow. Fowls which have yellow legs have also yellow skins. In this connection the almost universal assumption of orange feet by domestic guinea-fowls is significant. Normally the feet of these birds are black, and their natural African habitat is a dry one.

A grey or white colour appears to be correlated with resistance to cold. In birds this may perhaps be explained by the fact that the feathers in some light-coloured varieties are longer than in those of normally-coloured ones. Thus mealy-coloured canaries have longer feathers than brightly-coloured ones.

The Arctic Skua, having no enemies to fear, stands in no need of protective colouration. It would therefore seem that the white-breasted form of this bird becomes more numerous as it nears the north pole, not because of the closer assimilation of its plumage to the colour of the snowy surroundings, but because the bird has to resist the greater degree of cold the farther north it finds itself. Similarly, in the region of the south pole the albino form of the Giant Petrel (Ossifraga gigantea) becomes common. Both these birds are themselves predatory and not liable to be preyed upon.

The curious china-white legs of some desert birds—as, for example, coursers and larks—would seem to indicate a power of resisting the hot rays [363] radiating from the sand on which these creatures dwell.

White quills do not wear well either in domestic birds or in wild albinos. This may explain why it is that when a white wild species of bird has any black in its plumage the black is almost invariably on the tips of the wings.

White quill-feathers are one of the commonest variations observed in domesticated birds, nevertheless they are as rare as complete whiteness among birds in their natural state.

A chestnut or bay colour in mammals appears to be correlated with a high rate of speed, as in the thoroughbred horse. This perhaps explains why so many of the swiftest species of antelope, such as the hartebeests and sassaby (Damaliscus lunatus), are chestnut bay in colour. It is further a remarkable fact that in the Black-buck (Antilope cervicapra) and the Nilgai (Boselaphus tragocamelus) the females, which are faster than the males, are not black or grey like their respective males, but reddish.

Wild turkeys are bronze; tame ones are black more often than any other colour. This may be due to the fact that in them nigritude is correlated with the power to resist damp. Among human beings those races which live in very swampy districts are often intensely black.

It is a significant fact that those domestic animals which are bred for speed or for fighting [364] purposes do not assume all the varied hues that characterise those that are allowed to breed indiscriminately. Racehorses, greyhounds, and homing pigeons furnish examples of this. Even more remarkable is the case of the Indian Aseel or game-cock. This is bred purely for fighting purposes, and is required to display extraordinary powers of endurance, since the spurs are cut off in order to prolong the fight. Thus it is that this Indian race of game-cocks shows little variation when compared with the English breed, which fights in a more natural manner. The hens of the Indian form seem never to show the colouration of the wild jungle fowl, although the cocks may do so. It would appear that hens having the colouration of their wild ancestors cannot breed cocks possessed of the requisite courage. The Aseel is said to be of the highest courage only when the legs, beak and iris are white.

There is, we believe, not the least doubt that many other connections between colour and various characteristics have yet to be discovered. It is high time that competent naturalists paid attention to this subject. A study of the question will almost certainly throw much light upon many phenomena of animal colouration which hitherto have not been satisfactorily explained. It is quite likely that the sandy hue displayed by birds and beasts which frequent desert regions [365] may be due to a correlation with the power of withstanding intense dry heat rather than to its rendering them inconspicuous to their foes.

As other examples of correlation we may cite the correlation which seems to obtain between short canine teeth and the absence of a hairy covering to the body. This phenomenon is observed both in men and pigs. Hairless dogs almost invariably have their teeth but poorly developed.

Darwin called attention to the connection between a short beak and small feet in pigeons; we see the same phenomenon in the dwarf breed of ducks known as call-ducks.

A curious correlation exists between fowls' eggs with brown shells and the incubating habit. Fanciers have long tried in vain to produce a hen that lays brown eggs without becoming "broody" at certain seasons.

Among fowls, long legs are invariably correlated with a short tail, as is well seen in the Malay breed. This correlation may explain the short tails of wading birds. Short-legged fowls, like Japanese bantams, have long tails, and it is significant that the short-legged Weka Rails (Ocydromus) of New Zealand have unusually long tails for the family. In this connection we may say that the tail-like plumes of the cranes are not tail-feathers, but the tertiary feathers of the wings. As egrets also have long trains of [366] plumes growing from the back, it cannot be said that the short tail of the vast majority of the waders is due to the fact that these birds would be at a disadvantage were their caudal feathers long.

Isolation

Isolation is a most important factor in the making of species. It is a factor to which Darwin failed to attach sufficient importance, and one which has been to a large extent neglected by Wallaceians.

Divergence of Character

We have seen how a species can be improved or changed by natural selection. All those individuals which have varied in a favourable direction have been preserved, and allowed to leave behind them offspring that inherit their peculiarities, while those which have not so varied have perished without leaving behind any descendants. Thus the nature of the species has changed. The old type has given place to a new one. Instead of species A, species B exists. This is what Romanes has called monotypic evolution—the transformation of one species into another species. But any theory of the origin of species must be able to answer the question, Why have species multiplied? How is it that species A has given rise to species B, C, and D, or, while itself continuing to exist, has thrown off sister species B and C? How is it [367] that in the course of evolution, species have not been transmuted in linear series instead of ramifying into branches? This ramification of a species into branches has been termed by Romanes polytypic evolution. It is easy to see how natural selection can bring about monotypic evolution, but how can it have effected polytypic evolution? To use Darwin's phraseology, how is it that divergence of character has come about? Darwin's reply to this question is (Origin of Species, p. 136), "from the simple circumstance that the more diversified the descendants from any one species become in structure, constitution, and habits, by so much will they be better enabled to seize on many and widely diversified places in the polity of nature, and so be enabled to increase in numbers.

"We can clearly discern this in the case of animals with simple habits. Take the case of a carnivorous quadruped, of which the number that can be supported in any country has long ago arrived at its full average. If its natural power of increase be allowed to act, it can succeed in increasing (the country not undergoing any change in its conditions) only by its varying descendants seizing on places at present occupied by other animals: some of them, for instance, being enabled to feed on new kinds of prey, either dead or alive; some inhabiting new stations, climbing trees, frequenting water, and [368] some perhaps becoming less carnivorous. The more diversified in habits and structure the descendants of our carnivorous animal become, the more places they will be enabled to occupy. What applies to one animal will apply throughout all time to all animals—that is, if they vary—for otherwise natural selection can effect nothing." Darwin was, therefore, of opinion that natural selection is able to bring about polytypic evolution. Darwin tacitly assumes, in the illustration he gives, that the various races of the carnivorous animal are in some way prevented from intercrossing; for if they interbreed indiscriminately, these races will tend to be obliterated.

Isolation

"That perfectly free intercrossing," writes Professor Lloyd Morgan (on p. 98 of Animal Life and Intelligence), "between any or all of the individuals of a given group of animals is, so long as the characters of the parents are blended in the offspring, fatal to divergence of character, is undeniable. Through the elimination of less favourable variations, the swiftness, strength, and cunning of a race may be gradually improved. But no form of elimination can possibly differentiate the group into swift, strong, and cunning varieties, distinct from each other, so long as all three varieties freely interbreed, and the characters of the parents blend with the offspring. Elimination may and does give rise to progress in any given group, as a group; it [369] does not and cannot give rise to differentiation and divergence, so long as interbreeding with consequent interblending of characters be freely permitted. Whence it inevitably follows, as a matter of simple logic, that where divergence has occurred, intercrossing and interbreeding must in some way have been lessened or prevented.

"Thus a new factor is introduced, that of isolation or segregation. And there is no questioning the fact that it is of great importance. Its importance, indeed, can only be denied by denying the swamping effects of intercrossing, and such denial implies the tacit assumption that interbreeding and interblending are held in check by some form of segregation. The isolation explicitly denied is implicitly assumed."

This is very sound criticism, and is not very materially affected by the fact that the intercrossing of varieties does not necessarily imply a blending of their characters in the offspring; for, as we have seen, some characters do not blend. No matter what form inheritance takes, in order that natural selection may cause polytypic evolution it must be assisted by isolation in some form or other.

Thus isolation is an important factor in evolution, though probably not so important as its more extreme advocates would have us believe. Wagner, Romanes, and Gulick have, in insisting [370] upon the importance of the principle of isolation, rendered valuable service to biological science, but, in common with most men having a new theory, they have pushed their conclusions to absurd lengths.

As Romanes has pointed out, isolation may be discriminate or indiscriminate. "If," he writes, on p. 5 of vol. iii. of Darwin and after Darwin, "a shepherd divides a flock of sheep without regard to their characters, he is isolating one section from the other indiscriminately; but if he places all the white sheep in one field, and all the black sheep in another field, he is isolating one section from the other discriminately. Or, if geological subsidence divides a species into two parts, the isolation will be indiscriminate; but if the separation be due to one of the sections developing, for example, a change of instinct determining migration to another area, or occupation of a different habitat on the same area, then the isolation will be discriminate, so far as the resemblance of instinct is concerned."

Discriminate Isolation

Other names for indiscriminate isolation are separate breeding and apogamy. Discriminate isolation is also called segregate breeding and homogamy. The human breeder resorts to discriminate isolation in that he separates all those creatures from which he seeks to breed, from those from which he does not wish to breed. Natural selection itself is, therefore, a [371] kind of discriminate isolator, since it isolates the fit by destroying all the unfit, and, inasmuch as it kills off all those creatures which it fails to isolate, it differs from other forms of isolation in preventing the inter-breeding of the unisolated forms and their giving rise to a different race. Thus it is clear that natural selection, unless aided by some other form of isolation, can give effect to only monotypic evolution. This is a point on which Romanes rightly insists strongly.

There are several other forms of discriminate isolation. Sexual selection would be one of these. Suppose, for example, that in any species there are large and small varieties formed, and like tends to breed with like, then the small individuals will breed with other small individuals, while large ones will mate with large ones; thus two races—a large one and a small one—will be evolved side by side, provided, of course, natural selection does not step in and destroy one of them.

Another kind of discriminate isolation may be due to the fact that one variety is ready to pair before the other; thus two races are likely to arise which breed at different seasons. It is unnecessary for us to discourse further on the subject of discriminate isolation; those interested in the subject should read vol. iii. of Darwin and after Darwin, by Romanes.

Indiscriminate Isolation

It is impossible to deny the importance of [372] discriminate isolation as a factor in evolution. On this there can be no room for disagreement among biologists. It is when we come to the subject of indiscriminate isolation that we enter a region of zoological strife.

Is indiscriminate isolation per se a factor of evolution? Romanes, Gulick, and Wagner assert that it is, Wallace and his adherents assert that it is not.

As the burden of proof is on the former, they are entitled to the first hearing.

"We may well be disposed, at first sight," writes Romanes (Darwin and after Darwin, p. 10), "to conclude that this kind of isolation can count for nothing in the process of evolution. For if the fundamental importance of isolation in the production of organic forms be due to its segregation of like with like, does it not follow that any form of isolation which is indiscriminate must fail to supply the very condition on which all the forms of discriminate isolation depend for their efficacy in the causing of organic evolution? Or, to return to one's concrete example, is it not self-evident that the farmer who separated his flock into two or more parts indiscriminately, would not effect any more change in his stock than if he had left them all to breed together? Well, although at first sight this seems self-evident, it is, in fact, untrue. For, unless the individuals which are indiscriminately isolated [373] happen to be a very large number, sooner or later their progeny will come to differ from that of the parent type, or unisolated portion of the parent stock. And, of course, as soon as this change of type begins, the isolation ceases to be indiscriminate; the previous apogamy has been converted into homogamy, with the usual result of causing a divergence of type. The reason why progeny of an indiscriminately isolated section of an originally uniform stock—e.g. of a species—will eventually deviate from the original type is, to quote Mr Gulick, as follows:—'No two portions of a species possess exactly the same average character, and the initial differences are for ever reacting on the environment and on each other, in such a way as to ensure increasing divergence as long as the individuals of the two groups are kept from intergenerating.'"

The words of Mr Gulick require close scrutiny. We may admit that "no two portions of a species possess exactly the same average character," but why should the two, if prevented from interbreeding yet subjected to similar climatic and other conditions, present the phenomenon of "increasing divergence?" The reason assigned by Romanes is the "Law" of Delbœuf, which runs:—"A constant cause of variation, however insignificant it may be, changes the uniformity of type little by little, and diversifies it ad infinitum." [374] From this "Law" it follows, says Romanes, on p. 13 of vol. iii. Darwin and after Darwin, that "no matter how infinitesimally small the difference may be between the average qualities of an isolated section of a species compared with the average qualities of the rest of that species, if the isolation continues sufficiently long, differentiation of specific type is necessarily bound to ensue."

This deduction involves two important assumptions. The first is, that in each of the separated portions of the given species there is a constant cause of variation operating in one direction in the case of one portion and in another direction in the case of the other. This assumption is, unfortunately, not founded on fact. If we were to take one hundred race-horses and shut them up in one park and one hundred cart-horses and shut them up in another park, and prevent the interbreeding of the two stocks, we should, if Romanes's tacit assumption be true, see the two types diverge more and more from one another. We know that as a matter of fact they will tend, generation after generation, to become more like one another. Galton's Law of Regression, of which we have already spoken, and which is supported by ample evidence, clearly negatives this tacit assumption made by Romanes and Gulick. The second assumption upon which their reasoning is based is that there is no limit [375] to the amount of change which can be effected by the accumulation of fluctuating variations; but, as we have already seen (on p. 70), there is a very definite limit and this limit is quickly reached.

Thus the arguments of Romanes and Gulick are fundamentally unsound.

Mollusca of Sandwich Isles

But the fact remains, and has to be accounted for, that, as a general rule, when two portions of a species are separated, so that they are prevented from interbreeding, they begin to diverge in character, and the longer they remain thus separated the greater becomes that divergence. This is an observed fact which cannot be gainsaid.

It was the observance of this fact which led Gulick to insist with such emphasis on the importance of geographical isolation as a factor in evolution. He discovered that the land mollusca of the Sandwich Islands fall into a great number of varieties.

These islands are very hilly, and Gulick found that each of the varieties is confined not merely to one island, but to one valley. "Moreover," writes Romanes, on p. 16 of Darwin and after Darwin, "on tracing this fauna from valley to valley, it is apparent that a slight variation in the occupants of valley 2, as compared with those of the adjacent valley 1, becomes more pronounced in the next, valley 3, [376] still more so in 4, etc., etc. Thus it was possible, as Mr Gulick says, roughly to estimate the amount of divergence between the occupants of any two given valleys by measuring the number of miles between them. . . . The variations which affect scores of species, and themselves eventually run into fully specific distinctions, are all more or less finely graduated as they pass from one isolated region to the next; and they have reference to changes of form or colour, which in no one case presents any appearance of utility."

Hitherto three different attempts have been made to explain this and allied phenomena:—

1. That it is the result of isolation.

2. That it is the result of natural selection.

3. That it is the result of the action of the environment on the organism.

Let us consider these in inverse order.

Local Species

In the case of some organisms, more especially plants, invertebrates, and fish, the environment does exert a direct influence on their colouration. But, as we have seen, the changes in colour, etc., thus induced appear never to be transmitted to the offspring of the organisms so affected. They disappear when the offspring are removed to other surroundings.

On the other hand, local races or species—as, for example, the white-cheeked variety of sparrow found in India—usually retain their [377] external appearance when the environment is changed. In the one case the peculiarity is not inherited; in the other it is inherited.

The Wallaceian explanation is, of course, that the phenomenon is the result of natural selection. There must, say Wallace and his followers, be some differences in the environment, differences which we poor human beings cannot perceive, that have caused the divergence between the various isolated sections of the species. In the case of some local species this explanation is probably the correct one, but we have no hesitation in saying that natural selection is unable to offer a satisfactory explanation in a considerable number of instances. Take, for example, the case of the land mollusca of the Sandwich Islands. Mr Gulick worked for fifteen years at them, and states that so far as he is able to ascertain the environment in the fifteen valleys is essentially the same. "To argue," writes Romanes, on p. 17 of vol. iii. of Darwin and after Darwin, "that every one of some twenty contiguous valleys in the area of the same small island must necessarily present such differences of environment that all the shells in each are differently modified thereby, while in no one out of the hundreds of cases of modification in minute respects of form and colour can any human being suggest an adaptive reason therefore—to argue thus is merely to affirm an intrinsically [378] improbable dogma in the presence of a great and consistent array of opposing facts."

Men of science not infrequently charge the clergy with adhering to dogma in face of opposing facts; it seems to us that many of the apostles of science are in this respect worse offenders than the most orthodox of Churchmen.

The example of the mollusca of the Sandwich Islands is by no means a solitary one. D. Dewar cited some interesting cases in a paper recently read before the Royal Society of Arts (p. 103 of vol. lvii. of the Society's Journal):

"The Indian robins present even greater difficulties to those who profess to pin their faith to the all-sufficiency of natural selection. Robins are found in nearly all parts of India, and fall into two species, the brown-backed (Thamnobia cambaiensis) and the black-backed Indian Robin (Thamnobia fulicata). The former occurs only in Northern India, and the latter is confined to the southern portion of the peninsula. The hen of each species is a sandy brown bird with a patch of brick-red feathers under the tail, so that we cannot tell by merely looking at a hen to which of the two species she belongs. The cock of the South Indian form is, in winter, a glossy black bird, with a white bar in the wing, and the characteristic red patch under the tail. The cock of the northern species, as his name implies, has a sandy-brown back, which contrasts [379] strongly with the glossy black of his head, neck, and under parts. In summer the cocks of the two species grow more like one another owing to the wearing away of the outer edges of their feathers; but it is always possible to distinguish between

145

them at a glance. The two species meet at about the latitude of Bombay. Oates states that in a certain zone, from Ahmednagar to the mouth of the Godaveri valley, both species occur, and they do not appear to interbreed.

"It seems impossible to maintain that natural selection, acting on minute variations, has brought about the divergence between these two species. Even if it be asserted that the difference in the colour of the feathers of the back of the two cocks is in some way correlated with adaptability to their particular environment, how are we to explain the fact that in a certain zone both species flourish?

"A similar phenomenon is furnished by the red-vented bulbul. This genus falls into several species, each corresponding to a definite locality and differing only in details from the allied species, as, for example, the distance down the neck to which the black of the head extends. There is a Punjab Red-vented Bulbul (Molpastes intermedius), a Bengal (Molpastes bengalensis), a Burmese (Molpastes burmanicus) and a Madras (Molpastes hæmorrhous) species.

[380]
"It does not seem possible to maintain the contention that these various species are the products of natural selection, for that would mean if the black of the head of the Punjab species extended further into the neck the bird could not live in that country."

Thus, natural selection clearly is unable to explain some cases of divergence of character due to geographical isolation.

There remains the third explanation, that the divergence is the result of the simple fact of isolation.

We have already shown how insuperable are the objections to the view held by Romanes and Gulick.

It seems to us that explanation must lie in the fact that mutations occur every now and again in some species. If two portions of a species are separated and a mutation occurs in one portion and not in the other, and if the mutating form succeeds in supplanting the parent form in that isolated portion of the species in which it has appeared, we should have the phenomenon of two races or species differing in appearance although subjected to what appear to be identical environment.

This, of course, is pure conjecture. All that can be said of it at present is that it is not opposed to observed facts. That mutations do occur must be admitted. At present we are [381] totally in the dark as to what causes them. They arise at the most unexpected times.

In favour of the explanation based on "mutation" there is the interesting fact that geographical isolation does not by any means always cause divergence of character. This Romanes, with great fairness, freely admits. "There are," he writes, on p. 133 of vol. iii. of Darwin and after Darwin, "four species of butterflies, belonging to three genera (Lycæna donzelii, L. pheretes, Argynnis pales, Erebia manto), which are identical in the polar regions and the Alps, notwithstanding that the sparse Alpine populations have been presumably separated from their parent stocks since the glacial period." Again, there are "certain species of fresh-water crustaceans (Apus), the representatives of which are compelled habitually to form small isolated colonies in widely separated ponds, and nevertheless exhibit no divergence of character, although apogamy has probably lasted for centuries."

Cormorants

To these examples we may add that of the cormorants. These birds have an almost worldwide range. One species—our Cormorant (Phalacrocorax carbo)—occurs in every imaginable kind of environment. Isolation has not effected any changes in the appearance of this species. Yet in New Zealand there exist no fewer than fourteen other species of cormorant. New Zealand is a country where climatic conditions [382] are comparatively uniform, nevertheless it boasts of no fewer than fifteen out of the thirty-seven known species of cormorant. A possible explanation of this phenomenon may be found in the comparatively easy conditions under which cormorants live in New Zealand.[10] Under such circumstances mutants may be permitted by natural selection to survive, whereas in other parts of the world such mutants have not been able to hold their own.

Prof. Bateson has likened natural selection to a competitive examination to which every organism must submit. The penalty for failure is immediate death. The standard of the examination may vary with the locality.

Isolation, then, is a very important factor in the making of species, for without it, in some form, the multiplication of species is impossible.

Let us, in conclusion, briefly summarise what we now know of the method in which new species are made. We have studied the various factors of evolution—variation and correlation, heredity, natural selection, sexual selection, and the other kinds of isolation. How do these combine to bring new species into being, and to establish the same?

Natural Selection

Let us first consider the factor known as natural selection, since this is the one on which [383] Darwin laid such great stress. Natural selection, although a most important factor in evolution, is not an indispensable one. Evolution is possible without natural selection.

Let us suppose that there is no such thing as natural selection; that the numbers of existing species are kept constant by the elimination of all individuals born in excess of the number required to maintain the species at the existing figure, and that the elimination of the surplus is effected, not by natural selection, but by chance, by the drawing of lots. Under such circumstances there may be evolution, existing species may undergo change, but the evolution will be determined solely by the lines along which variations occur.

If mutations take place along certain fixed lines, and tend to accumulate in the given directions, evolution will proceed along these lines quite independently of the utility to the organism of the mutations that occur. An unfavourable mutation will have precisely the same chance of survival as a favourable one.

If, on the other hand, mutations occur indiscriminately on all sides of the mean, then those mutations which happen to occur most frequently will have the best chance of survival, and they will mark the lines of evolution. But suppose that no mutation occurs more frequently than the others. Under such circumstances there [384] will be no evolution, unless, by some cause or other, portions of the species are isolated, because in the long run the mutations will neutralise one another.

Let us now suppose that natural selection comes into play. The old method of determining by lot which forms shall persist is replaced by selection on the fixed principle that the fittest shall survive. The mutations appear as before, and as before, of the large number that occur, only a few are permitted to survive. But now the survivors, instead of being a motley crowd, are a selected band, composed of individuals having many characteristics in common—a homogeneous company. Thus one result of natural selection is to accelerate evolution, by weeding out certain classes of individuals and preventing them breeding with those it has selected. On the other hand, natural selection will tend to diminish the number of species which have arisen through mutation, inasmuch as it weeds out many mutants which would have perished had their survival been determined by lot.

Origin of the Fittest

From this the kind of work performed by natural selection should be obvious. Natural selection does not make new species. These make themselves, or, rather, originate in accordance with the laws of variation.

"You can," runs an old proverb, "bring a [385] horse to the drinking fountain, but you cannot make him drink." You may be able to bring a child into the world, but you cannot secure its survival. Variation brings into being mutants, which are incipient species, but variation cannot determine their survival. It is at this stage that natural selection steps in.

But because natural selection allows certain mutations to persist, it is not correct to say that natural selection has caused these mutations or made or originated the species to which they give rise.

The Civil Service Commissioners do not make Indian civil servants: they merely determine which of a number of ready-made men shall become civil servants. Similarly, natural selection does not make new species, it simply decides which of a number of ready-made organisms shall survive and establish themselves as new species. Nor does natural selection always do as much as this; for it is not the only determinant of survival. Its position is sometimes comparable to that of the Medical Board which inspects and rejects the physically unfit of the candidates which have already been selected by some other authority.

The examination conducted by natural selection may be compared to a competitive one. A separate, independent examination is held for each particular locality; consequently the severity of the competition will vary with the locality.

[386]
In each competition some candidates pass with ease: they gain an unnecessarily high total of marks. So in nature do certain organisms, as, for example, the Leaf-butterflies (Kallimas), appear to be over-adapted to their environment. Other candidates manage to pass only by a very narrow margin: these are paralleled in nature by those species which are barely able to maintain themselves, which become extinct the moment the competition increases in severity.

The great bulk of the candidates fail to obtain sufficient marks to gain a place among the chosen few; these unsuccessful candidates correspond to the mutating forms which perish in the struggle for existence, to those individuals which happen to have mutated in unfavourable directions.

Even as many candidates have acquired knowledge of subjects in which they are not examined, so do many organisms possess characteristics which are of no utility to them in the struggle for existence.

Wallaceians expend much time and energy in misguided attempts to explain the existence of such characters in terms of natural selection.

Nature's examination, like that held for entrance to the Indian Civil Service, is a liberal one, so that the qualifications of the successful candidates vary considerably. Provided a candidate is able to gain more marks than the other candidates for a vacancy, it matters not in what [387] subjects the marks are gained. So is it in nature. Natural selection takes an organism as a whole. One species may have established itself because of its fleetness, a

148

second because of its courage, a third because it has a strong constitution, a fourth because it is protectively coloured, a fifth because it has good digestive powers, and so on.

We thus perceive the part played by natural selection and other forms of isolation in the making of species. It is obvious that these do not make species any more than the Civil Service Commissioners manufacture Indian civil servants.

The real makers of species are the inherent properties of protoplasm and the laws of variation and heredity. These determine the nature of the organism; natural selection and the like factors merely decide for each particular organism whether it shall survive and give rise to a species.

The way in which natural selection does its work is comparatively easy to understand. But this is only the fringe of the territory which we call evolution.

We seem to be tolerably near a solution of the problem of the causes of the survival of any particular mutation. This, however, is merely a side issue. The real problem is the cause of variations and mutations, or, in other words, how species originate. At present our knowledge of the causes of variation and mutation [388] is practically nil. We do not even know along what particular lines mutations occur.

We have yet to discover whether one mutation invariably leads to another along the same lines—in other words, whether mutating organisms behave as though they had behind them a force acting in a definite direction. The solution of these problems seems afar off. The hope of solving them lies, not in the speculations in which biologists of to-day are so fond of indulging, but in observation and experiment, especially the last.

The future of biology is largely in the hands of the practical breeder.

[389]

FOOTNOTES

[1]The white, pied, and "Japan" individuals are not more different from the type than some variations occurring in wild birds.

[2]This short-legged type of dog is sometimes seen among the ownerless and unselected pariah dogs of Indian towns; and a short-legged variety of the fowl may occur sporadically in Zanzibar, where the long-legged Malay is the prevalent breed.

[3]"Effected" appears in the earlier editions, but in the later editions has given place to "affected," probably a printer's error.

[4]Some egrets, such as the rock-egrets (Demiegretta) of eastern tropical coasts, are normally grey, but may be white, and this whiteness may be confined in individuals to the young or adult states.

[5]After years of observation of these Indian geese, Finn is convinced they are now, at all events, pure Chinese; it is possible that they really were hybrids in Blyth's time, but that fresh importations of geese from China, such as still occur, may have ultimately swamped the blood of the common goose. The fertility of the hybrid geese was, however, known to such early writers as Pallas and Linnæus. Darwin himself, at a later date, bred five young from a pair of such hybrids (Nature, Jan. 1, 1880, p. 207).

[6]In this chapter we use the word Neo-Darwinism in its usually-accepted sense, i.e. as a name for that which should be called Wallaceism, for the doctrine of the all-sufficiency of natural selection.

[7]Animal Colouration, p. 125. A book full of valuable facts and ideas on this most interesting subject.

[8]Even these eggs, closely though they resemble in colouring the shingle, etc., on which they are laid, are discovered and eaten by gulls, as Mr A. J. R. Roberts points out in The Bird Book.

[9]Journal of the Bombay Natural History Society, Vol xv. (1903-4), p. 454.

[10]Hutton and Drummond record other examples of this in the valuable work entitled The Animals of New Zealand.

www.ingramcontent.com/pod-product-compliance
Lightning Source LLC
Chambersburg PA
CBHW070355290526
45790CB00004B/1506